Restoring the Soul of America Through
God's Plan for Your Marriage and Family

One Home at a Time

Dennis Rainey

PUBLISHING
Colorado Springs, Colorado

Library of Congress Cataloging-in-Publication Data
Rainey, Dennis, 1948-
    One home at a time: restoring the soul of America through
God's plan for your marriage and family/Dennis Rainey.
        p.   cm.
    Includes bibliographical references.
    ISBN 1-56179-545-3
    1. Marriage—Religious aspects—Christianity. 2. Family—
Religious aspects—Christianity. 3. Church renewal—United
States. 4. United States—History—Religious aspects—
Christianity. 5. Marriage—United States. 6. Family—United
States. 7. United States—Social conditions—1980- 8. United
States—Moral conditions. I. Title.
BV835.R346   1997   97-10893
277.3'0829—dc21   CIP

Published by Focus on the Family Publishing,
Colorado Springs, Colorado 80995.
Distributed in the U.S.A. and Canada by Word Books, Dallas,
Texas.

Most Scripture verses are from the *New American Standard
Bible.* Copyright © 1960, 1962, 1963, 1971, 1972, 1973, 1975,
1977 by the Lockman Foundation. Used by permission.

Other Scripture quotations are from *The Holy Bible, New
International Version* (NIV) © 1973, 1984 by International Bible
Society, used by permission of Zondervan Publishing House.

Focus on the Family books are available at special quantity dis-
counts when purchased in bulk by corporations, organizations,
churches, or groups. Special imprints, messages, and excerpts
can be produced to meet your needs. For more information,
write: Special Sales, Focus on the Family Publishing, 8605
Explorer Drive, Colorado Springs, CO 80920, or call (719) 531-
3400 and ask for the Special Sales Department.

Cover Design: Bradley Lind

Printed in the United States of America

97 98 99 00/10 9 8 7 6 5 4 3 2 1

*This book is dedicated to the men and women whose lives
are being spent in the cause of Family Reformation.
It is my privilege to work with you!*

*Merle and Lynn Engle
Don and Suzanne Dudgeon
Bob and Mary Ann Lepine
Steve and Angie Campbell
Roger and Barbara Craft
Dave and Diana Daggett
Bob and Marty Paine
Marty and Lora Schwieterman
Ken and Nook Tuttle
Blair and Debbye Wright*

*And to four additional couples who faithfully served with us for
many years at FamilyLife. Thanks for your friendship and service.*

*Mark and Lisa Schatzman
Jeff and Brenda Schulte
Lloyd and Lisa Shadrach
Jerry and Sheryl Wunder*

Contents

Acknowledgments

No book that I have written has ever been more challenging than this one. Perhaps this project has been more difficult because the message is so weighty and so important to so many. But my task was lightened by a battalion of committed warriors for the family. These front-line, battle-seasoned veterans have served with me in more than one spiritual skirmish. All deserve more thanks and appreciation than I could possibly express. But here goes . . .

First and foremost, thanks go to two men who helped me crystallize this manuscript and turn it into a book: Bruce Nygren and Rich Campbell.

Bruce Nygren, you, my friend, are an angel sent by God. Thanks for your heart for families and for the enormous weight you carried as we sharpened the original "tool." Your commitment to excellence and your long-suffering with me in the process are greatly appreciated. Thanks for the research, calls, and even last-minute changes that you helped me make—you never once complained, even though I did! I am so grateful to God for the good report on your wife Racinda's health that we received as we were finishing this book. Needless to say, neither of us dreamed we'd be finishing this book the way we did. Thanks for persevering.

Rich Campbell is one patient and faithful man who was sent by God for such a time as this. Really. I mean it! Your long hours, advice, gifted writing, and commitment are deeply appreciated. Thanks for stepping into a minefield and expending your life for a Family Reformation. I'd still be writing 8,000-word chapters and working on this beast if you hadn't joined the cause. Thanks.

A special thanks goes to Al Janssen of Focus on the Family. Thanks for your vision for families and your heart for God's work. By coming and locking arms with FamilyLife, you enabled two pro-family organizations to help one another make a difference. Also, many thanks to Keith Wall for his editorial encouragement.

And to Dave Boehi, a veteran of many of these "book birthings," goes another long and loud set of kudos. *Bo knows books*. And editing. And logic. And my writing style. Thank you for rescuing Rich and me from the impossible job of editing. You've saved my life before, and now you've done it again. I'm thrilled God has rewarded your years here at FamilyLife with the magazine *Real FamilyLife*. Thank you. Thank you.

Merle Engle is a servant-leader who made this book possible by managing the 200-plus FamilyLife staff. You have fought budget wars, battled fatigue from long meetings, suffered a mild heart attack (hastened, no doubt, by your relationship with me!), and anguished over personnel problems. Thank you for taking on the unending challenge of computers, endeavoring to train us, coaching us in excellence, and exhorting us to read the Bible and pray more. Merle Engle, you are one of a kind! Your legacy is, and will be, great.

Bob Lepine, Jeff Schulte, and Lloyd Shadrach—the three of you deserve medals for the philosophical and strategic edge you brought to the concept of Family Reformation. You men took the mandate and made it work. There would be no strategy without you!

To Mary Larmoyeux (the captain of the troops), Sharon Hill, Kathy Horton, Arlene Kirk, Matt Burns, and Fran Taylor, I offer incredible thanks for researching, editing, juggling the details, and running an office in my absence. Awesome! And to the new captain, Dorothy English, thanks for jumping in midstream and serving.

Kevin Hartman and Blair Wright are true leaders in the fight for the family and in the production of this book. Thank you for caring about the future of families, and for being "difference-makers" in tens of thousands of lives through materials like this one.

Chuck Bostwick, you took the challenge on the original cover design and surprised no one. Everything you do is superb. There aren't enough courageous men today, but you are one of them. Well done. Great job, too, on the layout of the rest of the original book.

Jeff Lord, you continue to grow and manage a very tough job. Thank you for your commitment to details over the years, details that generally go unnoticed unless there's a mistake. Thanks also for your commitment to excellence, and for serving with a willing spirit.

Julie Denker is once again a lifesaver in editing and proofing.

Additional thanks go to Dan Butkowski, Anne Wooten, Cyndi Warren, Sandy Harris, Mark Whitlock, and Betty Dillon for the quality work you did on this book, and on all the other projects I have sent your way.

Rob and Laurie Kopf, this ministry would be in big trouble at the distribution center if you hadn't come along and bailed us out. You both make all of us at FamilyLife proud by your sacrificial service to folks who order our books and resources.

Tonda Nations, your initial work on the "Family Reformation" radio broadcast helped fuel my creativity. And your backup research later saved me enormous amounts of time. Exponential thanks. Tom Clagett, your research is invaluable and helped to shape the strategy of this book. Thanks to both of you for your behind-the-scenes but all-important work.

Bill Howard, your studious, year-long contribution to the *Family Manifesto* will never be forgotten. Thank you. Beth Greenway and Mary Pierce, you both deserve a hearty thanks as well for your eleventh-hour editing contributions.

To Rebecca, Deborah, and Laura, thank you for allowing me to come home a little later in the midst of this assignment. You are the best kids in the world. And to my three collegians, Ashley, Benjamin, and Samuel, what a thrill it has been to see you becoming responsible young adults who love the Lord. It's been fun to have you back home recently. I love all six of you more than you'll ever know. You make me a proud papa! And when you get married, be sure to walk in the truth, love God with a whole heart, and challenge your generation to continue the Family Reformation.

And once again, I must say thanks to my wife, Barbara, my friend and companion for life. Thank you for all the healthy food that kept me going in the midst of this book. I love you and appreciate you for being an awesome mother and even better wife. I'd marry you all over again—10 times out of 10. I love you.

And finally, a heartfelt thank you to the hundreds of FamilyLife staff and the thousands of volunteers across the country and around the world who are igniting the flame of a Family Reformation!

Foreword

If you have been there—and I have—you know about the spasms of despair that wrench a kid whose home is "broken." It doesn't matter that other kids have the same problem; you know only the fear and the gnawing guilt that maybe you are the reason Mom and Dad fight and the family isn't together. You cry when nobody is looking, and you learn to tell the difference between the "God bless you" types and the one person who cares enough—and knows enough—to pull you to safety.

One Home at a Time is a salvage vessel. It escorts the reader through a no-nonsense tour of the slums of discordant and disjointed families. It touches the taproot of decay in our country—the most prosperous and blessed nation in the world's history. Ringing with authenticity, it calls divorce a national disaster, a killer of culture; then it leads the way to higher ground.

Dennis Rainey left my classroom more than two decades ago, a restless young reconnaissance man determined to find a formula for slowing the failure rate in American homes. He gave voice to FamilyLife, focusing intently on preventive care for married couples. Now this firebrand has declared war on the dissolution of home life. He has nailed his theses to America's front door and called for a Family Reformation.

A mystery story mixed with a construction kit, these pages build a framework for fulfillment in living. When disappointments undo our dreams, a whole new opportunity is waiting. Like the thaw in C. S. Lewis's Narnia, peace of mind melts our frustrations, even though we have been groping in the dark wardrobe of dysfunctional home life.

The Family Reformation happens, Dennis says, when life and truth collide. His truth streams from a biblical base; he explains that God's method has no factory of mass production. He touches one person, one family, one home at a time. There is no substitute for placing a clean person in a corrupt society and effecting change.

Dynamic living flowers from the timeless truths of the Scriptures to produce supernatural results.

It's not enough to count casualties; it's self-defeating to seek advice from marital escape artists. If we embrace immorality, if we try to redefine the family, if we shrug off husband-wife separation and lampoon loving commitment, then we simply hang a foreclosure sign on Western civilization.

Rainey's remedy confronts twenty-first century anxieties with a return to the One who wrote the rules, the Originator of marriage itself. His message engages husbands, wives, and children who want to reassemble their family structures. The payoff for choosing obedience to God's Word about families is an investment in future generations, as well as an immediate cessation of domestic hostilities. God's long-range promises are still redeemable. Every bride and groom past, present, and future needs to digest the nourishment of this timely message of marital retrieval.

Howard G. Hendricks
Distinguished Professor, Chairman
Center for Christian Leadership
Dallas Theological Seminary

CHAPTER ONE

The Silent Stirrings of Reformation

*The only real revolutions are those that change the
mind and the heart, and the only real revolutionaries
are the sage and the saint.*
—WILL AND ARIEL DURANT

Two different people, living on different continents, in different
times. One is famous, a brilliant theologian whose acts of
courage shook and transformed the world. The other unknown—a
young married woman struggling to keep her desperate life from
shattering into painful pieces. Yet their lives reveal common threads:
Both the celebrated monk and the broken woman experienced the
touch of God's grace and the power of reformation.

On a chilly fall evening in 1517, a light snow fell on the cobble-
stone streets of Wittenberg, Germany. A man in his early 30s, wearing the coarse, flowing robe of an Augustinian monk, trudged across
the grounds of a university, making his way absentmindedly toward
home. A blustery, unrelenting wind pricked at the exposed flesh on
his face.

A scowl cut deeply into the man's forehead, and his hands,

which often swung in rhythm to his steps, were still—buried inside the lining of his cloak. Oddly for him, he walked alone.

On most nights, Martin Luther journeyed the half mile from the classroom to his room at the monastery in the company of students. A professor of theology, he relished the repartee of theological debate and the camaraderie of bright acquaintances. Since his arrival at Wittenberg in 1511, Martin had become a social and spiritual magnet. Students devoured his lectures and sought his opinion on an array of theological topics. Always accessible, Martin did some of his best teaching outside the classroom. Strolling along, a flock of disciples in tow, the professor punctuated his points with shouts and waving arms.

Martin could be a showman. One night, to the applause and laughter of his audience, he hurled his floppy doctor's hat into the Elbe River to show contempt for the doctrine of papal infallibility. Another time, the monk opened his Latin Bible and tore out the books of the Apocrypha, charging that they didn't belong in Scripture. For those and other deeds of mischief, Martin Luther was viewed a renegade by his students. He loved it, and so did they.

But tonight there were no companions and no conversation, and that was just the way he wanted it. For Martin Luther, the brilliant professor of theology at the University of Wittenberg, needed more time alone to mull his options. The evening of October 30, 1517, would prove to be one of the longest nights of his life.

—

Across centuries, in a place much different from Martin Luther's sixteenth-century Germany, on an October evening, a woman in her 30s named Debi also contemplated an audacious act. Living in Milwaukee, Wisconsin, Debi was alone, too, deep in thought over an event that would not change the course of nations and world history. In fact, other than for a few friends and family members, who would even notice her obituary in the newspaper?

Martin Luther, in his earlier years, had worried that some single sin or group of sins would send him to hell when he died. Such things didn't bother Debi. She had already lived through hell. It was living that troubled her. She was putting the final touches on her suicide plans.

Debi had grown up in Georgia. Her family truly was dysfunctional, a term inadequate to describe the emotional holocaust of her childhood.

Debi's mother had married at 16, then within just a few years had divorced and remarried before Debi was born in 1956.

In a house where the adults are consumed with satisfying their lusts, a child becomes a victim.

Debi was no exception.

The stress and pain caused in Debi's family by drug abuse, sexual and emotional abuse, marital tensions, and infidelity wilted her tender heart. When she was still in preschool, Debi learned how to protect herself by mentally "crawling into a dungeon of despair and slamming a heavy metal door."

In a house where the adults are consumed with satisfying their lusts, a child becomes a victim.

School added to Debi's misery. Struggling just to stay alive in her home, she was not prepared to succeed with the three R's. In first grade she brought home a "bad report card" and was beaten.

As a child, Debi starved and shriveled from the absence of love. The pain became so great that when she was just eight, she looked in a mirror one day and vowed, "Debi, when you grow up, I promise you, you *will be loved.*"

Martin Luther paused to readjust his hat—a new one purchased by students to replace the one he'd pitched into the river. The dirt path ended, and Martin veered to the right on his trek home. He was now on the main road, at the northeastern edge of Wittenberg.

In contrast to his somber mood, the village bustled with festive activity. Preparations were under way for All Saints' Day, less than 48 hours away. The shopkeepers would labor into the night, stocking shelves to accommodate visitors from the surrounding countryside. Workmen raised carnival tents in the town square, while bands of young people, excited by the upcoming celebration, scurried to and fro, unfazed by the darkness.

On every November 1, All Saints' Day commemorated the great saints of the past. Though many people used the holiday as just another excuse to get drunk, the occasion retained some religious flavor.

But dead saints were not in Martin's thoughts. The state of the living church was more on his mind.

For months, Martin had been framing a theological criticism against the Roman Church's practice of selling indulgences. An indulgence was something of a spiritual pardon; a sinner could purchase a reduction in punishment for sins that otherwise would retain the poor soul longer in purgatory—a place of punishment, the Roman Church taught, between earth and heaven. For a financial contribution, a sinner could buy down the sentence—for himself and others—in purgatory. Martin was repulsed by this practice, labeling it a blatant violation of Scripture's teaching. He had a daring plan to declare his opposition.

—

Debi was still young when the many men—young and old—drifting through her home took notice of her. With her father usually absent and no one else around to look out for her, Debi became the sexual prey of an older stepbrother. He stalked her, seeming to be waiting behind every closet door.

When Debi's mother left the house, the stepbrother was put in charge and turned predator. If Debi and her younger siblings did not give him what he wanted, he had ways of making them pay dearly. And if she dared tell her mother, Debi was beaten because Mom sided with the young man.

Broken physically and mentally by the guerrilla warfare in her own home, Debi became sick as a teenager. She would awaken in the night with chest pain and in minutes be paralyzed from head to toe. Trying to help her handle the stress, Debi's mother gave her some of her own tranquilizers—a mistake because Debi's small body could not handle the adult-strength medication. She became addicted.

At 17, Debi married, hoping that a man would rescue her from her family's storm. Because of prior abuse, Debi was unable to enjoy normal sexual relations with her husband. Her marriage failing, she went to a doctor for help. After examining Debi, he asked her if she had ever been raped. "No!" she said. To her, rape happened when strangers abducted and harmed you.

The doctor shook his head. He told her there was something drastically wrong inside her body. Emergency surgery was performed that day. When Debi awoke in the recovery room, the doctor leaned over her and said, "You were all torn apart on the inside. Are you sure you are okay? Is there something about your family you want to tell me?"

"No. Everything's fine," Debi said.

In her family, you were warned not to tell outsiders about what went on at home. The family's dirty secrets were safe with Debi.

—

Martin Luther knew the risks were enormous. Defying the Roman Church could cost him his professorship, since profits from the sale of indulgences helped finance the university where he worked. He also knew that the church had little patience for dissenters. Heretics and infidels were punished, sometimes by death.

Tormented by his fears and doubts, Luther plodded on, past the shops, past the tents, past the laughing children, through the bustling village of Wittenberg, now covered with a film of snow. At the edge of town, he ascended stairs to the second floor, pushed open the oak door of the small room, and kindled a fire to chase away the cold.

Martin sat near the flickering fire, praying for strength, but feeling only dread. Go through with this tomorrow, and his life would change forever. He glanced at the document lying on the table. *Throw it into the fire,* the voice of doubt whispered. Torn between self-preservation and righteous indignation, Martin reached for the parchment. *Maybe I'm just a fool,* he thought. *Am I the only one troubled by this affront to God?*

The monk read the words he had written—ideas prayed and agonized over for months. A spirit of resolve stirred his mind, and warmth spread through his breast. Yes, tomorrow he would do this, regardless of the cost.

Late into the night, Luther sat by his fire in tiny Wittenberg, no longer alone but blessed by the presence of almighty God. Torments fled, fear abated, strength returned. And long after midnight, assurance came.

—

It took months for Debi to recover from her surgery. Eventually, several years later, she did become pregnant. But by then the relationship with her husband had deteriorated into a separation.

Alone, broke, and expecting a baby, Debi at last made significant contact with her father. After spending some time in jail, he lived in Wisconsin. He offered Debi a place to stay, and with few options, she moved north and settled in with her dad.

After the birth of her baby, a girl named Carla, Debi and her husband briefly reunited. The reconciliation failed, though, and the couple divorced when Carla was 16 months old.

Debi drifted from one relationship to another. One of the men was an alcoholic—and a batterer. Little Carla often heard the screams and saw her mother's blackened eyes and swollen mouth. All of Debi's fingers were broken, and surgery was required twice to mend wounds. Her weight fell to 89 pounds.

She became pregnant again, but hating the thought that the child would have an abusive father, Debi aborted the baby during the fifth month.

Debi worked as a cocktail waitress at Captain Jack's West bar in Pewaukee. The bar life meant many free drinks, and Debi accepted her share. Alcohol became her best friend.

Now and then a man named Jim Godsey stopped at the bar and sat in a corner, draining beer after beer. Jim was laid-back, and in the barroom clamor, Debi didn't notice him. But Jim took note of Debi. Watching her from afar, and making mental notes on all the unsuccessful come-ons to Debi from other customers, he quietly fell in love with her.

But Debi was no more impressed with Jim than all the other men she met at the bar. He asked her out on dates, but she stood him up repeatedly. He persisted. Finally, hoping to get Jim to leave her alone, Debi agreed to a date—a party that turned into an all-night drug spree.

Jim drove them to the party in Debi's car. When he made a sudden stop, an object slid from under the seat and banged Jim's foot. Curious, Jim reached down and grabbed a small loaded handgun. It was Debi's. Because she had been hurt so many times, she always carried her own protection.

Debi's opinion of Jim didn't change. She tried to get rid of him by encouraging Jim to drink and dance with her friends at the bar. No deal—he had eyes only for her. Eventually, she gave in and let him move in with her.

When Jim showed up, Debi's daughter was three—a very worldly wise three. Carla, at times, was more stable than her 25-year-old mom. Night after night, the tiny daughter had held her mother as Debi cried herself to sleep. Since Carla had seen other men do bad things to her mom, she warned Jim, "If you ever hit my mom, I'll hit you back!"

One day, while Jim and Debi walked beside a railroad track, she asked, "Do you ever think of throwing yourself in front of a train?"

"No, I don't!" he answered, wondering what was going on in her head.

For Debi, suicide wasn't something shameful, but just the ultimate painkiller—another option for dealing with your problems.

With little shared love holding them together, Debi soon tired of Jim and kicked him out. She was not a one-man kind of woman. Having Jim around interfered with other options.

But Jim loved Debi. He continued to show up at Captain Jack's, sitting at a table in the back, watching Debi, and often breaking into tears as she rebuffed his affection.

Jim persisted and Debi let him move back in—only to kick him out again. The cycle continued for two years until Debi said, for no good reason, "Let's get married." She wasn't in love but thought maybe another marriage would heal her wounds.

After the honeymoon, Debi went back to her job at the bar, night after night fending off the men who were now hitting on a married woman. Jim sat in the corner, downing his beers, sulking over the pawing and clamoring Debi always created.

Their relationship grew ugly, filled with angry shouting matches. Debi slid deeper into her private hole—that dungeon she had built when just a child.

———

Hours passed in Martin Luther's spartan room. The fire faded. A mouse scurried across the hardwood floor. It paused momentarily, picking at stale crumbs under the table, then scampered along the wall before disappearing into the darkness. The rodent's tiny claws scratched the floor and roused Martin from his preoccupation.

"Tetzel, is that you?" inquired Luther, a note of glee in his voice. The joy of resolution had chased away his early evening gloom.

He rose from his chair, placed the document on the seat behind him, and laughed out loud. He tossed a log on the fire and rubbed his hands over the expanding flame. Dubbing his late-night visitor "Tetzel" had provided him with much merriment. But the name also made him angry. The similarities between Tetzel the mouse and Tetzel the priest were obvious: Both were shrewd thieves. Tetzel the mouse regularly invaded Luther's cupboard, stealing his food. Johann Tetzel the priest invaded the local parishes, stealing money from God's people.

An emissary for the pope, Tetzel marketed indulgences among the naive citizens of Germany. Forbidden to enter Saxony for political reasons, Tetzel hawked his wares just across the border. Members of Luther's parish (Martin was both a professor and a preacher) traveled regularly over the border to buy what they thought were spiritual favors from God.

A superb salesman, Tetzel even coined a jingle that was particularly offensive to Luther. When he entered a village with pomp and pageantry, Tetzel would cry out, "As soon as the coin in the coffer rings, the soul from purgatory springs!"

Martin tolerated the mouse, but he could not accept such an offensive Dominican priest.

Anger surged in Luther's veins. The night was now short. There were only a few more hours until daylight, not enough time to sleep. Martin walked to his bed, grabbed a blanket, and returned to the fire. He stretched the blanket over his solid frame, leaned back in his chair, and prayed that when the sun rose tomorrow, he would still have the courage to confront the darkness.

—

After two years of struggle, the Godseys decided in January of 1990 to get a divorce—no hard feelings, just end it.

The death of the marriage was more evidence for Debi that she was out of hope. She became serious about ending her life.

The court date for the divorce was set for June 1990. Early that month, Debi moved out. Happy to be rid of her, Jim hauled her belongings to the house of her new boyfriend. Debi was so unstable emotionally that she willingly left Carla with Jim, who had adopted Carla and would take custody of her after the divorce.

"If there is a God, then You need to show me who You are!"

The judge postponed the divorce date from June until July, then delayed it once more to October 29, 1990.

In August, Debi reached the end of her emotional rope. Before the breakup with Jim, she had thought he was the source of her pain. With him gone, she ached as never before. Although she had long ago given up on God, Debi murmured one day, "If there is a God, then You need to show me who You are!"

She waited . . . a day, a week, a month. No answer came from God. She set the date for her suicide—October 29, 1990, the same day her marriage to Jim would officially terminate.

She knew precisely how she would do it. Near her home was a busy two-lane highway. The night of October 29, she would drive her Honda Shadow motorcycle onto that road, accelerate to 85 miles per hour, then veer into the path of an 18-wheeler.

Quick, certain death.

The end of a lifetime of hurt.

Debi had forgotten her prayer to God. But He hadn't. An emissary of hope named Mark Jorgenson had been dispatched.

Mark was Jim Godsey's brother-in-law, married to Jim's sister Patty. The Jorgensons' marriage had nearly disintegrated, too, until they attended a FamilyLife Marriage Conference. God had intervened, and after seeing his own marriage and family rescued, Mark set out to help the Godseys. He decided they needed to attend the weekend conference.

First, Mark cornered Debi, taking her to lunch. After Mark explained the conference as a great place to get help with all relationships—sort of a self-improvement course—Debi showed interest.

"Jim will never go, though," she said, thinking that would get Mark off her back.

"Will you go if Jim says he'll go?" Mark asked.

"Yeah, I'll go if he goes," Debi said, but thinking, *Fat chance that will happen.*

Next, Mark paid a visit to Jim, taking him to a restaurant where he argued passionately with Jim for hours about the need to give the conference a try. Finally, with Jim so frustrated that he was ready to slug him, Mark played his final card: "Jim, if you agree to go to this conference, I will never say another word about this to you."

"Okay, I'll go to the conference!" Jim exclaimed.

The next day Jim and Debi met.

"Well?" Debi said.

"Well, what?" said Jim.

"Are we going to the stupid conference?"

"Yeah, we're going to the stupid conference!"

"Well, thanks a lot, you —," Debi said. She stormed out.

I can't believe I'm going to a marriage conference with that woman! Jim thought.

God works in mysterious ways, Jim.

—

On the morning of October 31, 1517, the sun burst through the single window of Martin Luther's flat in Wittenberg. Martin sat listlessly for a moment and then perched himself upright in his chair. A pool of sunlight warmed the wood floor. The doubts of the previous night had been disarmed by conviction.

Eager to act, Luther rose to his feet, stretched his arms, and rubbed the shaved portion of his head. He put on his coat and picked up the hammer and a nail lying by the fireplace.

As Martin glanced at the cold ashes, his mind raced with the new day's plans. He would take the document to the door of Castle Church in Wittenberg. The door not only kept the German winter out of the sanctuary, but also was used to disseminate information, serving as a forum for communication, dialogue, and debate—a medieval bulletin board. For his ideas to influence others, Luther knew he must post his document for all to read on that door.

Out his door and down the stairs he went, retracing his path from the previous evening. He strode briskly through the deserted streets. At the opposite end of town, Martin Luther mounted the steps of Castle Church. A few early morning worshipers glanced in his direction but said nothing.

Luther faced the massive door, cradling the document in his left hand. He reached into his pocket for the tools of revolution. Holding the parchment against the door with the nail, he raised the hammer and struck the rusty shaft. The nail penetrated paper and wood, the sharp "crack" echoing down the empty streets. Four more blows finished the job.

Relieved, and pleased with his obedience, Martin Luther turned and headed home.

The Reformation had begun.[1]

—

The marriage conference was scheduled for October 19-21—just a few days before Debi Godsey's divorce and planned suicide.

Friday afternoon, Jim and Debi drove to the conference hotel and checked in, making sure there were two beds in their room; it was not stacking up as a romantic getaway.

The conference began (I was one of the speakers) that evening, and one topic presented was "The Five Steps in the Death of a Marriage." As the other speaker, Stu Weber, listed the steps, Debi and Jim realized that their marriage had been through all five; it was already a corpse.

They left the meeting and went to their room. Jim wanted to talk. Although he agreed their marriage was a disaster, he speculated that if the speakers at the conference knew what killed a marriage, they must also know how to heal one.

Debi would not hear of it. "Don't you ever listen?" she said wearily. "We are beyond the death of a marriage. There's nothing left. Divorce is the right thing. Leave me alone." She crawled into her bed, and as she drifted off to sleep, she heard Jim crying.

When I first saw her, I thought, I'm looking into the eyes of a dead woman.

The next morning the Godseys showed up with the other 300 couples. Throughout the day they were told about God's purpose for marriage and His blueprint for building a relationship. They heard the gospel and learned how no one can have a God-honoring marriage without first knowing Jesus Christ.

Then, with heads bowed in prayer, the couples were asked to raise their hands if they wanted to commit themselves to Christ. Debi, hoping her husband wouldn't notice, timidly put her small hand in the air. Jim, not wanting his wife to know what he was doing, quietly lifted his hand.

Later in the afternoon, Debi approached me, wanting to talk. When I first saw her, I thought, *I'm looking into the eyes of a dead woman.* Debi told me that she wanted to commit her life to Christ, but then she explained the problems she was having with Jim. Since we had just finished a session on forgiveness, I talked to her both about her need to accept Christ and about her need to forgive her husband.

Debi left and, while riding the elevator to her room, decided on a plan. She would first ask Jim for forgiveness—even though she wouldn't mean it, of course. Then she would find me and have me help her commit her life to Christ. Having so neatly settled matters with God, she could kill herself a week later and avoid going to hell. The conference was a stroke of good luck. In her own contemporary way, Debi was looking for an indulgence.

Debi arrived at the room and Jim said, "I have something to ask you."

"No, I have something to ask you!" Debi said. The two began to fight like grade-schoolers. Finally, Debi blurted out, "Jim, I need to ask you to forgive me."

Jim walked across the room, gently grabbed Debi's shoulders, looked into her face, and said, "No, I'm supposed to ask you to forgive me."

Debi began to cry. She had never expected to hear words like these from anyone. For years, her life had resembled a dam with a small hole—in which she had plugged her finger. She thought that if ever she pulled that finger out, the small hole would become a crack, the crack a fissure, and the fissure would burst—destroying the dam and releasing a flood of water. Debi would drown.

In that hotel room, with her husband beside her, Debi Godsey eased her finger out of the hole, and the dam broke. She and Jim wept and talked for hours.

Around 11:00 P.M., their eyes red and cheeks puffy, Jim and Debi stopped, looked at each other, and laughed. They had forgotten about dinner, and room service was closed. Out they went to find food, stopping at one of the few places open—a bar. They ordered sandwiches, and the bartender added a touch of romance by placing a candle on their table.

Back in their room, Jim went to sleep. Debi, though, lay in bed, sleepless, staring at the ceiling. Her spirit tingling, the night suspended in time, for hours she gazed beyond the confines of a hotel room, and through her imagination, she looked into the sky, marveling at the stars, the moon, an entire creation on display just for her.

She whispered, "How come I never saw Him before? He's seeing me. I'm noticing Him. I think He likes me! Check this out . . . I'm talking to the God of the universe!"[2]

A Family Reformation had begun.

CHAPTER TWO

Do You Feel the Heat?

*I think our country sinks beneath the yoke;
it weeps, it bleeds; and each new day a gash
is added to her wounds.*
—MALCOLM IN WILLIAM SHAKESPEARE'S MACBETH

A renegade monk from the 1500s attempting to redirect his beloved church.

A modern-day couple attempting to break free from the clutches of drugs and despair.

Your family and mine—living in an out-of-control world.

Sometimes God uses one person's life to begin the process of changing the world. I would like to speak to you—heart-to-heart—about that process.

I have no idea what your circumstances are in life—whether you picked up this book as a pastor who seeks help, as a layman or lay-woman who yearns for your marriage and family to be godly, or as one who is broken, looking for hope in the midst of another day's chaos.

Perhaps you need a God-sized miracle. Or a new vision for your life. What can be learned from the lives of Martin Luther and Debi and Jim Godsey? What themes link them together? Let me suggest three:

First, *all faced hopeless situations.* From a human perspective, each had reason to despair.

In the sixteenth century, the Catholic church had no rival or equal in power and influence. Who was Martin Luther anyway? Just a man, living in a nondescript village in Germany, far away from the power center in Rome. Why would anyone heed his novel interpretations of Holy Scripture?

As for Debi and Jim Godsey, what better word to describe their situation than *hopeless?* They were dealt a cruel hand by dysfunctional families and surrounded by a council of fools, and their own choices compounded their miseries. Who would have given this desperate couple a chance? Flawed and bitter, they were about to become a divorce statistic. Again.

The most important battle being fought today is for the soul of America.

Second, *this unlikely trio is united by their bedrock courage.* God invaded their souls and gave them a holy grit. Turning from the lies of their age, each discovered and embraced the truth of God's Word. Instead of playing it safe, they chose to seize the truth.

Finally, *their courageous stand helped others also embrace God's truth and follow Him.*

Luther's posting of his 95 Theses on a church door sparked a fire of reformation that not only inflamed hearts, but also altered the history of nations.

The Godseys' decision to surrender their lives to Christ ignited a fire of love in the ashes of their marriage, a fire that would soon spread to their daughter, to their friends, and to needy families in urban Milwaukee.

Martin Luther and Debi and Jim Godsey decided to take God at His Word and stop drifting with the flow of their culture. They did not see themselves as special. But they were willing to believe that God could make a difference in their lives and, eventually, in their world. (I'll be telling more of the Luther and Godsey stories throughout this book.)

With all of my heart, I believe God longs to make a difference in our lives and our world. And just as the church and world needed a reformation in the sixteenth century, I believe our culture desperately needs a reformation today. The most important battle being fought today is for the soul of America. And the battle for the soul of our nation begins at home. That's why we urgently need a Family Reformation, *one home at a time.*

Concerning America, Billy Graham recently said, "The greatest nation in history stands on the brink of self-destruction."[1]

William Bennett, the secretary of education during the Reagan Administration, wrote:

> America now finds itself at or near the top of the industrialized world in rates of murder, rape, drug use, divorce, abortion, child abuse, and births to unwed mothers. Our elementary- and secondary-education system often places us at the bottom of the industrialized world. Much of our popular culture is vulgar, violent, mindless, and perverse. Many of our character-forming institutions are enfeebled. . . . Large segments of America are characterized by moral confusion, indolence, indifference, distraction, self-pity, self-absorption.[2]

A national magazine surveyed its readers concerning our nation's moral and social decline. More than 1,000 people responded. Summing up the results, the editor wrote: "Perhaps the most alarming result of our unscientific survey is that not one person disputed the premise that American society is decaying. What also comes across is a real sense of urgency about the need to get things back on track." One reader added, "We're over the edge and slipping fast into chaos."[3]

Our country is in trouble. Yes, the United States is a world power, and even with our problems, we are one of the greatest nations in history. God has blessed this land, and I would not want my home address anywhere else. But above my loyalty to country is my loyalty to the King.

The God of the ages says much in Scripture about what will

happen when individuals and nations ignore His ways. As a nation, we are ignoring God's ways. And if we choose not to change our ways, this nation will face the consequences. God will not abandon His people, but life as we have known it will disintegrate, and we'll have a cultural blowup.

THE DANGER OF A BLOWUP

To a firefighter, one of the most terrible words in the English language is *blowup*. A blowup is a very uncommon, but lethal, occurrence in forest fires.

While scientists don't fully understand the dynamics of this strange phenomenon, they do know that it occurs when an explosive fuel source combines with two deadly counterparts: fire and oxygen. This combination of earth, wind, and fire can suddenly transform a manageable forest fire into an inferno that rages through trees at up to 30 miles per hour, faster than an Olympic champion sprinter like Michael Johnson can run.

We know little about blowups, because few firefighters trapped in them have lived to tell the story. One rare survivor described a blowup as "a terrific draft of superheated air of tremendous velocity [that] swept up the hill exploding all inflammable material, causing a wall of flame six hundred feet high. . . . This wall covered three thousand acres in ten minutes or less."[4]

As you can imagine, a firefighter in the path of a blowup quickly becomes a traveler on the way to eternity.

To me, blowup is an appropriate description of what is happening to American society. At some point in the last decade, elements combined into a lethal fireball of destruction that now engulfs all of our institutions, including the most precious structure of all—the family.

In the midst of this cataclysmic inferno, what once was a manageable experience—a mom and a dad raising their kids—became an ordeal. A matter of life and death. After consuming the arts, media, and other segments of the broader culture, the blowup now rages down Main Street. No longer do we just read about "the fire" in the newspaper. Now it's in our neighborhoods.

You see the sky red with flames when . . .

- Your child is invited to a slumber party with a friend whose family you don't know, and you wonder about that family's values and if your child will be safe.
- You pull up at a stoplight, glance at the driver in the car next to you, and wonder, *Does he have a gun?*
- You watch television sitcoms and see the traditional family ignored, mocked, and ridiculed.

You hear the fire's crackle when . . .

- You pick up the local newspaper and read about another young girl who was raped, abducted, molested, or murdered.
- You are single and it seems not another person on the planet shares your values and wants to have a God-centered marriage.
- You are deciding where to send your child to school and find yourself thinking more about safety than academics.

You smell smoke when . . .

- You attend your high school reunion and learn how few of your classmates are still married to their first spouse.
- You see story after story about homosexual couples bearing and raising kids.
- Your son falls in love with a young woman, and you know the home she was raised in was far from ideal.

You feel the heat when . . .

- You are in a blended marriage, and your ex-spouse is undermining your discipline with the children.
- You miss another of your child's soccer games, because your supervisor asks you to spend another Saturday working on the big project.
- Your daughter marries, then you find out the guy who was Prince Charming is an alcoholic who beats her up and has run up credit card bills of $20,000.

The inferno rages on all sides. We're all feeling the heat. As America moves into the third millennium, the charred victims of a cultural blowup litter the landscape. I've met thousands of them while conducting seminars and speaking to hundreds of groups on marriage and family issues for the past 25 years. The epicenter of all this pain is the American family.

In 1996, for example, I addressed more than 700 college students at a conference in Dallas, Texas. At the beginning of my message, I asked everyone who had been affected by divorce—through the immediate or extended family—to stand. Approximately *80 percent* of the young men and women rose to their feet.

There they stood, the next generation of husbands and wives and moms and dads, a generation scarred by divorce. It was eerie. My soul filled with sadness—for what could and should have been experienced in their families.

After my message, a tall young man spoke to me. His handsome face marred by pain and confusion, he told me about his parents' divorce just two weeks before Christmas. His father was a leading pastor in an evangelical denomination.

"Dennis, my dad was my hero," he said. "He taught me everything I know. And now he's gone. I'm the only one left in my family who is still walking with God."

With his family background, this young man should have felt confidence and hope. Instead, his voice quaked with fear as he asked, "What can I do?" His family had been obliterated. He was homeless.

Other young men and women stood in line that day to tell their stories of abuse, desertion, dysfunction, and divorce. They shared openly about their dreams for intimacy in marriage and their desire for a happy family. But they were scared. Really scared. Wanting desperately to move beyond their fear, anger, and hopelessness, they had no assurance that more family pain would not blight their future.

Their faces haunt me.

The young are supposed to be the eager idealists, the next generation of visionaries gazing expectantly at the future. But it is not so. Instead, many young people are seared and scarred by the heat of a cultural blowup, paralyzed by their wounds.

Our culture—the church included—is full of people like this. The heartache is pervasive. We all feel the heat.

LEADING SPIRITUAL INDICATORS

How did we get to where we are today? How did the American family become a triage unit, filled with shattered and disfigured patients?

In 1993, William Bennett developed what he called The Index of Leading Cultural Indicators. Bennett's study traced the decline of American society by showing the correlation between rising rates of social problems—such as crime, out-of-wedlock births, abortion, divorce, child abuse, teenage suicide—and cultural decline.

Without question all of these social issues are symptoms of serious societal decay, and we need to respond to them intelligently and forcefully. But when I analyzed Bennett's indicators, I concluded that more serious, underlying spiritual issues lay beneath these distressing indicators.

To answer my own question—"Just what in the world is happening in this country?"—I created an index of my own that I called Leading Spiritual Indicators. I believe the withering of these core values has kindled the cultural blowup that now chokes, smothers, and incinerates the family and consumes our culture.

These six indicators are not surface issues. They represent the real reason, the root cause, that explains why our culture has no conscience and few convictions, and finds itself perilously close to disaster.[5]

Spiritual Indicator #1: We Have Lost Our Fear of God

"The fear of the Lord is the beginning of knowledge; fools despise wisdom and instruction" (Proverbs 1:7).

At the core of our moral meltdown is a society that does not fear God. As a people we have rejected the rules because we have lost our respect for the Ruler.

The fear of God is reverential awe and respect for Him. It is a heartfelt conviction that He is not only loving and personal, but holy and just as well. It is the awareness that God sees and knows everything I think, feel, and do. When I fear God, He becomes preeminent in my life.

As the proverb says, "The fear of the Lord is the beginning of knowledge." The fear of God is the basis for all authority and accountability. If there is no God, who has authority to establish absolute standards, and to whom am I ultimately accountable? And if I am accountable to no one then I can do as I please. Why keep my promises? Why fulfill my vows? Why carry out my responsibilities?

But in much of our culture God is ridiculed and not even recognized, much less held in reverential awe. Can it be said that a nation fears God when it declares that it is illegal to post the Ten Commandments in the Cobb County Courthouse in Atlanta, Georgia? Can a nation that refuses to protect a helpless unborn baby from the selfish whim of a pregnant woman and the knife of an abortionist be known as a nation that fears God and His judgment?

Can it be said that our nation fears God when its constitutional rights have been elevated above the authority of God and His Word? Under the guise of free speech, our nation has allowed the arts and the media to desecrate Christ, mock moral goodness, and promote perversion.

Imagine for a moment that our nation was about to be born—today. Can you imagine the national outrage that would be expressed if someone on the founding committee suggested that "In God We Trust" be stamped on every coin and bill for the new country?

Regardless of how closely the religious beliefs and practices of the founding fathers parallel our own (many were ardent believers; others were not), it is evident that respect for God and the truth of Scripture were the cornerstones supporting the country's foundation.

Listen to the perspective of our nation's second president, John Adams: "Our Constitution was meant for a moral and a religious people. It is wholly inadequate for the governance of any other."[6]

All of our nation's institutions—public and private—were permeated with a biblical perspective of life—what's right, what's wrong; how you treat others; the value of each person; and on and on. Our nation's first universities and colleges, now some of our most prestigious schools, such as Princeton and Harvard, assumed that Christian theology was *the* core subject—"the queen of the sciences."

So much of this has changed. Now, many faculty members at these same universities—without concern for consequences—ridicule faith in God and dismiss the study of theology as irrelevant.

Will and Ariel Durant wrote, "There is no significant example in history, before our time, of a society successfully maintaining moral life without the aid of religion."[7]

It's not surprising there's no fear of God in society, because even in the Christian community we are strangely silent on the subject. There is little teaching on His judgment of sin, His wrath, or His anger. We haven't rejected God, but we have conveniently reduced and re-created Him to our specifications. A. W. Tozer summarized our predicament when he observed that "this low view of God entertained almost universally among Christians is the cause of a hundred lesser evils everywhere among us."

Once I was listening to a highly respected Christian radio station. I found it troubling that the station had sold a 30-minute spot to a secular author to hawk her books, videos, and tapes. Not once did she refer to the Scriptures. But she did refer to God—in vain, a half dozen times in fewer than 10 minutes. And that was on a Christian station! However troubling that was to me, I was unprepared for the response from the station manager when I called him a couple of days later. He told me I was the *only person* who had called and objected.

Do we even discern what is offensive to God? Are our consciences numbed and seared by compromises? Or do we in the Christian community *respect God enough to confront sin?*

The unchanging God of history does notice our sin. He will deal with it. He is the God to be feared.

Spiritual Indicator #2: We Have Abandoned Absolute Truth

"If you abide in My word, then you are truly disciples of Mine; and you shall know the truth, and the truth shall make you free" (John 8:31-32).

As part of the campaign to introduce the new Windows 95 software in August 1995, the Microsoft Corporation ran a two-page advertisement of two children running with a kite. Smiling, the girl and boy romped across a deep green field with no fences. Emblazoned on those pages were two words that promised what every human being has desired since Adam and Eve: No Limits.

That advertisement could serve as a metaphor for modern America. It captures brilliantly the lie of our age: "You can be free, living a life with no fences. Why submit to the old boundaries? You are in charge of your destiny. The only rule you need to know is that there are no rules."

An editor at *USA Today* magazine wrote, "Probably the greatest loss of respect in our time is that for truth itself. The absolute has become relative, and the relative has become absolute. Supposedly, there are no facts in history, only interpretations. Truth has become opinion and, in these egalitarian times, one opinion is as good as another—at least in academe."[8]

Augustine wrote, "When regard for the truth has broken down—all things become doubtful."

Tolerance has become the supreme national virtue. According to this philosophy, everyone is free to decide what is moral and true. Josh McDowell declared, "Tolerance has arisen as the sole virtue of Western culture, and intolerance the sole vice. Tolerance is extolled as the new measure of morality. It has become synonymous with goodness and open-mindedness; intolerance has come to connote bigotry."[9]

With such an inane philosophy, how can a society possibly determine what is right or wrong? And woe to the Christian who might dare to declare that Christ alone is "the way, and the truth, and the life" (John 14:6). How narrow-minded and intolerant!

A revealing way to check the moral pulse of a nation is to examine its media. For example, in the last decade we have seen a steady disintegration of standards on network television programming. As Steven Bochco, cocreator of *NYPD Blue* and *Hill Street Blues,* said, "There's no such thing as broadcast standards today. It's really what you can get away with. Then it becomes a standard."[10]

As hard as it is to believe, as recently as 1970 it was considered too controversial to have a divorced man as the main character in a weekly comedy.[11]

Just how opposed to the biblical standard of sex only in marriage are TV shows in the 1990s? Scenes of premarital sex now outnumber incidents of sex within marriage eight to one.[12]

Immersed in a godless culture that has no ultimate reference points, we become indifferent, and few things really shock us anymore. When actor Hugh Grant was arrested for indecent exposure, most Americans were astonished—not by the act itself, but because he already had an attractive live-in girlfriend. Was anyone shocked that Grant was living with his girlfriend? Of course not! In our "anything goes" culture, fornication has become the norm.

The esteemed social commentator and author Michael Novak observed, "The intellectual/political class in this country has for some decades been falling into moral disorientation. The two concepts fundamental to the American system, *truth* and *liberty,* have been corrupted. If one cannot oppose power with truth, only power is left."[13]

Is it any wonder that our moral slide is greased by our rejection of absolute truth and the one true God who established it? Near the bottom of this slippery slope we find a nation without a national conscience, which has spawned a generation with few convictions and a soul stricken with moral poverty.

Spiritual Indicator #3: We Accept Divorce

"'For I hate divorce,' says the Lord, the God of Israel" (Malachi 2:16).

A recent headline in our local newspaper brought instant perspective: "Bejing, China Divorce Rate Soars to One Percent." The story told of how troubling it is to the Chinese that *so many* of their marriages are breaking up! And concerned they should be.

When I was a boy in grade school back in the mid-1950s, only one of my classmates had parents who divorced. Just one. Although my friend's father was successful in business, he lost the respect of the community because he failed to keep his commitment to his wife and children.

The U.S. Census Bureau gives us a chilling historical backdrop to what has become a national epidemic.

In 1900, 1 divorce for every 10 marriages.
In 1920, 1 divorce for every 7 marriages.
In 1940, 1 divorce for every 6 marriages
In 1960, 1 divorce for every 4 marriages.
In 1972, 1 divorce for every 3 marriages.
In 1976, 1 divorce for every 2 marriages.[14]

A Chinese proverb says, "In the broken nest there are no whole eggs." What a provocative summary of the negative impact of divorce.

I am thankful that some voices in our culture are beginning to agree. For example, the Council on Families in America—made up of some of America's most prestigious citizens from a variety of disciplines—issued a landmark report "Marriage in America" in 1995. The opening lines of the report's executive summary read: "The divorce revolution—the steady displacement of a marriage culture by a culture of divorce and unwed parenthood—has failed. It has created terrible hardships for children, incurred insupportable social costs, and failed to deliver on its promise of greater adult happiness."[15]

Divorce is destroying our children, our churches, and our culture. We have become a culture of divorce. The national media have begun to speak out in various articles about the need for commitment in marriage. But there is an awkward silence concerning the social consequences of divorce. Even the church is hesitant to confront this issue.

Why the silence? Perhaps because most of us know people who are divorced: They are our friends, our family members, our associates, our brothers and sisters in Christ. We don't wish to condemn them.

Perhaps our motives are right. But unfortunately, our reluctance to speak out against divorce has unwittingly created a moral climate that not only *accepts* divorce, but *expects* it as well. One study revealed that when a friend gets married, 64 percent of those surveyed expect the marriage to end in divorce. Only 31 percent expect it to last forever.[16]

Harvard historian and sociologist Pitirim Sorokin watched with horror as the divorce rate escalated during his lifetime. He was deeply disturbed by the destruction of the family unit: "An illiterate society can survive, but a thoroughly anti-social society cannot. Until recently, the family was the principal school of socialization for the newborn human animals rendering them fit for social life. At present this vital mission is performed less and less by the family."[17] He wrote that in 1948! What would Sorokin say if he were alive today?

Spiritual Indicator #4:
We Have Lost the Clear Distinctives in Male and Female Roles

"And God created man in His own image, in the image of God He created him; male and female He created them" (Genesis 1:27).

Over the last three decades, the lines between manhood and womanhood have grown more opaque and convoluted. This gender blending has resulted in fewer and fewer people recognizing the unique roles of men and women and increasing social confusion. John Piper details the consequences:

> The tendency today is to stress the equality of men and women by minimizing the unique significance of our maleness and femaleness. But this depreciation of male and female personhood is a great loss. It is taking a tremendous toll on generations of young men and women who do not know what it means to be a man or a woman. . . . The consequence [of this confusion] . . . is more divorce, more homosexuality, more sexual abuse, more promiscuity, more social awkwardness, and more emotional distress and suicide that come with the loss of God-given identity.[18]

The radical feminist movement, which was birthed in the '60s, nurtured in the '70s, and matured to adulthood in the '80s, completely redrew the lines and blurred the distinction between masculinity and femininity. If you go to any high school or college classroom today and ask women, "What is your primary goal in life?" very few will respond by saying, "To be a wife and a mother."

It's even becoming unusual for younger girls to express a wish to grow up to be a mom. I wish there were more like seven-year-old Kayla Schatzman, the daughter of a coworker, who wrote for a Brownie project: "When I grow up, I'd like to be a mother and help my children do what is right. . . . I hope by the time it comes to being a mother that I have learned the right thing to do. I hope that I'm a wonderful mother just like my mother."

Unfortunately, this important role, which is critical to social stability, for many women has become passé.

At the same time, the radical homosexual movement is steadily succeeding in its primary goal—to convince Americans that homosexuality is common and healthy. In any given week, you'll find this philosophy continually promoted in newspapers, magazines, television shows, and movies. A growing number of youth are experimenting with bisexuality in order to determine their sexual identity.

Case in point: The November 4, 1996, issue of *Newsweek* ran a cover photo of two women snuggled up. The headline read, "We're Having a BABY." The copy line asked, "Can Gay Families Gain Acceptance?"

Would you have imagined that a major newsmagazine would dare to cover such a story—much less put it on the cover—even 10 years ago? How far we have slid down the slippery slope.

Spiritual Indicator #5: We Abandon Our Children

"Behold, children are a gift of the Lord; the fruit of the womb is a reward" (Psalm 127:3).

No other parents in the industrialized world spend *less* time with their children than American fathers and mothers. According to the *Wall Street Journal,* American parents spend, on average, "less than fifteen minutes a week in serious discussion with their children."[19]

This lack of involvement is hastened by rising divorce rates, out-of-wedlock births, and working mothers. Parental abandonment—and most notably, fatherlessness—tears like a fault line at American culture. "Studies of young criminals have found," reports *Time* magazine, "that more than 70 percent of all juveniles in state reform institutions come from fatherless homes."[20] Says David Murray, "Neighborhoods without fathers . . . are seedbeds for predators. Without a female *and* a male who consider themselves responsible for children, the stable features of social continuity are not constructed."[21]

But the problem runs deeper than that. Even in many stable homes, parents are neglecting their children by failing to provide the moral and spiritual guidance they need.

A recent report from the Carnegie Council on Adolescent Development sounded an alarm about parents who—through ignorance, selfishness, or fear—fail to remain involved in the lives of their children after they reach early adolescence:

> Barely out of childhood, young people ages ten to fourteen are today experiencing more freedom, autonomy, and choice

than ever at a time when they still need special nurturing, protection, and guidance. Without the sustained involvement of parents and other adults in safeguarding their welfare, young adolescents are at risk of harming themselves and others. . . . Many reach adulthood ill-equipped to participate responsibly in our democratic society.[22]

Writer James Lincoln Collier holds that America's abandonment of parental responsibility is "unmatched in human history."[23] We can't abandon one generation of children without altering the social, moral, and spiritual landscape of the *next* generation. But this is precisely what we've been doing for 30 years.

At a time when the Christian community should be calling parents to renewed spiritual, emotional, and moral involvement, too often there is silence. It's no wonder the culture invests so little in the next generation when we in the spiritual community are afraid to speak up and lead out because of private compromise in our own families.

Spiritual Indicator #6: We Feel Powerless to Effect Change

"I can do all things through Him who strengthens me" (Philippians 4:13).

Of all the spiritual indicators, this one is the most subjective and the most subtle. But how else to explain our retreat from the battlefield?

Far too many people feel impotent to make a difference in their own homes, much less in their communities. The battlefront is so vast and the problems are so overwhelming that many have resolved that redeeming our nation is impossible.

National polls consistently show that Americans are pessimistic about our country's future, and I believe this pessimism leads to a feeling of powerlessness. Most of us believe there is too much sex and violence in today's movies and television shows, but few of us contact our local theaters and stations to object to specific films or shows. We feel some in government are corrupt, but rather than vote out corrupt politicians, we don't even exercise our right to vote.

This pessimism is tragic for Christians, for it betrays a lack of faith in the power of God. Christians who are controlled by unbelief will never see God work in and through their lives. Unbelief caused nearly an entire generation of Israelites to perish in the wilderness.

Unbelief begins with dangerous assumptions; it concludes that the problem is too big for God, that God doesn't want to act on our behalf, and that we might as well eat, drink, and be merry, for tomorrow we die. Unbelief is the parent of a mundane, business-as-usual Christian life that knows little of the supernatural workings of God.

—

These six Leading Spiritual Indicators clearly describe our root problems. Like me, you may be deeply troubled by the fireball of destruction sweeping across our land. And in reflective moments you may ask yourself, *Is there really any hope for my family? Can I do anything to escape the blowup and possibly even save others in the process? Is there a solution?*

I believe there is, and our hope is closer to home than we might want to admit. Too long as a society we have hoped that a super-tanker from Washington would fly over and extinguish the inferno. What folly! Since 1965, the federal government has spent $5 *trillion* on social programs, and things are worse, not better. As Senator Phil Gramm has noted, "If social spending stopped crime, America would be the safest country in the world."[24]

Government is not the answer. If somehow we could make every politician, judge, and leader in Washington, D.C., a Christian (which would be wonderful), it would not eliminate the need for individual spiritual reformation in your life and mine. *I want you to read that last sentence again.*

No, the answer is not "out there"; it's "in here"—with *us*. If you and I will submit ourselves, our marriages, and our children to the Holy Scriptures and the Lord Jesus Christ, then we can take the first step toward beginning a Family Reformation! The gospel is still the most profound, effective solution to humankind's ills (see Romans 1:16).

If you feel threatened by the blaze consuming today's culture, it's time to start a fire of your own.

FIGHTING FIRE WITH FIRE

On August 5, 1949, a fire ignited in a remote forest in the Montana wilderness. A crew of 15 young firefighters parachuted into the area, ready to extinguish what looked like a manageable fire.

No one anticipated a blowup.

Strung out in a line, the firefighters climbed the south side of Mann Gulch. The blaze was above them on the hillside. Traversing the slope, which was densely covered with Douglas fir and ponderosa pine, they moved closer to the fire line. But the foreman, Wag Dodge, didn't like the angle. And something about the look of the fire bothered him. Dodge instructed his men to retreat and cross the gulch on the north side.

The terrain on the north side of Mann Gulch was different. Dense stands of timber gave way to waist-high fields of "bunch" grass and "cheat" grass. Fire moves slowly through timber, but it races through open fields.

With Dodge leading the way, the crew finished the traverse of the north slope and stopped for a breather. As they gazed across the gulch at the fire, which now looked less manageable, the flames jumped to their side of the gulch and began licking through the grass. Later, one of the smoke jumpers reported, "Below in the bottom of the gulch was a great roar without visible flames but blown with winds on fire."[25]

A blowup.

In panic, the men broke for the ridge above them. The 76-degree angle of the slope made escape all but impossible. Howling, spitting, and convulsing behind them, the fire beast lapped at their heels, the intense heat melting their lungs. One by one, the inferno consumed its victims.

Only three of 15 men lived. Miraculously, two of them beat the fire to the top of the ridge. More amazing, however, is how Wag Dodge survived.

Unlike the others, Dodge realized early that escape on foot was impossible. So with the fire dragon roaring toward him, Dodge did the unthinkable: He bent down on one knee, struck a match, and ignited a fire that, pushed by the wind, burned quickly up the hill. The foreman then stepped into the hot ashes of his own fire and found refuge. He waved for his crew to join him, but no one did.

Quickly passing over Dodge, the firestorm looked hungrily for combustible fodder elsewhere.

The two other survivors both testified that "the whole crew would probably have survived if they had understood and followed Dodge's instructions."[26]

There is a great lesson for us here: *To escape the fire, you must ignite a fire.*

A fire for Christ. You can't outrun a blowup. You must understand that flight from our cultural inferno is impossible; safety for you and your family lies only in the flames of divine truth. The prophet Jeremiah knew this. He wrote, "'Is not My word like fire?' declares the Lord" (Jeremiah 23:29).

Like Wag Dodge, you and I must kneel in humility, strike a match, and burn a piece of ground. We must ignite the fire of biblical truth in our *hearts,* our *marriages,* our *homes,* and our *communities.* This act of courage will nullify the cultural blowup by denying a fuel source. We will create a place of refuge amid the destructive fires of life.

To escape the fire, you must ignite a fire.

This book is intended to provide some fuel for your fire for Christ. My goals in writing are straightforward: First, I want to help you build a distinctly Christian marriage and family. Second, I wish to encourage you—to instill *courage in you* for the journey. And finally, I desire to cast a vision of how we in the Christian community can lock arms and labor together to reform and rebuild the family—to the glory of God!

The only true reformers in our day will be common men and women with the uncommon courage of Martin Luther and Debi and Jim Godsey—dads and moms, singles and single parents—who will ignite the fire of personal reformation, regardless of the cost. The battle must be fought up close, heart by heart, marriage by marriage, home by home, community by community.

The time for waiting is past. You have two choices: You can flee for the ridge, or you can light a fire.

What will you do?

A Reformation Moment

THE RIDE HOME

Still stunned by the events of the previous night, on
Sunday morning, October 21, 1990, Debi and Jim Godsey set
out from their hotel room to finish the marriage conference.

While riding the elevator, Debi in her thoughts asked,
*Well, God, where were You for 33 years? Why did I have to
go to hell and back so many times?*

In her heart, she heard God whisper back, *Because I
have a job for you to do.*

Debi thought, *Wow! This is weird.*

The morning session of the conference began with the husbands and wives divided into separate groups. The women's topic was a wife's role and responsibility in marriage. Debi's enthusiasm waned: "I thought on the other side of the curtain they were telling those guys that now they could tell us what to do. Jim would think he could start lording it over me." But Debi remembered her dramatic, loving encounter with the Lord the night before and reasoned, *Well, maybe I need to give this submission thing a shot.*

The conference ended in midafternoon, and Jim and Debi loaded the car and left the hotel. A topic emphasized at the conference had been "husbands and wives should pray together," so they agreed to give it a try.

Jim blurted, "Okay, God, You've got eight days to show us this marriage can work."

Debi nodded in agreement. Their divorce court date was just over a week away.

As the miles ticked by, Debi remained quiet. Based on past experience, Jim assumed she was angry and expected her to blow up at any moment.

What have I done wrong now? he wondered. Finally, the silence was driving him crazy. "Deb, what's going on? Are you okay?"

Debi looked out her window and did not speak.

Oh, boy, look out! Jim thought.

Several more miles passed. Debi was never this quiet. The suspense was so thick that Jim said, "Deb, you've got to say something. What's going on?"

In a calm voice, carefully choosing her words, Debi finally spoke, "I'm waiting for you to tell me what to do."

"What?" Jim said, nearly running off the road. "Give me a break! You've never listened to a man in your life. What makes you think you're going to start now? No way!"

"No, really, try me," Debi said. "Give me an order. See if I can obey it."

Fighting his skepticism, Jim considered what he might say. He settled on an idea he was sure she would angrily reject.

"Okay . . . move out from your boyfriend's house and move back in with Carla and me."

Debi didn't speak.

Another mile rolled by.

Then she replied simply, "Yes."

CHAPTER THREE

One Family at a Time

*Whatever else may be said about the home, it is the bottom line of life,
the anvil upon which attitudes and convictions are hammered out. It is
the place where life's bills come due, the single most influential force in
our earthly existence. . . . It is at home, among family members, that we
come to terms with circumstances. It is here life makes up its mind.*
—CHARLES SWINDOLL

A few years ago, a friend and I were invited to city hall in Dallas, Texas, to receive awards for our work in the area of marriage and family. The building was being remodeled, and as we walked into the lobby, it became evident we would not find the room without directions.

We spotted a custodian and asked him for help. Immediately, I knew we had asked the wrong person. The man paused and shook his head. He then pointed across a mass of construction debris to a hallway across the lobby. Looking confused, he declared, "But you can't get there from here."

Later, after we found our room, my friend said to me, "You know, I almost asked that custodian, 'Well, if we can't get there from *here,* is there a place we can go so we can get there from *there?'*"

Every time I recall our encounter with the custodian, I smile.

But there is nothing cute or amusing about America's moral and family dilemma. We know the problems to solve, evils to eliminate. Our objective is clear.

But we don't seem to know how to get there from here.

Since the early 1970s, I've watched our society decay from the inside out. For a few years, I thought that deliverance was *out there:* We needed to reform Hollywood, clean up television, elect politicians with a certain ideology, and change laws. These actions are *absolutely essential,* but we must take a far more important step.

I am convinced, as never before, that reformation must begin— can *only* begin—with individuals. With me. With you.

John Adams, our second president, made the following observation: "No matter how heedless, insensate, materialistic, selfish, unjust, and greedy a society may be, if there can be found in it a few clear and powerful voices that speak out unafraid against its corruptions, the spirit and the hope of reform can persist."[1]

When enough Christians kneel on the ground, strike a spiritual match, and light a fire for Christ, then—and only then—will real reform begin in America. The fire ablaze in our culture will lose its carnal fuel; decency and morality will return to our land.

The real problem is this: We are trying to reform society without reforming ourselves.

The spiritual reformation of America needs a focal point, a rallying cry. I believe that focal point is the family. The pivotal national issue today is not crime; neither is it welfare, health care, education, politics, the economy, the media, or the environment. *The* issue today is the *spiritual and moral condition of individual families.*

When Jim and Debi Godsey heard about God's blueprint for marriage, that truth—and the God of truth—began to change their personal lives, their marriage, and their family. They chose to believe that God offered hope. They applied His Word by forgiving each other and by asking Christ to heal their relationship.

If a spiritual reformation does not occur at the grassroots level— in individual homes like the Godseys'—then the outcome of the battle for our families and our culture is in serious jeopardy.

WHEN THE STITCHES FRAY

Each family in America is an irreplaceable stitch in the fabric of social order. When one stitch frays, the fabric is weakened. When several stitches fray, the fabric tears: And when most of the stitches fray, the fabric disintegrates.

Even people outside the Christian faith recognize the importance of the family. Consider what the Chinese philosopher Confucius said: "The world is at war because its constituent states are improperly governed; these are improperly governed because no amount of legislation can take the place of the natural social order provided by the family."[2]

The sound of stitches fraying is heard every day: An anguished wife discovers her husband's adultery; a teenage girl looking for love gets pregnant; another father leaves home.

Many of these rips are muffled—not even worth a sound bite on your local evening news. Other rips sound more like screams—big news of family heartache.

- Two physicians, formerly married, appear in court because the husband refuses to send child support. The judge warns the man that unless he obeys the court order, he will be sent to jail. "You can send me to jail," the ex-husband replies defiantly, "but I will not pay!" As the man she once loved is taken into custody, the woman weeps. "What have I done?" she asks. "This is the father of my children. What will I tell them at dinner?"[3]
- In Butte, Montana, 11-year-old Jeremy Bullock is standing in line outside his elementary school. Another fourth-grade boy walks up and fires a .22 semi-automatic pistol three times. Two bullets miss. The third strikes Jeremy behind the ear; he is dead before he hits the ground. Later, the 10-year-old killer sits in the principal's office, no hint of remorse on his face of stone. He does utter three revealing words about his life and family: "Nobody loves me."[4]
- Construction workers discover a man hanging by his neck in a grove of oak trees. When a police officer arrives, he sees an older man, half-running and half-stumbling toward the trees. His face disfigured by anguish, the man asks, "Is it Mark? Is it my son? Where is he? Where's my son?" The officer can't allow the man to

see his son, so he lets the father talk. He says that Mark left home the night before and never returned. The father admits they never did get along well, then looks the officer in the eye and says, "I guess we never did have a very good family life."[5]

Do you hear the fabric tearing in those voices of despair?

"What have I done? This is the father of my children. What will I tell them?"

"Nobody loves me."

"I guess we never did have a very good family life."

These are the sounds of America's tattered families, firsthand witnesses to the rapid decline and relentless disintegration of our culture.

What could possibly halt this unraveling? Can we *really* get there from here?

RETURNING TO THE TRUTH

The map from "here" to "there" is found in an old but timeless book. The Old Testament reveals three simple yet seminal themes related to the family.

First, *God gave us His Word to help us survive in a hostile world.* As Psalm 119:105 says, "Thy Word is a lamp to my feet, and a light to my path." His Word is *truth*. If we are to experience change in our families, we must admit we are lost and need to find our way to the truth of God's Word.

I often hear Christians complain that the Bible can't be read in public schools. But do we faithfully read it in our own homes? The lamp cannot light a dark pathway if it's lying, covered with dust, on an end table in the family room. The sad reality is that the *real* altar in Christian families today, which gets hours of attention, is the television.

Second, *God blesses those who honor and obey His Word.* He told His people in Joshua 1:7-8:

> Be careful to do according to all the law which Moses My servant commanded you; do not turn from it to the right or to the left, so that you may have success wherever you go. This

book of the law shall not depart from your mouth, but you shall meditate on it day and night, so that you may be careful to do according to all that is written in it; for then you will make your way prosperous, and then you will have success.

The Bible is replete with stories showing how God blesses people who obey His commandments. The eleventh chapter of Hebrews reminds us of a select few: Noah, Abraham, Sarah, Jacob, Moses—these all-too-human heroes "trusted and obeyed" and were blessed by God.

This pattern of God's blessing the obedient didn't end in biblical times. In recent decades we've seen that when churches, denominations, and Christian organizations do what the Bible says and point people to repentance and obedience to God, they flourish and change the world.

The same pattern holds true in families. When a man and a woman are married in a holy, lifelong commitment to God, and when they raise a family according to God's principles, they receive His blessing. Psalm 119:2 asserts, "How blessed are those who observe His testimonies, who seek Him with all their heart."

Does this mean they never have problems? Of course not. We are all soldiers fighting battles in enemy territory against a fierce opponent. Your family and mine will take hits. But our setbacks are temporary when we do things God's way.

Third, the Old Testament shows how *God established the family as His primary way of passing on the truth of His Word from one generation to the next.* Psalm 78:5-8 declares:

> For He established a testimony in Jacob, and appointed a law in Israel, which He commanded our fathers, that they should teach them to their children, that the generation to come might know, even the children yet to be born, that they may arise and tell them to their children, that they should put their confidence in God, and not forget the works of God, but keep His commandments, and not be like their fathers, a stubborn and rebellious generation, a generation that did not prepare its heart, and whose spirit was not faithful to God.

The implication is clear. When parents don't pass on a godly legacy to their children, the entire nation suffers.

You may remember a time when our families and our nation were guided by biblical principles; a time when divorce was a disgrace, when the roles of men and women were clearer, when fathers and mothers were more tuned in to their children. Even most Americans who did not know Christ as Savior believed in a morality based on the Bible.

At some point, the family began to deteriorate. Homes broke apart, and more children grew up with Mom or Dad absent. The biblical chain of one generation passing its godly values to the next snapped. The culture drifted from its moral moorings.

Why? Because, as my friend and pastor Dr. Robert Lewis states, "Family is culture." One family plus one family—multiplied exponentially—creates a culture. The family is the most important element in any decent and just society.

Societies are destroyed one family at a time; they are rebuilt the same way.

You may feel powerless to fix crime, welfare, health care, education, politics, the economy, the media, or the environment. But you *can* do something about your family.

DEFINING A FAMILY REFORMATION

The Protestant Reformation began with a return to a standard— the Word of God. In the same way, a Family Reformation begins when people reshape and reform their marriages and families according to a standard—the truths revealed in the Bible.

A Family Reformation really begins when life and truth collide.

Life has a way of editing the truth of Scripture. For example, we know God's Word teaches that marriage is a covenant. But life begins to edit that truth when a grown daughter calls her parents and says through her tears that her Christian husband is verbally abusing her and the children. "Mom, Dad, I don't know how much longer I can take this!" she says.

At that moment we would do anything to free her from her pain. "After all," we conclude, "there will then be peace instead of hostility.

Wouldn't that be better for the kids?" But if we react only with our hearts, we may forget about God's Word and resort to the world's solution—divorce. These are defining moments that clarify what we really believe. In these real-life situations the truth of Scripture can too easily be set aside for the sake of expediency.

A *Family Reformation* occurs when, at the point where life and truth clash, you courageously choose the truth.

Such circumstances are extremely difficult, requiring intense prayer and godly wisdom. I'm not trying to dismiss the problem by giving a simple, cut-and-dried theological answer. But we must not rush to accept the world's solutions and ignore a careful examination of the *full* counsel of God. Our compassion in such situations must be informed and guided by *all* the truth of Scripture.

A Family Reformation occurs when, at the point where life and truth clash, you courageously choose the truth. Simply stated, *a Family Reformation involves knowing, applying, experiencing, embracing, and proclaiming God's truth about marriage and family.* It's a lifelong process of forming our life, marriage, and family according to Scripture. Each component of this definition possesses special significance:

Knowing God's truth means learning the biblical blueprint for marriage and family. The world advances countless ideas about values, morality, marriage, family, and parenting. These ideas—the changing philosophies of human beings—usually collide head-on with the unchanging truth of Scripture. The problem is that too many Christians do not know the Bible. As a result, many marriage and family problems in the Christian community can be traced to this biblical illiteracy.

Applying God's truth requires following God's blueprint for your own life and family relationships. You apply God's truth to your life when you measure your attitudes and actions against the yardstick of God's Word. You believe God's ways are absolute, unchanging, and always best. This belief demands application, a strong step of faith and obedience—believing that God's Word is more trustworthy than your feelings or opinions.

Experiencing God's truth occurs as you apply His Word repeatedly in your family. When God blesses your faith and obedience—in trials and triumphs—you will see changes in your family. Following Christ will not be some sacred theory or once-a-week tradition, but a day-by-day experience with the living Creator of the universe. What could be more thrilling, for example, than praying for needs as a family and then watching those prayers answered? And when you make choices and decisions based on the absolute standard of Scripture, you will enjoy the benefits: peace, harmony, and hope.

In the final two stages—*embracing* and *proclaiming* God's truth—your convictions take root and emerge. When you proclaim publicly what you embrace privately, you take a huge step toward maturity and godliness. No longer are you satisfied with just seeing God work in your life and family, but now you become a soldier for truth, a conduit of love, grace, and life change in others. As a result of these deeply held convictions, an individual family's reformation thirsts to touch the lives of others. When God's truth is no longer just head knowledge but a living, transforming power in your family, you will be compassionately compelled to share it with others.

Unfortunately, large segments of the Christian community have become silent—a convictionless, middle-of-the-road subculture. When it comes to upholding godly marriage and family beliefs and ideals, most are absent from public discourse and debate. Fearing that we will be labeled "intolerant," we rationalize that our convictions are "private matters." Our lives become a gray world with few operative absolutes. Consequently, we fade into the background and have little influence on others.

Thus the salt loses its flavor.

It does not have to be this way.

With the Holy Spirit's help, you and I can courageously live lives based on the standard of God's Word. Just like Martin Luther, we also must have our list of "95 Theses"—convictions based on His absolute, unchanging truth that will reform our lives as well as spark a Family Reformation inside the walls of our homes. And in the homes of others.

THE FOUR PILLARS OF FAMILY REFORMATION

Following Martin Luther's lightning strike at the Castle Church door in Wittenberg, the original issue of indulgences quickly took a backseat to the more substantive issue of *authority*. Luther charged that the popes of the Roman Church had usurped the authority of God. By restricting biblical interpretation to the pope alone, and preventing the common person's access to the Scriptures, the pontiff was, according to Luther, undermining God's authority.

As the Protestant Reformation spread, the movement embraced four pivotal convictions that still constitute the heart and soul of evangelical Protestantism. The four convictions the Reformers fought and (in many cases) died for were: *sola Christi,* Christ alone; *sola Scriptura,* Scripture alone; *sola fide,* faith alone; and *sola gratia,* grace alone. These "*solas*" (Latin for "only" or "alone") established the preeminence of Christ, Scripture, faith, and grace in God's redemption of humankind.

A Family Reformation is also based on four pivotal convictions. These *solas,* which I will refer to as "pillars," constitute the heart and soul of God's plan for the family. As you support a Family Reformation by seeking to *know, apply, experience, embrace,* and *proclaim* God's truth, these four pillars will provide the spiritual infrastructure of your family.

Pillar #1: Personal Repentance and Purity

Family Reformation begins in the heart—my heart and yours. It will not begin as a broad-based social movement; it is first and foremost a *spiritual* movement in an individual's life. A Family Reformation is kindled when husbands and wives, singles and single parents, kneel before God—in absolute humility—and cry out, as the prophet Isaiah did centuries ago, "Woe is me, for I am ruined! Because I am a man of unclean lips, and I live among a people of unclean lips" (Isaiah 6:5).

Personal repentance—admitting and turning away from our pride, selfishness, arrogance, and compromise—is the critical prerequisite for Family Reformation. God's truth will never be applied, experienced, embraced, and proclaimed by Christians who are proud and selfishly hang on to rights. Christians who desire to turn to God must first repent from self-sufficiency and independence. We must become broken and contrite in heart if we are to truly experience the presence and power of God.

From the ashes of personal repentance, God forgives and refashions a new individual—one who seeks to obey His will in all of life, including His will concerning the family. God, through the guiding power of the Holy Spirit, then takes and turns the *repenter* into a *reformer*—a family reformer.

Pillar #2: The Sacred Covenant of Marriage

Individual Christians must embrace the sacredness of the marriage covenant. A covenant is a binding and solemn agreement between two parties. But the word has even richer meaning to Christians because of the covenants God has made with humankind. To God, the word *covenant* doesn't just mean two people have agreed to terms on some issue, but their fundamental integrity is involved. A covenant is a solemn *promise,* a very serious matter.

Couples used to marry with the *expectation* that the relationship would last a lifetime. Divorce was not an option. But today, too many couples marry with a *hope* that their marriage will last a lifetime. If the relationship doesn't work out, they figure, at least subconsciously, they can always try again.

The Bible states emphatically that marriage is a sacred vow, a public declaration of a holy covenant between *one* man and *one* woman and *their* God for a *lifetime.* To succeed, a Family Reformation must embrace a return to this timeless truth.

Keeping a marriage covenant is more than just pledging to remain married. It also involves making a holy promise to God and your spouse to care for, love, and remain faithful to your spouse for life. It means making your marriage all that God intended it to be.

Pillar #3: The Sanctity of God-Ordained Roles

A Family Reformation will not occur without recognition of the unique, biblically prescribed responsibilities of men and women in the marriage relationship. Among other things, the Bible champions the husband's role as a servant-leader and the wife's role as a lover-helper. Tragically, many Christian men have failed to lead, love, and serve their wives. Many Christian women, too, recognize their failure to lovingly support and encourage their husbands and to nurture their children. There is a stirring within both to return to the truth of Scripture.

For almost three decades, the feminist movement has undermined the family by blurring the lines between manhood and womanhood. Families are suffering today because the Christian community has significantly conformed to feminist ideology. This philosophical intrusion has left its mark: Many Christian parents are not training their sons and daughters to become godly husbands and fathers, wives and mothers.

This feminist "Trojan horse" called equality has been pushed (and in some cases even welcomed) into the church. A thousand lies have invaded our families, paralyzing men and seducing women. Left in the wake of this ideology is a generation of Christian young people who are sexually confused and more committed to careers than family.

A Family Reformation will reestablish the biblical mandate of defined masculine and feminine roles.

Pillar #4: A Legacy of Spiritual Vitality for the Next Generation

"Behold, children are a gift of the Lord," proclaims Psalm 127:3. They are indeed a gift and a responsibility. Sociologist Neil Postman wrote, "Children are the living messages we send to a time that we will not see."[6] For most of us, our greatest legacy in life will be our children—these living messages now eating at our tables, devouring our resources, and testing our patience.

A Family Reformation calls parents to recognize the inherent value of these generational messengers and seeks to infuse them with love, godly values, and Christian character. A Family Reformation occurs when you and I return to the truth about children—that they are image bearers of God and perhaps our most important assignment. They are the conscience, character, and message bearers of the gospel to the next generation.

THE BATTLE FOR THE FAMILY

During the critical Civil War battle at Gettysburg, a key engagement occurred near the crest of a hill called Little Round Top. On that wooded hillside, Yankees from Maine and Confederates from Alabama slaughtered and maimed one another in one of the bloodiest skirmishes of the war.

Commanding the Twentieth Maine Regiment was a young colonel named Joshua Lawrence Chamberlain, who was a featured character in the movie *Gettysburg*. Prior to the Confederate attack, Colonel Strong Vincent explained to Chamberlain the importance of defending their position on Little Round Top.

"I place you here," Vincent told him. "This is the left of the Union line. You understand. You are to hold this ground at all costs."[7]

Chamberlain was well aware that the troops of his regiment were the end of the Union line and could not withdraw under any circumstances. If the Confederates could breach or flank his unit, the rear of the Union army would be exposed, the battle would probably be lost, and the forces of the South would have an unobstructed route to the capitol in Washington. The small piece of turf on a Pennsylvania hillside had to be defended to the last man.

That's precisely what Chamberlain and his men did. Again and again rebel soldiers stormed their position. Again and again the regiment from Maine held the high ground. They didn't retreat. And they didn't surrender. The unwavering bravery of those men helped seal the victory for the Union.[8]

I believe we are now embroiled in the most pivotal battle of our generation, the fight for the soul of America. Our "Little Round Top" is the family. And like Gettysburg, this battle demands courage—the courage of husbands and wives who will turn from the seductive voices of the culture and make their marriages work; the backbone of dads and moms who will reject the poisons of materialism and shape the conscience and character of the next generation. We need courage, not merely to hold our high ground, but to advance our colors and enlist others in the most important battle we may ever fight: the battle for the family. The battle for *your family,* for *my family.*

There is hope! With *God's* help, we can get there from here.

A Reformation Moment

"HERE I STAND!"

In early April of 1521, a nondescript convoy left
Wittenberg, headed for the distant city of Worms, Germany.
In one of the two-wheeled carts, dressed in a simple
hooded cloak, rode a high-spirited monk. His dark brown
eyes flashing, he regaled his comrades with jokes and lively
conversation. Observers could not have guessed that the
jolly monk, named Martin Luther, was on a trip that might
cost him his life.

In Worms, at a Diet—a regional meeting of religious and government leaders chaired by Emperor Charles V—Luther would either recant what he had written against the Roman Church and its pope or face serious consequences.

As the cart rocked along the rutted road, the horses snorting and sniffing the fragrant spring air, Martin recalled events in the years since he had pounded the 95 Theses to the Castle Church door. Opposition had intensified, and while continuing to teach and preach, Martin had also authored controversial books defending his convictions.

In October of 1520, Martin had learned of his excommunication from the Roman Church. Although he had known this was likely, he still was saddened.

But the bone-jarring journey across Germany encouraged Martin. Although the official church was dead set against him, the people of Germany greeted him as a national hero. Word of his trip spread, and more and more of the common folk—peasants and tradesmen—gathered in villages to cheer and clap as his cart rolled by. Martin loved the attention and smiled broadly—calling out greetings and blessings, his eyes dancing in the spring sunshine.

The cheers galvanized Martin's courage. He would need it. The days ahead were to be a severe test of his faith.

The trip took two weeks, and on April 16, Martin and his companions neared Worms. As they approached a city gate, a trumpet rang out from the central cathedral, announcing the arrival of an important visitor. It was lunchtime, and thousands of the city's residents took to the streets to welcome the celebrity.

At 6:00 P.M., Martin appeared before the Diet. The setting was impressive. In addition to the emperor, the princes of Germany and representatives of the Roman Church sat in pomp and majesty.

Auspiciously, in the center of the room, a table sat piled high with books—Martin's books.

After the hubbub quieted, an inquisitor asked Martin two simple questions. "Are these books yours?" He paused, then dramatically asked, "Will you recant of what you have written in these books?"

Martin was subdued. The gravity of the moment settled fully on his mind and heart. Softly, he said, "Yes, these are my books. But before I answer your next question, allow me time to ponder my answer."

An uproar filled the hall. The inquisitor asked loudly why someone of Martin's ability needed more time to respond to such a simple question. But the Diet agreed to give him until the next day to answer.

Once again Martin faced long hours of prayer and reflection, much like that night in Wittenberg when he had reviewed the theses. This time, though, Martin was not wondering what action to take. He just wanted to prepare the most compelling answer possible. After weighing his words, he asked for God's blessings and slept soundly.

The next day it was again late when Martin appeared before the Diet. The sun had set, and large torches were lit in the grand assembly hall. So many people crowded the room that only the emperor had a seat. Pointing to the pile of books, the inquisitor repeated his questions.

"You must give a simple, clear, and proper answer to the question. Will you recant or not?" the inquisitor pressed.

The room was silent. With his eyes flashing and thunder in his voice, Martin's answer filled the huge hall: "Unless I am instructed and convinced with evidence from the Holy Scriptures or with open, clear, and distinct grounds and reasoning—and my conscience is captive to the Word of God—then I cannot and will not recant, because it is neither safe nor wise to act against conscience."

Above the roar of voices, Martin shouted, "Here I stand! I can do no other. God help me! Amen."

Martin Luther walked briskly from the great hall. Another seed of reformation had been courageously planted.[1]

CHAPTER FOUR

Needed: A Good Housecleaning

To reform a world, to reform a nation, no wise man will undertake; and all but foolish men know, that the only solid, though a far slower reformation, is what each begins and perfects on himself.
—THOMAS CARLYLE

E very year during my childhood, when the gray days of winter dissolved into the therapeutic warmth of spring, my mom would reenact the grueling ritual of spring housecleaning. It was a duty she took seriously. Very seriously.

Blankets were stripped unceremoniously from the beds, taken outdoors, shaken, hung over clotheslines, and beaten with a broom mercilessly. Storm windows that had held wintry blasts at bay were decommissioned for the season and stacked in the basement. Screens were latched in place to allow the fresh breezes of spring into our home.

No dust mite, cobweb, or dust ball was safe from Mom's unrelenting eye. Like a soldier on a search-and-destroy mission, she methodically probed every corner and closet. From the most hidden nook in the ceiling to the darkest cranny behind the couch, she proceeded with unbending resolution.

All the while, the fresh Ozark sunshine bathed our living room with warmth, and a cool, pure breeze rushed through those screened windows, announcing a new season.

After days of backbreaking labor, the task was completed. Our house was clean. I felt it.

—

Spring . . . 1994. Early one morning, I stood before a small group of men at our FamilyLife office in Little Rock. I had invited them to discuss the concept of Family Reformation.

I had no idea a different kind of housecleaning was about to begin. In *my* house.

On the chalkboard, in large letters, someone had written the words *Family Reformation.* We talked about those two words and what it would take for a Family Reformation to occur in America. We identified the needs of families. Observations bantered back and forth like balls in a tennis match. A stream of ideas poured forth. We were hopeful and optimistic.

But an hour into our discussion, the tone of the meeting changed dramatically. Staring at the chalkboard, each of us, one by one, fell silent.

Instead of dreaming about all the things that must occur "out there" in the culture, we gradually realized something had to happen "in here" and "in us" first. A daunting question had silenced us: "Lord, what needs to change in *my life* for a Family Reformation to occur in *my home?*"

Not much else was written on the chalkboard. Instead of crafting a resounding battle cry for the masses, we ended up with individual introspection, earnest prayers, and somber hearts. *What does God expect of me?*

The meeting adjourned early.

FROM "OUT THERE" TO "IN HERE"

I deeply appreciate the work of the Spirit of God at that first meeting, for on that day, the *real* issue became clear. I realized that the beginning—the flash point—for Family Reformation is *individual and personal repentance.* Family Reformation is an intensely personal matter.

God must work *in* us before He can work *through* us.

Prompted by the Holy Spirit, I began to repent—a deeper repentance than I've ever experienced.

The familiar challenge of Deuteronomy 6:5-7 became my mandate and invigorated my spirit:

> And you shall love the Lord your God with all your heart and with all your soul and with all your might. And these words, which I am commanding you today, shall be on your heart; and you shall teach them diligently to your sons and shall talk of them when you sit in your house and when you walk by the way and when you lie down and when you rise up.

The phrase "shall be on your heart" means "to be burdened by" or "to carry a heavy load." Although I've felt this weight in the past, now I am burdened daily with my responsibility to pray for my wife and children, to read and instruct them in the Scriptures, to protect them from evil. I'm continually challenged to be the man of God they need me to be.

I have also been convicted to practice regularly the spiritual disciplines of prayer and fasting. I confess that I'm just a beginner at fasting, one of the more important, yet neglected, aspects of the Christian life. But God is using these disciplines to strip away layer after layer of selfishness in my life.

Now, years after that abbreviated meeting, it is clear that a return to God *alone* is our only hope for Family Reformation. The psalmist says it best: "Unless the Lord builds the house, they labor in vain who build it" (Psalm 127:1). There are no solutions to our family problems until our individual relationships with Jesus Christ are set right and our lives are under the control of the Holy Spirit.

Hard Questions

Spiritual housecleaning begins with introspection. As individuals and as the church, we who are followers of Christ need to ask some hard questions.

Why is the divorce rate *inside* the church nearly identical to the divorce rate *outside* the church? And why is there so much silence from the evangelical community on this important issue?

Why do so many Christian men perform aggressively at work and remain disengaged and passive at home?

Why are so many Christians negative about having and rearing children?

Why do so many Christians say their secular job is their ministry, but then *show* so little fruit for their efforts?

Why do Christians talk about family values while their lifestyles are virtually identical to those of average non-Christians?

Why do so few Christians possess confidence that they are on a divine mission?

Why have so many Christians in full-time ministry washed out because of immorality and impurity?

Why is the fifth commandment—to honor our parents—neglected by large numbers of Christians?

Why are we nonchalant about the legacy we will leave our children?

Why do less than 10 percent of all Christians regularly tell others about God's forgiveness and the new life found in Christ?

If Jesus Christ changes lives, why do 50 million Americans claiming to be born again have such a marginal impact on society?

More than ever before, the church desperately needs a spiritual housecleaning.

The prophet Jeremiah asked similar questions about the "church" of his day. He observed they were a people with stubborn hearts (see Jeremiah 3:17) who pursued "emptiness" (2:5). Incredibly, as their evils mounted, the people of God "refused to be ashamed" (3:3). "They did not even know how to blush" (6:15). The spiritual leaders ignored the truth of God's Word and ruled on their own authority (see 5:30-31). And just like in our generation, the deceived, distracted "believers" sat contentedly in the house of God, week after week, listening to the teaching of Scripture but refusing to repent and seek personal purity.

In one of the most scathing condemnations in all the Bible, Jeremiah relayed God's thoughts on spiritual mediocrity: "Will you steal, murder, and commit adultery, and swear falsely, and offer sacrifices to Baal, and walk after other gods that you have not known, then come and stand before Me in this house, which is called by My name, and say, 'We are delivered!'—that you may do all these abominations?" (Jeremiah 7:9-10).

Inevitably, Jeremiah and other Old Testament prophets returned again and again to the only solution to Israel's problems: repentance. Jeremiah 7:3 tells us: "Thus says the Lord of hosts, the God of Israel, 'Amend your ways and your deeds, and I will let you dwell in this place.'"

Today, however, this spiritual decay in the church is not always easy to recognize. Because we're good at using "God talk" and playing church, we can mask an unrepentant heart. Jerry White perceptively points out:

> No one is so empty as the man who has stopped walking with God and doesn't know it. He smiles at church, serves on boards, even teaches the Bible, but he is an empty shell. He lives on past knowledge and correct doctrine. He says and does the right things. But there is a hollow ring to his life. No one really notices, however, because there are so many other hollow rings around him.[1]

More than ever before, the church desperately needs a spiritual housecleaning.

The great reformations and revivals of history all have begun with repentance. In his outstanding book *The Spiritual Awakeners,* Keith J. Hardman says that, as a prelude to revival, "an individual or a small group of God's people becomes conscious of its sins and backslidden condition, and vows to forsake all that is displeasing to God."[2]

History supports Hardman's observation. For example, when Peter preached on the day of Pentecost, his message was primarily about repentance. Acts 2:37-38 depicts the scene: "Now when they heard this, they were pierced to the heart, and said to Peter and the rest of the apostles, 'Brethren, what shall we do?' And Peter said to them, 'Repent, and let each of you be baptized in the name of Jesus Christ for the forgiveness of your sins; and you shall receive the gift of the Holy Spirit.'"

America's first Great Awakening (1740-45), ignited by the preaching of Jonathan Edwards and George Whitefield, was fueled by confession and repentance. Edwards had been troubled by the townspeople's "frequenting of taverns and lewd practices."[3] But after the Spirit of God changed many hearts, the preacher testified to "a glorious alteration in the town."[4] Repentance changed the way people lived.

The second Great Awakening (1790-1840) altered the structure of American society, spawning antislavery and temperance movements, prison reform, Scripture distribution, and missionary endeavors.[5] This great movement of God, which transformed an entire nation, began with repentance. Could not the same result be prompted today by repentance in the church?

A number of years ago, in support of a friend, I attended an Alcoholics Anonymous meeting. The room was crammed with 300 men and women from every socioeconomic and ethnic background. Their differences were startling. Their unity was riveting.

The group of strugglers had one important thing in common: All were transparent and brutally honest about their addiction to alcohol. I was stunned by their sincerity. My friend noticed my surprise and said, "Dennis, there are no facades here. We have all admitted we are alcoholics. We freely acknowledge that we need one another."

There were no masks and no pretenses, just real, broken people acknowledging their need. For many of them, the meeting was an issue of life and death—and it showed as they hugged each other and spoke words of encouragement.

What will it take for us in the church to get real, to strip away the pretense of spiritual success, and to admit we need cleansing? Perhaps God is using the blazing inferno of our base culture to bring us to our knees, to humble us so we will seek His healing.

TURNING FROM SIN

What is repentance? The Greek word for repentance is *metanoia,* which means "a change in mode of thought and feeling."[6] According to John Calvin, repentance is "a true turning of our life to God, a turning that arises from a pure and earnest fear of Him."[7] Repentance involves a turn *from* sin and a pursuit *of* righteousness. We do not argue with God; we admit our wickedness, turn away from it, and endeavor to live wholly for Him.

The repentant man or woman allows the Spirit of God to scrutinize every relationship, every habit, every goal, and every thought. J. I. Packer got to the heart of the matter: "The repentance that Christ requires of His people consists in a settled refusal to set any limit to the claims which He may make on their lives."[8]

When God's people turn from their sin through repentance, God's peace and forgiveness replace turmoil and shame. Consider 2 Corinthians 7:10: "Godly sorrow brings repentance that leads to salvation and leaves no regret" (NIV).

Keith Lynch, a coworker in our broadcast ministry, shared the story of an incident in his home that is uncomfortably familiar for many of us. He had a choice one morning to go his own way or to go God's way and respond with a repentant spirit. Keith wrote:

> Even as we finished the breakfast rush and got the kids to school, I could feel the tension mounting. I had wronged my wife, Jonell.
>
> I watched, somewhat amused, as we circled each other warily. I have developed the fine art of winning the argument at any cost, especially when I am in the wrong! My mind clicked into action as she began to accurately recite the liturgy of my error.
>
> As I caught my breath, readying my tongue for the task, something happened. Just at that moment, God did one of those surprising things it seems He loves to do. As I revved up my brain for a great "discussion" (read "argument"), I was suddenly dumbstruck. No words came. I watched her fall silent in turn, as she waited, girding herself for my self-defense.
>
> But this time, to our mutual surprise, it didn't come. In place of my impeccable logic, the intricate dissection of detail, five simple words came out of my mouth: "I'm sorry. I was wrong."
>
> Jonell smiled, and that smile shouted from the rooftops, "You are the most godly man to me, for you love *me* more than your logic, your process, and your need to win." There were no more words between us.
>
> Husband, don't argue with your wife from a position of authority, or gifting, or power, or capacity. Don't "win" just because you can. Simply apologize.[9]

Repentance is not easy—it's even bitter at times. But the fruit is sweet: Husbands and wives forgive each other and discover fresh joy, hope, and oneness in their relationship. Children regain loving, attentive parents and are raised to fear God and keep His commandments. The estranged are reconciled. The haughty are humbled. The guilty find relief and freedom. A Family Reformation begins.

THE BEAUTY OF REPENTANCE

In July of 1995, my wife, Barbara, and I traveled to Fort Collins, Colorado, for the U.S. Staff Conference of Campus Crusade for Christ. More than 3,000 staff members and volunteers had made the pilgrimage from campuses, cities, and homes across America and from abroad to join forces and celebrate the cause of Christ.

Our first three days together were memorable.

The last three were unforgettable.

On the fourth day of the conference, Nancy Leigh DeMoss, writer and speaker for Life Action Ministries, gave a message that ignited a fire. She spoke of our desperate need to turn from pride to humility, our need for spiritual brokenness and confession. Nancy described the differences between proud people and broken people to help call us to repentance. Here's a portion of her list:

Proud People	Broken People
Focus on the failures of others	◆ Overwhelmed with sense of their own spiritual need
Look down on others	◆ Esteem all others as better than self
Independent/self-sufficient spirit	◆ Dependent spirit/recognize need for others
Maintain control; must be my way	◆ Surrender control
Have to prove that they are right	◆ Willing to yield the right to be right
Claim rights	◆ Yield rights
Demanding spirit	◆ Giving spirit
Self-protective of time, rights, reputation	◆ Self-denying
Desire to be served	◆ Motivated to serve others

Proud People	**Broken People**
Desire to be a success	◆ Desire to be faithful to make others a success
Desire to be recognized/appreciated	◆ Sense of unworthiness; thrilled to be used at all; eager for others to get credit
Think of what they can do for God	◆ Know that they have nothing to offer God
Feel confident in how much they know	◆ Humbled by how much they have to learn
Self-conscious	◆ Not concerned with self at all
Keep people at arms' length	◆ Risk getting close to others/willing to take risks of loving intimately
Quick to blame others	◆ Accept personal responsibility—can see where they were wrong
Unapproachable	◆ "Easy to be entreated"
Defensive when criticized	◆ Receive criticism with a humble, open heart
Concerned with being "respectable"	◆ Concerned with being real
Concerned about what others think	◆ All that matters is what God knows
Find it difficult to share their spiritual needs with others	◆ Willing to be open/transparent with others
Have a hard time saying, "I was wrong—please forgive me"	◆ Are quick to admit failure and to seek forgiveness
When confessing sin, deal in generalities	◆ Deal in specifics
Remorseful over their sin—got caught/found out	◆ Repentant over sin (forsake it)
Compare themselves with others and feel deserving of honor	◆ Compare themselves to the holiness of God and feel desperate need for mercy
Blind to their true heart condition	◆ Walk in the light
Don't think they have anything to repent of	◆ Continual heart attitude of repentance[10]

Following Nancy DeMoss's hour-long address, God orchestrated what became three days of holy introspection, confession, and cleansing. Individuals streamed to the platform in the field house, one after one asking God publicly to forgive them for their sins. Hundreds of others found fellow staff members and, face-to-face, sought forgiveness and prayed for healing and reconciliation in their relationships. The cavernous building became a temple filled with the presence of God and the sorrow of individuals.

Scheduled meetings were canceled, and speakers who traveled in from across the country returned home without presenting their messages. Men and women repented of their sins: Lies, deceit, bitterness, hidden compromises and immoralities were confessed—publicly and privately.

Staff members made phone calls seeking forgiveness for years of bitterness harbored against a parent, brother, sister, or friend. Brokenhearted parents sought prayer for wayward sons and daughters.

Barbara and I sobbed in anguish as we stood beside a friend who confessed to a life of deceit and adultery. More than 100 believers streamed from the bleachers to surround this man and his wife and to pray for healing in their marriage and protection for their children.

For three days, the entire conference asked God to "search me . . . know my heart, and see if there be any hurtful way in me" (Psalm 139:23-24). As people confessed sin publicly, there was little inclination to judge. All of us knew we were sinners and were publicly or privately coming clean and turning back to God.

The experience left us with an unforgettable impression of our own sin-sick depravity, a fresh perspective of God's grace, and a new resolution to obey God. And the effects remain. Later, I sought out a friend, face-to-face, and I admitted my bitterness toward him, asking for his forgiveness. Barbara met with our children the following Thanksgiving and tearfully confessed her pride and an attitude of selfishness. The fruit of repentance is a sweet cleansing that purifies the conscience and releases joy.

As Barbara and I left Fort Collins, we pondered if the same spiritual cleansing could visit the church. Most pastors, church leaders, and laypeople will never choose or have the opportunity to set aside a week to seek God's grace, mercy, and forgiveness. Most will find it difficult to be still long enough to hear the convicting work of the Holy Spirit and repent. But this cleansing needs to occur. Where do we begin? What does God expect of us?

SACKCLOTH AND ASHES

You will recall that only three men survived the Mann Gulch fire I described in chapter 2. Two men sprinted to the ridge; one of them, the foreman, ignited a fire. After the blaze roared up the hill, Wag Dodge lay down in the hot ashes of his own fire.

In a spiritual sense, repentance is also climbing into the ashes— our own ashes of pride and selfishness, of greed and immorality, of fear and apathy. Repentance, too, is painfully hot—singeing our flesh, burning out the rotting evil in our hearts.

But unlike the raging inferno in Mann Gulch, the fire of repentance restores life! It sears away our layers of independence and pride, and it prepares our hearts to receive the truth.

God is calling you and me into the ashes—the ashes of personal repentance. It's time to quit running. The ridge is too far away. Attempting to outrun a blowup is futile.

God has prepared a place of refuge amid the flames. Throw yourself on the ground. Confess your sin. Experience the cleansing fire of repentance. You won't be consumed! Instead, you will be changed. Forever.

Let me ask some questions: Is there shame in your life? Do you feel guilty because of some wrong you committed? Is there a corner of your soul that is tainted with remorse, a guilt that you know you must deal with someday? Is that *someday* right now? Why delay?

Has God's Spirit been convicting you of a compromise? *Repent.*

Have you been looking at pornography? *Repent.*

Have you lied? *Repent.*

Have you deceived another? *Repent.*

Are you cheating on your spouse? *Repent.*

Are you cheating on your income tax or expense reports? *Repent.*

If you are single, are you morally compromised in any relationship? *Repent.*

Has anything or anyone taken God's rightful place as your Lord and Master? *Repent.*

Is there someone you've refused to forgive? *Repent.*

If you are divorced, are you holding grudges against your former spouse? *Repent.*

Have you spoken harshly to another? *Repent.*

Have you robbed God by not giving as you have received? *Repent.*

But there's more. Have you omitted a responsibility or duty? *Repent.*

Have you failed to pray daily with your wife and lead her spiritually? *Repent.*

Have you failed to support your husband and lovingly nurture your children? *Repent.*

Have you failed to pray with and for your children? *Repent.*

Have you ignored the reading of the Bible with your spouse and children? *Repent.*

Have you been lazy around the house, failing to help your spouse with household chores and duties? *Repent.*

Have you ignored your spouse's needs for relational intimacy? *Repent.*

Have you withheld sexual intimacy from your spouse? *Repent.*

Have you failed to provide for your family? *Repent.*

What is God saying to you? Have you come clean before God? If not, then you will not experience a true reformation in your life or your family's life until you confront your sin.

The first step toward a Family Reformation is repentance.

THE GLORY OF REPENTANCE

During the past two decades, I've counseled a number of people caught in adultery. Many of these men and women have lied about it or denied it. While I've watched some self-destruct, I've seen others repent. One woman's story stands out as an example of the power of repentance.

She had been married nearly 40 years when she told me of adulterous relationships that had occurred nearly a decade earlier. Her husband had no idea of her unfaithfulness.

The more we talked about her infidelity, the more I became

convinced that if her repentance and healing were to be complete, she must go to her husband and tell him what she had done. She had sinned against God and her husband. Their marriage would never be what God had intended if she kept this breach of trust a secret.

Yet long before I told her what I felt she needed to do, God had been working in her heart, burdening her with her deceit and unfaithfulness. Over a period of several months, her heart softened, and she agreed that she *needed* to tell her husband.

Some days later, broken and ashamed, she confessed the adultery to her husband. She came clean. She uncovered the decay that had polluted her heart and relationship with God and her husband for years.

She repented of her sin.

As you can imagine, there were tears, shock, and anguish. Feelings of betrayal and anger. And more tears.

But there was also forgiveness, real forgiveness from God and, in time, from her husband. A spiritual housecleaning took place, and God broke through in their lives. This couple isn't just playing church anymore. Now God is real. God's grace and mercy are real. God's Word is real. And their relationship is real.

To experience a sweeping transformation in our culture, Christians must come clean. Family Reformation begins when God's people cry out, as David did, "Create in me a clean heart, O God, and renew a steadfast spirit within me. . . . Restore to me the joy of Thy salvation" (Psalm 51:10, 12).

Family Reformation begins in your heart—with repentance.

REFORMATION CHECKUP

All of us can benefit from a checkup on our spiritual health. Check your answer to each question, then refer to Scoring below.

1. Based on the regularity of your personal devotional/prayer time, how would you rate the place of these activities in your life?
   _____ Very Important
   _____ Somewhat Important
   _____ Not That Important

2. Considering your giving of time, spiritual gifts, money, and other resources to a local church or other ministries, how would you rate the place of such giving in your life?

_____ Very Important

_____ Somewhat Important

_____ Not That Important

3. When you do something wrong or hurt another person, how often do you make an apology and ask forgiveness?

_____ Very Often

_____ Somewhat Often

_____ Not That Often

4. When you are struggling with a sin issue in your life, how often do you discuss/confess that sin with your spouse or another person?

_____ Very Often

_____ Somewhat Often

_____ Not That Often

5. Based on how often you go before the Lord and engage in honest evaluation or soul-searching concerning the quality of your spiritual life, how would you describe this activity?

_____ Very Important to Me

_____ Somewhat Important to Me

_____ Not That Important to Me

Scoring: If you answered most of the questions with a "Very" response—great! Thank the Lord and persevere on the journey. If most of your answers were in the "Somewhat" or "Not That" categories, spend some time with the Lord asking for His insight on the current vitality of your spiritual walk with Him.

REPENTANCE RETREAT

After reading this chapter, you may wish to spend some time seeking God's cleansing through repentance. Here are some suggestions on how to proceed:

- Set aside a block of time—at least a couple of hours or up to a 24-hour day—and go to a place where you will not be distracted. You may wish to fast as part of your preparation. Take your Bible and a notepad with you.
- Begin your retreat with an extended time of prayer and meditation on Scripture. Some suggested Scriptures include Psalm 46; Psalm 139; Psalm 51; 1 John 1:1-10; and Romans 8:1-39. Be still; wait on God. Ask Him to reveal to you areas of sin that need your repentance. List significant items on a piece of paper, which you may choose to destroy later in your time with the Lord.
- Pray through your "repentance list." Ask God for forgiveness of each item. Claim His assurance of forgiveness (see 1 John 1:9), and thank Him for cleansing you of all unrighteousness.
- Take the sheet of paper listing the sins you have confessed and repented from and write "1 John 1:9" across the page. You may even wish to find a secluded spot outdoors and burn the paper, symbolizing God's forgiveness of your sin. If you struggle with guilt from confessed sin, consider covering the ashes from your paper with several rocks to form a landmark that will remind you of God's forgiveness.
- In your journal, write down any action points you need to perform that will give evidence of your repentance. For example, if you have wronged someone, you may need to make restitution. You also may wish to share issues from which you repented with a friend who will hold you accountable in the future.
- If your repentance involves confessing a sensitive sin (such as adultery) to another person, seek counsel from godly individuals who can guide you through this step.
- Conclude your retreat in prayer, asking God to give you the strength to turn away from sin and evil and do what is right. Ask Him to help you keep short accounts with Him so that you will confess and repent regularly rather than allow your sin to build up and become a barrier between you and God.
- Share with your spouse what you learned through this process. Pray for each other.

A Reformation Moment

A FAMILY AGAIN

Still shaking his head in amazement, Jim Godsey drove
with his wife, Debi, to pick up their daughter, Carla. Just two
days before—prior to the marriage conference weekend—
the couple had despised each other's company. But now
Debi was giving up her boyfriend and coming home.

The couple stopped to pick up Carla, who had spent the
weekend with her aunt and uncle, Patty and Mark
Jorgenson.

"I'm moving back in with Jim and Carla," Debi announced. "We found God at the conference."

Mark and Patty were delighted, but Carla frowned. She had lived through similar scenes too many times, only to have her hopes smashed by the next verbal brawl.

The Godseys headed on to Jim's house. The fall evening was crisp. As the Renault scattered leaves on the darkened streets, Debi reflected on the changes in her life. Only 24 hours after releasing her life to God, she felt so different, but why?

Then the realization struck Debi like lightning—her depression had lifted! As long as she could remember, a dark cloud of emotional pain had hung over her life. Now the dull, empty ache was gone, replaced by exhilarating freedom and peace.

The threesome arrived at Jim's place, a small Cape Cod-style house in an older, inner-city neighborhood of Milwaukee. Eleven-year-old Carla was grumpy about the turn of events. Since her mom had moved out four months earlier, a relative calm had replaced the tension caused by her parents' angry shouting matches—and she'd had Jim all to herself.

With a divorce looming, Debi and Jim had grown lenient with Carla, and she was making the most of it. Now, after the marriage conference, her mom was back in the house.

Confused and skeptical, Carla pouted. She gave the new arrangement a couple of weeks at best, then, she feared, the whole lousy scene would repeat itself.

Something strange was definitely happening, though. Jim and Debi constantly consulted their conference manuals to see "how to do things right," and within a day or two they visited a bookstore and bought Bibles.

Later Debi remembered, "I couldn't get enough of the Word. I'd been thirsty so long, and now I had found the well."

On Friday, October 26, Debi called the judge's office to ask for another postponement of the divorce hearing scheduled for the following Monday. Both she and Jim were encouraged about their refurbished marriage but still wary after so many years of marriage problems. They had agreed to ask the judge to delay the divorce action for six months—they hoped enough time to see if things would work out.

The judge's secretary was adamant—take the divorce now or forget it.

"You're fooling yourself!" the woman told Debi forcefully over the phone. "I've seen too many alcoholic husbands convince their wives that they won't drink anymore. The woman postpones, then he goes back on the bottle. Why not do it after waiting so long?" the secretary asked.

Debi groped for an answer but could only mumble, "I found God at a marriage conference." Her thoughts whirled. Her life had changed, but it was all so new. Would the bubble burst? Would she come crashing to earth when the excitement wore off? Debi was scared—maybe she was crazy not to go ahead and divorce Jim.

But she was gripped by a wondrous thought: *If God is as big as I think He is, He can take care of this marriage!*

Over the weekend Debi and Jim discussed what to do. They had waited so long to be rid of each other—were they about to blow a great opportunity? No, too many good things had happened.

On Monday, Debi called the judge's office and canceled the divorce action.

That night, October 29, 1990, on 38th Street in Milwaukee, Wisconsin, a Honda Shadow motorcycle, owned by Debi Godsey, remained parked in the family garage.

A date with an 18-wheeler and death had been canceled by an encounter with the living God. New life in Jesus Christ had given birth to hope.

CHAPTER FIVE

Restoring Dignity to the Covenant

*To call me a judge is something of a misnomer. I am really a sort
of public mortician. In the past 11 years I have presided over the
final obsequies of 22,000 dead marriages. The trouble is:
I have buried a lot of live corpses.*
—A JUDGE ON THE COURT OF COMMON PLEAS, TOLEDO, OHIO

We have become a culture of divorce. Not so long ago, marriage
breakup was the exception to the norm—a shameful blight to
a family. Now, after we have spent years observing what the ax of
divorce has done to the family tree, the marriage that *lasts* feels like
the exception.

Divorce is sabotaging America and ought to be considered a subversive act. Consider some of the evidence:

EXHIBIT A: A father crafts a letter to his teenage son explaining
the rationale for why he divorced the boy's mother:

> Dear Jim,
>   Before I start this letter to you, I must tell you that I
> love you and none of what happened or is going to hap-
> pen is in any way your fault. If I had been as good a father
> as you are a son, there would be no need for me to write
> to you now.

77

Over the years I have been unfaithful to your mother in thoughts as well as in deeds. Because your mother had complete trust in me, I was able to cover up by lying to her. Last May I met a woman in San Jose. Her name is Elizabeth. I am going to leave your mother and go live with her. This does not mean you no longer have a home. Your mother and I still both love you very much. I want you to know that your mother and I will always receive you into our homes with love that is unconditional.

What I have done is morally wrong, and I hope you will not follow in my ways. When you meet the right woman, make a lifelong commitment to her. I was never able to do this, and it has caused much sorrow.

Please do not allow this to change your feelings about your mother and me.

We love you very much and both need your love now more than ever. We will always be your family and will be here for you, even though we will be living apart.

I love you,

Dad

EXHIBIT B: The book is titled *How to Dump Your Wife.*

The author, whose pen name is Lee Covington, clearly states the purpose of his book. He dedicates it to "all the men who lost it all—their kids, their careers, their reputations, their freedom, even their lives. Because of a wife." *How to Dump Your Wife* is an avowed "tutorial" for the man whose singular goal in life is freedom from a bad marriage.

Covington imparts toxic advice on such topics as dealing with the guilt of divorce, hiding a girlfriend until the divorce is final, and concealing money from your spouse. Included in the book's pages are flights of convoluted logic ("If we go backwards and force people to stay together, who really gets hurt? That's right, the kids.")[1] and outright denial ("Many kids cope with divorce. Kids have been coping with it for decades. They function. They see their dads; they stick it out and make it all right.").[2] Interspersed in all this, the reader finds the book's premise: If you're not happy in your marriage, then leave. The author states, "One steady principle applies to most guys who are dying to get out of a marriage: You are not happy. . . . If you were happy, you wouldn't be dumping your wife. You're just not happy. . . . This is your happiness we're talking about, for once."[3]

EXHIBIT C: Susan teaches sixth grade in a public elementary school. In class one day, a 12-year-old named Todd wrote an essay describing his parents' troubled marriage. Without editing Todd's work, this is what he said:

> Families are beuatiful.
> One thing I care about is my family.
> Something you want to hold on to.
> Families are like glass,
> you let go it will brake.
> My glass slipped
> and I'm trying to catch it.

Todd's family did slip. Shattered by the divorce, his world cracked. At age 15, he ended his pain with a single bullet to the brain.

A Devastating Impact

What makes a child four times more likely to commit a violent crime?

What increases the likelihood of a child's living in poverty, dropping out of school, and becoming a juvenile delinquent?

What increases the probability of a child's abusing alcohol, taking drugs, becoming sexually promiscuous, and committing suicide?

What cripples hundreds of thousands of young people when they marry and creates fear, insecurity, and a higher likelihood that their marriages will not last a lifetime?

It's divorce, divorce, divorce. And divorce is killing both America and the church.

Broken promises . . . mistrust . . . instability . . . shattered people. Divorce has created a national disaster. An enemy.

Just like a grenade exploding in a crowded room, the white-hot, twisted shrapnel of divorce maims all participants—children and adults. Everyone bleeds. Divorce permeates every facet of life—disrupting communities, obstructing education, and dividing families. Divorce kills a culture.

Judith Wallerstein, an international authority on divorce, has studied the effects of marital breakdown over time. After completing research done on families 10 years after a divorce, she reported the following:

> I expected that most adults would say that divorce was a closed book. For children, it would be ancient history. . . . I did not expect the experience to endure so fully for so many, with high drama, passions, vivid memories, fantasy relationships, jagged breaks in development, intense anger, and profound discrepancies in quality of life. Nor did I anticipate the problems that so many young people would encounter upon entering young adulthood. Although I thought I was being realistic, nothing prepared me for what I found.[4]

One woman wrote after her divorce, "Our divorce has been the most painful, horrid, ulcer-producing, agonizing event you can imagine. . . . I wish I could put on this piece of paper for all the world to see, a picture of what divorce feels like. Maybe my picture would stop people before it's too late."[5]

But the children are the true victims of this social calamity.

Author Gary Sprague recorded the experiences of children in his moving book *My Parents Got a Divorce*. The children's voices echo across the scorched landscape, melding into a chorus of scarred lives and incinerated futures.

> It feels like a hurt that won't go away. I felt like my mom was pulling on one arm and my dad was pulling on the other arm.[6] —Kelly, age 11

> When my parents got a divorce it hurt bad. I thought I was going to die. I took the blame on myself. That was what made me mad. It was like my family was falling apart.[7] —Chris, age 11

I feel sad that my mom and dad are separated. I don't have two prayers at night; I just have one prayer at night. I feel scared at night.[8] —Joseph, age 9

The evidence is conclusive: Divorce—because it destroys families—destroys a culture. Harvard sociologist Armand Nicholi III concluded, "Divorce is not a solution, but an exchange of problems." In a more personal way, novelist Pat Conroy said of his own marriage breakup, "Each divorce is the death of a small civilization."[9]

For the sake of the children and for the sake of civilization, we *need* a Family Reformation.

MARRIAGE IS A COVENANT

Early in our marriage, Barbara and I came face-to-face with a minor problem: Our garbage can wore out. Because the defective product had a lifetime warranty, we confidently returned the can to the place of purchase and exchanged it for a new one.

The department store honored our warranty, but to our surprise, the new garbage can didn't come with the same lifetime guarantee. Instead, it was guaranteed for only six years. And to add insult to injury, the store deducted the four years we'd already had the first garbage can from the new can's six-year guarantee! The moral of the story: Our culture seems to say, if your product is flawed, redefine the terms of your original agreement.

This is precisely what is taking place with the sacred covenant of marriage. Marriage is being redefined—after the fact—as an agreement or a contract. One company, attempting to cash in on this new approach to the marriage covenant, has created a unique wedding gift called Divorce Insurance. Like life insurance, a divorce insurance policy is given to the newlyweds so that if their marriage doesn't work out, they can collect the proceeds to pay for the legal expenses of their divorce!

More and more couples are preparing prenuptial agreements. Although this custom has long been popular with the rich and famous, now ordinary folk are in on the act. One couple decided to split all expenses in their marriage 50/50—even dinners in restaurants.

The husband said revealingly, "Money has never been an issue for us. But neither has trust."[10] Another couple, embarking on marriage after several previous divorces, drew up a 16-page prenuptial agreement. It specified how often they would have sex, what time they would go to bed, which gasoline they would buy, and more.[11]

Marriage is not a private experiment, littered with prenuptial agreements and an attitude of "Try it! If it doesn't work, you can always bail out!"

Marriage is not just a convenient relationship based upon "what's in it for me."

Marriage is not some kind of social contract—something you just "do" for as long as you both shall "love."

It's none of those.

Marriage is a sacred covenant between one man and one woman and their God for a lifetime. It is a public vow of how you will relate to your spouse as you form a new family unit.

The traditional wedding vows used by most couples constitute a *covenantal oath,* not a two-party contract. The vows I shared with Barbara went like this:

> I, Dennis, take you, Barbara, to be my lawful wedded wife. I promise and covenant, before God and these witnesses, to be your loving and faithful husband; to stand by you in riches and in poverty, in joy and in sorrow, in sickness and in health, forsaking all others, as long as we both shall live.

When we spoke these words, Barbara and I weren't agreeing to provide some personal services via a contract that could be terminated if one of us defaulted. Instead, we were entering into a *covenant*—the same type of sacred, binding obligation that God made with His children on several momentous occasions, such as with Noah after the Flood.

Any covenant—including the marriage covenant—is a *binding, weighty* obligation. In Proverbs 20:25, we read, "It is a trap for a man to dedicate something rashly and only later to consider his vows" (NIV).

Deuteronomy 23:23 offers this advice: "You shall be careful to perform what goes out from your lips, just as you have voluntarily vowed to the Lord your God, what you have promised." Jesus said that "every careless word that men shall speak, they shall render account for it in the day of judgment" (Matthew 12:36).

God takes the wedding covenant seriously, even when we do not.

RECLAIMING THE SANCTITY OF MARRIAGE

Christians must reaffirm and reclaim the sanctity of marriage. God says, "I hate divorce" (Malachi 2:16). The Lord didn't stutter when He spoke these words. It is time for each of us to embrace and proclaim God's sacred view of marriage, as well as His corresponding hatred for divorce.

Reclaiming the sanctity of marriage begins with several commitments:

Commitment #1: Do Not Get Married Unless You Plan to Keep Your Vows

It's time to take what some people will view as radical measures to restore meaning to marital vows, commitment, and the covenant of marriage. Both churches and individuals have a holy trust and responsibility to do this.

1. *The church.* According to the U.S. Census Bureau, nearly three-fourths of all couples still get married in a religious institution.[12] I believe it's time for the church to aggressively assume its responsibility of exalting and protecting the marriage covenant through the following:

- Refuse to marry couples who will not take a church-prescribed marriage preparation course.
- Craft a fresh marriage covenant that spells out the permanence of the marriage covenant, the responsibilities of both husband and wife to love each other, and a pledge to never divorce. Marry only couples who agree to sign and be held accountable to such a public document.
- Rewrite the marriage ceremony, including the vows, to reflect this return to the truths of God's Word. Read the

signed marriage covenant publicly during the ceremony. Publicly charge the marrying couple and those in attendance to embrace and proclaim their marriage pledge.

- Assign an older marriage and family mentoring couple to all newlyweds before they get married. (More will be shared on this topic in chapter 11.)
- Refuse to marry individuals who have divorced for unbiblical reasons and who have not sought reconciliation.
- Discipline when needed. Divorce needs to become shameful again, and church discipline needs to be resurrected for those who are not fulfilling their vows.[13]

2. *Individuals.* A couple who marry must take important steps to exalt and protect their marriage covenant. They must:

- Agree to faithfully fulfill all the church's requirements for marriage preparation, including the signing of a marriage covenant.
- Refuse to sign any type of prenuptial agreement.
- Pledge to each other, to one's new extended family, and to the community to never divorce and to solemnly fulfill the marriage vows.
- Be accountable after marriage to a marriage and family mentor.

By no means is this a comprehensive list of all that needs to be enacted, nor will it eliminate failure, but it does give us a helpful, proactive starting point.

Commitment #2: Fulfill Your Vows by Staying Married

If you are married, you have a sacred covenant obligation. Fulfill it.

Too many marriages begin to unravel when one of the spouses mentally entertains the possibility of divorce. The notion that divorce is a solution must be rejected. We must fight tenaciously to restore the ideal of marriage for a lifetime. Marital commitment demands perseverance.

Winston Churchill once commented on perseverance, "The nose

of a bulldog is slanted backwards, so that he can continue to breathe without letting go." For a Family Reformation to occur, Christians must not let go of their marriage covenant. The church needs to restore the model of one man and one woman bound together before God for a lifetime.

We need more couples like J. L. and Hilda Simpson, godly Christians who wrote me a profound note:

> September 9, 1995, made us 46 years together. I was 15 and J. L. was 17 when we married. We are now 61 and 63. We could have divorced dozens of times but because we love each other deeply, and because God hates divorce, we didn't want to bring the curse of divorce into our family, so we didn't.[14]

Barbara and I have been married since 1972, and we have had our share of illness, tragedy, and disagreements—but we have not mentioned divorce. That word has never passed through our lips. May I challenge you to do the same?

You need to keep your covenant. You *must* keep your covenant. Your children's marriages, your legacy, and the strength of the church depend upon it.

Commitment #3: Fulfill Your Vows by Praying Faithfully with Your Spouse

Why do so few Christian couples pray together? What could seem more natural—husband and wife talking intimately together with the One who provides the glue to hold a relationship together? Yet prayer is one of the most challenging disciplines for any married couple to practice.

I think I know why. The enemy of our souls, Satan, also knows how effective prayer is. He'll do anything to prevent it in a marriage. And our flesh gets in the way, too, because prayer demands humility before God. It's hard to be in the midst of some selfish behavior and then pray with your spouse—I know, I've tried and failed! But Barbara and I have found that no other spiritual discipline works better in placing God in the center of our marriage.

I believe that daily prayer prevents divorce and makes marriages stronger. A national survey on marital satisfaction and happiness that FamilyLife commissioned in 1995 discovered that couples who pray together frequently (at least three times per week) have higher levels of marital satisfaction than those who don't.[15]

What would happen to the divorce rate in the church if husbands and wives would consistently pray together? I believe that the number of divorces could be cut in half within months, and that within a decade, divorce would be uncommon in the Christian community.

If you want to divorce-proof your marriage, then make a commitment today to begin praying with your spouse.

Commitment #4: Fulfill Your Vows by Caring Faithfully for Your Spouse

I once had the privilege of speaking at a memorable dinner party in Miami. The guests of honor were Allen and Ida Morris; the occasion was their 55th wedding anniversary. The Morris children honored their parents by presenting them with a book, a tribute that chronicled their life together.

The priceless pages were filled with pictures and memorable quotations marking their journey of more than half a century. I leafed through their story and came across one quotation in particular that summarized their feelings for each other. Of his dear wife, Allen said, "We have been married 55 years and we still tell each other 'I love you' all the time. We say it first thing every morning, and it's the last thing we say to each other before we go to sleep. My only regret is that, since Ida is most likely to outlive me, I won't always be around to take care of her. I know the Lord will do it, but in the meantime, I'm glad He uses me."

Couples who affirm the sanctity of marriage *care faithfully for each other.* They meet each other's needs for affection, for emotional and sexual intimacy, for protection and affirmation. And they never stop caring—long after the summer has turned to winter and the vigor of youth is mellowed by old age.

Winston Churchill had this devotion for his beloved wife, Clemmie. Once at a banquet in London, Churchill and the other dignitaries were asked, "If you could not be who you are, who would you like to be?"

Naturally, everyone was curious to know how Churchill would reply. When the great man's turn came, Churchill rose slowly and said dramatically: "If I could not be who I am, I would most like to be"—and here he paused to take his wife's hand—"Lady Churchill's second husband!"[16]

I may not have the charm of the prime minister, but frequently, I let Barbara know how much I care by telling her, "I'd marry you all over again." I've learned that this kind of affirmation freshens our marriage vows and communicates the depth of my affection for her.

Commitment #5: Fulfill Your Vows by Maintaining Emotional and Moral Fidelity

For too many people—Christians included—adultery is the first step out of a marriage. An emotional or sexual attachment to someone *other* than your spouse creates intense passions that sabotage trust and steal marital intimacy. Proverbs 6:27-29 details the consequences of playing with fire:

> Can a man take fire in his bosom, and his clothes not be burned? Or can a man walk on hot coals, and his feet not be scorched? So is the one who goes in to his neighbor's wife; whoever touches her will not go unpunished.

Adultery, as alluring as it may seem, fails to live up to its promises. Peter Blitchington, in his outstanding book *Sex Roles and the Christian Family,* cites a study by the Research Guild that measured sexual satisfaction. The guild found that "compared with the 67 percent of men and 55 percent of women who find marital sex very pleasurable, only 47 percent of the men and 37 percent of the women with extramarital experience rate its sexual aspect very pleasurable."[17]

The grass is *not* greener on the other side of the fence.

The glistening highway of adultery is actually a rutted back road littered with loneliness, guilt, and broken hearts. Adultery supplants loyalty and trust with fear and suspicion.

Will you commit to emotional and moral fidelity to your spouse, no matter how hopeless your marriage may feel? Two steps are critical:

First, *maintain a healthy sexual relationship.* Lovingly study your mate to learn what will keep him or her interested and satisfied in your sexual relationship. Cultivate the fine—and often forgotten—art of romance. Pursue your spouse with the same creativity and energy that characterized your dating relationship.

Second, *guard your heart in relation to the opposite sex.* According to Jesus, the eyes are the doorway to the heart (see Matthew 6:22-23). For this reason, restrict your gaze and refuse the temptation to look longingly at members of the opposite sex. Don't fantasize about someone else. Proverbs 4:23 advises, "Watch over your heart with all diligence, for from it flow the springs of life." Build boundaries around your heart by making yourself accountable to a friend for your secret thoughts.

In many marriages the alluring mistress of pornography undermines trust, divides loyalties, and destroys intimacy. The use of pornography by men may be the most pervasive, powerful, and deadly addiction largely ignored by the Christian community today.

If you feast your eyes on pornography, you need to *turn away* from this evil and *turn to* a real relationship with your God and your spouse.

Commitment #6: Fulfill Your Vows by Finishing Strong

In the 1968 Olympics, Tanzanian marathon runner John Stephen Akhwari limped into an empty stadium more than an hour after all other runners had crossed the finish line. When asked why he had not given up, the gutsy competitor replied, "My country did not send me to Mexico City to start the race; they sent me to finish the race."[18]

America has become a culture of great starters and poor finishers. Many relish initiating new projects but drop out long before completing them. This pattern also occurs in marriage. Americans are quick to walk the aisle—and also quick to run away when the marriage gets rough. We need to heed the words of Charles Spurgeon: "It was by perseverance that the snail reached the ark."

Commit yourself to finishing strong with your vows.

In November of 1995, I spoke to nearly 60,000 men at a Promise Keepers rally at Texas Stadium near Dallas. I urged the men to finish strong in their marriages, and I concluded with the story of Dr. Robertson McQuilkin and his wife, Muriel.

Dr. McQuilkin was president of Columbia Bible College and Seminary (now Columbia International University) in Columbia, South Carolina, for 22 years. All those years, Muriel was his biggest fan and chief supporter. They were a dynamic ministry team: Robertson presided over the college and seminary, and Muriel hosted a local Christian radio show.

But in 1984, Muriel's health deteriorated. Tests confirmed the worst: She had Alzheimer's disease. Over the next few years, she slowly failed, losing many of her basic skills. She couldn't speak clearly, and she lost her ability to reason. Muriel no longer could feed herself, and Robertson had to dress and bathe her.

With Muriel's needs escalating and his responsibilities at the college unchanged, Robertson faced a gut-wrenching decision: Should he place Muriel in an institution? After all, he had been called by God to the ministry, and now caring for his wife encroached upon his duties at the college. In an article in *Christianity Today,* Dr. McQuilkin wrote,

> When the time came, the decision was firm. It took no great calculation. It was a matter of integrity. Had I not promised, 42 years before, "in sickness and in health . . . till death do us part"?
>
> This was no grim duty to which I was stoically resigned, however. It was only fair. She had, after all, cared for me for almost four decades with marvelous devotion; now it was my turn. And such a partner she was! If I took care of her for 40 years, I would never be out of her debt.[19]

In 1990, Robertson resigned as the president of Columbia Bible College and Seminary so he could care for his beloved Muriel.

While telling this story to the men at the Promise Keepers rally, I recalled how I had phoned Barbara when I first read the McQuilkins' story. After I shared it with her, there was a long silence, then with her voice breaking Barbara asked, "Dennis, will you love me like that?" Without hesitation, I responded, "Yes, sweetheart, I will."

The men listening to me at Texas Stadium started to applaud. But I stopped them and said, "Guys, the issue is *not* what I've committed to do; the real issue is what *you* are willing to do. Are *you* willing to commit yourself to love *your* wife, unconditionally, as long as you both shall live?"

I then asked all the married men to stand and recite their wedding vows. Across the stadium they rose to their feet in a huge wave. A dull hum rose to a roar as thousands joined to recite the most important vow any man will ever make to another person—a commitment to the sanctity and permanence of his marriage.

In early 1996, Robertson McQuilkin—still caring for Muriel—wrote, "I think my life must be happier than the lives of 95 percent of the people on planet earth."[20]

That's the reward given to those who obey God and persevere in marriage.

REFORMATION CHECKUP

A marriage is never static—the relationship is either moving forward or losing ground. These questions will help you assess the vitality of your marriage. Check your answer to each question, then refer to Scoring below.

1. How would you describe the closeness and intimacy of your marriage?
   _____ Very Close and Intimate
   _____ Somewhat Close and Intimate
   _____ Not That Close and Intimate

2. How committed are you to the idea of the marriage covenant—one spouse for your lifetime?
   _____ Very Committed
   _____ Somewhat Committed
   _____ Not That Committed

3. How often do you share your deepest thoughts and feelings with your spouse?

    ____ Very Often

    ____ Somewhat Often

    ____ Not That Often

4. How frequently do you pray with your spouse?

    ____ Very Often

    ____ Somewhat Often

    ____ Not That Often

WOMEN ONLY

5. Based on recent experience, how important is it to you to do something special for your spouse—like cook a favorite dish or excuse him from his "Honey-Do List"?

    ____ Very Important

    ____ Somewhat Important

    ____ Not That Important

MEN ONLY

5. Based on recent experience, how important is it to you to do something special for your spouse—like bring her flowers or give her a night off?

    ____ Very Important

    ____ Somewhat Important

    ____ Not That Important

Scoring: How many questions did you answer that begin with "Very"? The more the better! If most of your answers began with "Somewhat" or "Not That," you should prayerfully consider if some unwanted distance has invaded your marriage. Would it be wise to spend some concentrated time with your spouse renewing the communication and closeness?

AReformation Moment

SIR GEORGE THE KNIGHT

The ordeal at Worms over, Martin Luther and companions boarded their two-wheeled "limousines" on April 26, 1521, and headed for Wittenberg, their departure unnoticed.

His spirits no longer buoyed by crowds, Martin was circumspect. After much back-room debate and negotiation, the Diet had ruled that the church's actions against him must stand. Luther was barred from further preaching or writing—he was considered an outlaw. The Diet had promised him only three more weeks of official protection, enough time for the return trip to Wittenberg. After that, anyone could kill him and not face charges for murder.

Creeping along the road, which was just a rocky path, the caravan entered a quiet wood, dense with spring foliage. Abruptly, several armed horsemen rushed from the trees and stopped the wagons.

"Is one of you Martin Luther?" the leader shouted.

Martin's driver panicked and pointed at the stocky monk. Three of the intruders grabbed Luther and wrestled him to the ground. Before being dragged away to a waiting horse, Martin snatched two of his most precious books—the Hebrew Old Testament and the Greek New Testament.

Word spread quickly about the kidnapping. Martin Luther's whereabouts were unknown, and many feared he was dead. Albrecht Dürer, an influential artist, wrote in his diary: "Whether he lives, or whether they have murdered him—which I do not know—he has suffered this for the sake of the Christian truth. . . . O God, if Luther is dead, who will now present the gospel to us so clearly?"

In reality, the abduction was a carefully executed plot with one of Martin's traveling companions in on the ruse. With his life seriously in danger after the Diet of Worms, some of Luther's supporters decided to hide him near Eisenach at a castle called the Wartburg.

To maintain the hoax, Martin discarded his monk's clothing and let his hair and beard grow. He dressed as a knight and took the name of Sir George.

Although it may sound romantic, Wartburg castle was not a five-star lodge. It was cavernous and drafty, and Martin shared his quarters with owls and bats. Worse for Martin, though, was the loneliness. A gregarious, energetic man, Luther now had more time for thinking, praying, and writing than he wanted. The abundance of time alone led to a bout with depression, and Martin had digestive and other physical problems, too. He compared the experience to what Elijah endured after defeating the prophets of Baal.

"I can tell you in this idle solitude there are a thousand battles with Satan," Martin said.

In spite of his problems, Martin wrote furiously. After just three weeks at Wartburg Castle, he had completed a commentary on Psalm 68 and had begun a translation of the New Testament for the German people.

During his "captivity," Luther's books and other publications were burned in the Netherlands and elsewhere. In Germany, though, his disappearance made Luther and his ideas even more popular.

For amusement Luther sneaked out of the castle to go hunting, gather strawberries, and even meet with Franciscan brothers—but always in disguise. One day on a hunt, a rabbit tried to escape the dogs by running up Luther's pant leg! Before the crazed animal could be removed, the dogs bit and killed it through the cloth.

Luther completed translating the New Testament into German in just 11 weeks, a prodigious rate of more than 1,500 words per day. The translation was so masterful that ultimately it heavily influenced even today's German language. Now everyone—from nobles to peasants—could read God's Word with as much ease as they read pamphlets or the newspaper. For a man who loved Scripture as intensely as Luther, that may have been the supreme gift he gave to his people.

While at Wartburg Castle, Luther clandestinely communicated with friends in Wittenberg. The reformation fires were hot, burning nearly out of control. While cooped up, Martin learned that a number of his Augustinian brothers had left the monastery and married. Other events were escalating at an alarming speed. Martin wanted to go home, to rejoin the action, but the danger was too great.

CHAPTER SIX

Role Call

*I do not deny that women have been wronged and even tortured; but I
doubt if they were ever tortured so much as they are tortured now
by the absurd modern attempt to make them domestic empresses
and competitive clerks at the same time.*
—G. K. CHESTERTON

The dark and murky Blackwater River meanders through cypress
groves and lonely swamps in northern Florida. During the day,
this pristine wilderness is alluring. But when the sun sets, daylight
yields authority to the blackness of night, and an eerie transformation occurs. Moonlit shadows creep across the twisted cypress
groves like corpses. The strange cries and guttural shrieks of animals penetrate the silence, evoking primal fears and childhood
nightmares.

Local residents once feared the Blackwater River at night. And
for good reason since strange things happened down by the river.
Over a period of two decades, a number of prized hunting dogs,
worth thousands of dollars, vanished without a trace. Their owners
were at a loss to explain the disappearances. Some residents thought
thieves were snatching the dogs; others believed a swamp creature
was the culprit.

In August of 1995, after Rufus Goodwin's dog, Flojo, disappeared, the strange case was finally solved. Flojo was wearing an electronic collar when she vanished, so Goodwin was able to track the collar's signal. He followed the signal deep into the swamp, to a hole near a game trail.

Goodwin knew immediately that the culprit was an alligator.

A few days later, the 10-foot, 500-pound alligator was captured and killed. When the gator was cut open, the hunters found Flojo's collar and half her remains. Incredibly, they also found *six* other dog collars, one of which belonged to a dog missing since 1981!

Goodwin and others figured out the tactics of the ingenious 50-year-old alligator. Deliberate, crafty, and voracious, the gator "would come out of his hole, come up the creek 200 yards and sit on the trail." Blinded by the darkness and unaware of the imminent danger, the dogs ran right into the monster's gaping jaws.[1]

THE GAPING JAWS OF FEMINISM

For the last 30 years, men and women in our culture have run blindly into the jaws of something equally dangerous and life-threatening: a deliberate and voracious philosophical "alligator" called feminism. Perched on the path of mainstream America, feminism has devoured families and imperiled children. Promising freedom, rights, and liberation, feminist doctrine has blurred the lines between male and female, seduced the church, and confused a whole generation of young adults.

Sociologist W. Peter Blitchington argues that "the most important component of the family is the husband-wife relationship. Any changes in that relationship will produce far-reaching effects upon the community as a whole."[2] Feminism has completely altered the expectations, roles, and responsibilities in vast numbers of American homes—both secular and Christian.

Why is feminism such a threat? Why must we Christians denounce, and even root out, the tenets of feminist ideology in our homes, churches, and communities? Two reasons are paramount:

First, *the goal of feminism is a genderless society.* Writer Susan Moller Okin bluntly articulates the secret passion of these social engineers. Read her words slowly. They describe an ideal future feminist society:

A just future would be one without gender. In its social structures and practices [read "family"], one's sex would have no more relevance than one's eye color or the length of one's toes. No assumptions would be made about "male" and "female" roles; childbearing would be so conceptually separated from child rearing and other family responsibilities that it would be a cause for surprise, and no little concern, if men and women were not equally responsible for domestic life or if children were to spend much more time with one parent than the other.[3]

A quick glance at American life shows the rapid progress that feminists have made toward their genderless objective. "In nurseries and schools, in athletics and home economics, in sex education and social life," writes Harvard sociologist George Gilder, "the sexes are thrown together in the continuing effort to create a unisex society."[4]

Yet this approach to sexual roles just does not work. Esteemed anthropologist Margaret Mead concluded, after studying multiple societies, "If any human society—large or small, simple or complex, based upon the most rudimentary hunting and fishing, or on the whole elaborate interchange of manufactured products—is to survive, it must have a pattern of social life that comes to terms with the differences between the sexes."[5]

After studying more than 2,000 cultures that have existed in world history, Dr. Charles Winick of City University of New York determined that femininity and masculinity blurred in only 55 of them. And not one of these unisex societies survived more than a few years.[6]

Second, *feminism devalues marriage and child rearing.* Simone de Beauvoir, one of the philosophical mothers of feminism, states the matter all too plainly:

I think a woman should be on her guard against the trap of motherhood and marriage. Even if she would dearly like to have children, she ought to think seriously about the conditions under which she would have to bring them up, because being a mother these days is real slavery. . . . If a woman still wants a child in spite of everything, it would be better to have one without getting married, because marriage is really the biggest trap of all.[7]

Driven by this subversive philosophy, millions of American women have sprung from the "trap" of motherhood and marriage into the "liberating" surroundings of the workplace. Career-minded mothers have surrendered their children to day-care, believing they could have it all—success at work and at home. Many other mothers have been forced by their husbands to join the workforce—often at the expense of their children—for the sole purpose of a desirable lifestyle.

Never before in our nation's history has a woman's role centered on economics and the fulfillment of a career—at the expense of the family. Because of this focus, our national birth rate has slid to only 1.7 births per couple, the lowest in history.

I find it fascinating that the feminists and others who have so devalued motherhood and children now sponsor an annual Take Your Daughter to Work Day. This national observance is supposed to build self-esteem in daughters by showing them how they can find value and self-worth in the workplace.

Strangely absent from the organizer's list of valued occupations for women are those of wife, mother, and homemaker. I am not opposed to women having the opportunity to use their God-given gifts and abilities to pursue careers outside of marriage and the home. But why are we so silent about the value of a woman choosing the esteemed full-time occupation of wife and mother? I believe that millions of teenage girls today are struggling with a deficient self-image *because* their fathers and mothers gave themselves to careers and material pursuits instead of investing in the next generation.

The feminist message *is* being heard by this generation. At my teenage daughter's school, Take Your Daughter to Work Day was celebrated and a career poll was taken. Not one of my daughter's classmates *wanted* to be a mother.

At the beginning of this century, President Theodore Roosevelt spoke to the National Congress of Mothers in Washington, D.C. The truth of his words rings just as clearly now as we enter the twenty-first century:

No piled-up wealth, no splendor or material growth, no brilliance or artistic development, will permanently avail any people unless its home life is healthy . . . unless the average woman is a good wife, a good mother, able and willing to perform the first and greatest duty of womanhood, able and willing to bear, and to bring up as they should be brought up, healthy children, sound in body, mind and character. . . . Into the woman's keeping is committed the destiny of the generations to come after us.[8]

A SUBTLE ATTACK

Why is feminism so hostile to the traditional family? A significant factor is the tragic childhood family experience that several key feminist leaders endured. When the modern feminist movement was gaining momentum in the '60s and the '70s, three prominent spokeswomen were Betty Friedan, Germaine Greer, and Gloria Steinem. Author Brenda Hunter persuasively argues in *Home by Choice* that "all three came from troubled families. Friedan and Greer had openly rejecting mothers, and Steinem, an absent father and an emotionally ill mother."[9]

Each of these women would play a role in "reinventing" womanhood and emasculating manhood. Hunter writes, "How ironic that three unnurtured women with distorted views of men and marriage have influenced our current notions of family and motherhood. Speaking from their woundedness, these three have disparaged marriage and the traditional woman. . . . A whole generation of women has marched to their misguided anti-marriage, anti-male, and anti-family music."[10]

Feminist ideology pervades and poisons our culture. George Gilder correctly observed that "society can resist epidemics of physical disease, [but] it is defenseless against diseases of the mind."[11] More distressing, though, is how the Christian community has failed to challenge much of feminist ideology with the clear teaching of Scripture.

The family is God's primary institution for achieving a host of vital objectives, the most important one being the nurturing and training of children. Through the family, children *best* learn the essence of biblical masculinity and femininity and what it means to be husband, wife, father, and mother.

The family achieves optimum success in nurturing children when a father and a mother willingly embrace clearly defined roles in the home: the father sacrificially loving, leading, and protecting; the mother sacrificially nurturing and caring.

Feminism overturns this equation by demeaning the man's uniqueness and importance and denying the woman's invaluable, incomparable role of nurturing mother and helping wife.

My parents, Ward and Dalcie Rainey, were married for almost 45 years. I was fortunate that my mom and dad were untainted by the tenets of feminism. My mother worked in the home, nurturing two rambunctious boys. She loved and cared for us with the tenderness and the tenacity of Mother Teresa. My father, a private man with a great sense of humor, built his own business and his family as well. Although his father had deserted him and his family when he was a boy, my dad provided the moral and spiritual backbone for our family through his model of integrity. Dad loved Mom.

I am the man, husband, and father I am today because I had a *mother* and a *father* who lived out biblical roles in front of me and loved me faithfully and sacrificially. Virtually everything about me— my identity, my character, my personality—was formed through their influence.

Feminism would have castigated my dad for his active role as the head, the leader of our home. My mother would have been made to feel inferior for her career at home and devalued for the enormous amount of time spent nurturing her sons. To the feminist, fatherhood is irrelevant, and full-time motherhood is a limiting endeavor, a "trap," and a burden to avoid.

My mom and dad would have vehemently disagreed!

God Made Them Male and Female

Have you ever listened carefully to an evangelical pastor or conference speaker teach on the subject of roles in marriage? Even if his theology is biblical—affirming the husband's role as servant-leader and the wife's role as helper-nurturer—he inevitably feels the need to defend his position. I've heard speakers say things like:

"No, I'm not being sexist."

"Of course, a number of Christians interpret this passage differently."

We apologize. We backpedal. We dilute the truth.

Some skirt the issue altogether.

The biblical understanding of sexual roles is essential to the survival and success of the Christian family.

Although in discussing this topic I feel like a soldier crossing a minefield while under intense enemy fire, now is not the time to be bashful about what the Bible teaches concerning roles in marriage. Husbands need to be called out of their passivity or dictatorial headship and challenged to lead by laying down their lives for their wives and families. Wives need to be called back to being helpmates to their husbands and nurturing, affirming mothers to their children.

A Family Reformation requires husbands and wives who know what the Bible teaches, who live out their roles and responsibilities without shame, and who pass on a biblical model to the next generation.

The biblical understanding of sexual roles is essential to the survival and success of the Christian family. And the centerpiece of our theology is a six-word statement by God in the first chapter of Genesis: *"Male* and *female* He created them" (v. 27, emphasis added).

Two timeless truths are embedded in this powerful statement.

First, *male and female are separate and distinct genders.* The sexes are *different.* Not interchangeable, but unique. And the differences are much more than merely physical. From birth, boys and girls exhibit distinctive characteristics that derive from their unique, divinely created *biological* natures. Generally, boys tend to be more aggressive and physical in their behavior; girls tend to prefer more sedate activities, such as playing house or dressing dolls.

At age six, the average boy has about 7 percent more vital energy than the average girl.[12] The difference in energy increases to 35 percent at the onset of puberty.[13]

Developments in modern science support the variety of biological differences between male and female. For example, researchers have discovered subtle differences between the brains of men and women—in both structure and function.[14] Generally, certain skills come easier to one gender than the other: Women are better at interpreting the emotions of people in photographs,[15] while men are statistically better at solving mathematical problems.[16]

Also note that God created *two* genders to reflect His image, not three or four. Unisex, homosexuality, and other sexual perversions are a direct assault on the image of God. A "genderless marriage" cannot reflect the image of God. A Family Reformation calls men and women to reflect God's image by rejecting distortions of male and female sexuality.

Second, *God created the two sexes with distinct purposes in mind.*

The characteristics of your gender are not, as feminists contend, a result of cultural conditioning. God gave both men and women a divinely imprinted, biologically mandated set of gifts and abilities that enable them to contribute invaluably to the lives of others.

If you are a married *male,* then you have been *created by God* to love and lead your wife, and to provide for and to protect your family.

If you are a married *female,* then you have been *created by God* to nurture your children and to support your husband.

I love the illustration related to the distinction in sexual roles used by authors John Piper and Wayne Grudham: "Every wife knows that something is amiss in a man's manhood if he suggests that she get out of bed 50 percent of the time [at night] to see what the strange noise is downstairs."[17]

The irony is that in every marital relationship, a husband and a wife settle into some sort of social and organizational arrangement.

There are no roleless marriages.

The question we must answer is, "What standard will we use to define roles in our marriage?"

The Bible is the only standard! Our greatest joy and fulfillment in life come when we embrace the roles God created for us. But today there is a revolt against God and these roles. Why? Because these roles require accountability and submission to authority.

In a genderless world, where the structure and lines of authority in the family are unclear, both husbands and wives inevitably must fall back on their own flawed human wisdom. A "roleless marriage" will never fully reflect the true image of God.

A NOBLE ENDEAVOR

When my daughter, Rebecca, was 11, the two of us were driving home one evening after gymnastics practice. Ever the inquisitive dad, I asked Rebecca what she wanted to be when she grew up. Her response didn't surprise me; I'd heard it a number of times before.

"Dad, when I grow up," she said with great determination, "I want to be a gymnastics instructor!"

I pondered her answer for a while before saying, "Rebecca, that's a good goal, and if God calls you to be a gymnastics instructor, nothing would make me happier. But I want you to know that if, when you grow up, God calls you to marry a young man and become a mother, your mom and I would be just as proud of you. Rebecca, you need to make your home your primary focus and commitment."

A couple of months later I overheard Rebecca and Barbara discussing the subject of careers. Barbara asked Rebecca what she wanted to be when she grew up. I cocked my head to listen.

"Mom," said Rebecca, "when I grow up, I think I want to be a wife and mother."

YES!

CONFORM OR REFORM?

There are those in the Christian community who cringe as I tell this story. How narrow of me to "push" my daughter toward being "just a wife" or "only a mother." Some might say that I am trying to resurrect the Ozzie and Harriet home of the '50s.

To those who criticize my exhortation to my daughter, I would ask a couple of questions: When we point our daughters to the world to find fulfillment at the expense of the family, are we following God's design for the family? (The same would be true for our sons.) Or to put it another way, what kind of wife do you want for your son? What kind of mother do you desire for your grandchildren? Isn't the present chaos in the family enough evidence that the feminist social experiment with the family has tragically failed?

Why would anyone criticize parents who raise their daughters to be first and foremost a wife and mother? Have we gone mad?

A famous entertainer, whose mother died when she was six years old, said in an interview: "When I see my girlfriends with their mothers even now I can't imagine—it's unfathomable what that sort of nurturing would have done for me. Let's face it. I probably wouldn't be sitting on this couch here talking to you now if I'd had a mother. I really miss it. My role models who nurtured me when I was growing up were all men."[18] This woman's name is Madonna.

At this point, in the most heartfelt words I can muster, I must address an extremely critical issue: Never before in the history of the church have we raised our daughters with such a preoccupation to achieve successful careers. Think of what's happening. The church is now staggering under the weight of broken homes, yet we continue to push our daughters toward the marketplace—at the expense of the family.

The Christian community needs to repent of its conformity to the world and resolve to train the future generation of children—both sons and daughters—in what is required first and foremost to be successful at home. Then, and only then, will we have something distinctive to offer the world.

To become a husband-father or wife-mother, according to the scriptural mandate, is a noble endeavor. The time has come for Christians to reaffirm these biblical roles. We must give the next generation a vision of God's structural design for families.

THE BIBLICAL ROLE FOR MEN: SERVANT-LEADER

What is the husband's role in the marriage relationship? When you collate, analyze, and synthesize the biblical record, you arrive at a clear definition: The husband's role is servant-leader. The husband is the head of his home. Paul summarized well the man's position in Ephesians 5:23-25: "For the husband is the head of the wife, as Christ also is the head of the church, He Himself being the Savior of the body. But as the church is subject to Christ, so also the wives ought to be to their husbands in everything. Husbands, love your wives, just as Christ also loved the church and gave Himself up for her."

Just how did Christ love the church?

Self-denial: Jesus Christ stepped out of eternity into time and laid aside the privileges of deity. He denied Himself, even to the point of death. Servant-leaders deny themselves for the good of their families.

Sacrificial action: Christ gave His life for those whom He loved. Husbands are called—daily—to give up their desires and die to "self."

Servant's heart: Jesus continually set aside His own desires to serve others. In the same way, husbands should surrender their own agendas—and their hobbies—to serve their wives and meet their needs.

I believe one reason feminism has made such inroads in our culture is that for too many years, husbands have ignored the biblical imperative of servant-leadership. We have not loved our wives as Christ commanded; as a result, many women have sought fulfillment outside the family unit. Even today, many Christian husbands act like dictators in their homes; they think only about their own needs and expect their wives to serve them.

By pointing to Christ's servant-leadership, however, Paul gave a radically new definition of leadership. What wife would not want to be loved like this?

Even though Barbara and I have been married since 1972, I am still learning the art of servant-leadership. Over the years, Saturdays have proven to be a test of my true priorities. After a wearisome workweek, I long for a quiet, unstructured weekend. I love to hitch my boat to my car, drive to my favorite fishing hole, and drown a few worms.

I still recall one Saturday, many years ago, when I did just that. Barbara didn't want me to go; she had just finished a hard week at home with the kids and needed a break. But I went anyway, ignoring her pleas.

My son and I fished for a few hours. But I was miserable. I started the boat motor and headed back to the dock. Benjamin asked why we were leaving.

"Son, your father has made a bad choice; your mom needs me at home," I said. I went back home and apologized.

God calls us men to deny ourselves, live sacrificially, and lead with a servant's heart. To do anything less is to be disobedient to God. To the unrepentant man, these ideals are foolish and burdensome. But to the man who has surrendered himself to Christ, they are weighty responsibilities that lead to life and success in marriage.

At the core of a Family Reformation are husbands and fathers who sacrifice time, energy, and their lives for their wives and families.

HOW TO BE A GOOD HUSBAND

Nearly 100 years ago, a publication entitled *A Bond of Love* was issued by a small religious publishing company in Chicago. Not long ago sections of this book were brought to my attention. The language is a bit dated, of course, but the ideas resonate with truth and exhibit a tone of servanthood and caring that I wish would permeate marital relationships today.

In a later section, I will present "How to Be a Good Wife," but here are excerpts on how men can love and cherish their wives.

Honor your wife. She must be exalted and never dethroned.

Love your wife. The measure is, as Christ loved the church and gave Himself for her.

Show your love. All life manifests itself. As certainly as a live tree will put forth leaves in the spring, so certainly will a living love show itself.

Suffer for your wife, if need be. Christ suffered for the church. Consult with her. She is as apt to be right as you are, and frequently able to add much to your stock of wisdom.

Study to keep her young. It is not work, but worry, that wears. Keep a true heart between her and all harm. If you will carefully walk in the way of righteousness you can shield her from cankering care. Providence will not be likely to bring upon her anything that is not for her good.

Help to bear her burdens. Bear one another's burdens, and so fulfill the law of love.

Make yourself helpful by thoughtfulness. Remember to

bring into the house your best smile and sunshine. It is good for you and cheers up the house.

Study your own character as a husband. Transfer your deeds, with the impressions they might naturally make, to some other couple and see what feelings they would waken in your heart. . . . Are you seeking to multiply the joys of your wife, as well as to support her? Are you an agreeable associate among your companions? . . . If you can, make yourself a role model husband, that will help your wife to be a model wife. . . . Your home [will be ensured] against shipwreck and your happiness against decay.

Seek to refine your nature. It is no slander to say that many men have wives much more refined than themselves. Preserve the gentleness and refinement of your wife as a rich legacy for your children, and in so doing you will lift yourself to higher levels. Be a gentleman as well as a husband. . . . The soul of gentlemanliness is a kindly feeling toward others that prompts one to secure their comfort.

Level up. If your wife has the advantage in culture and refinement—and this is a quite a common condition, as girls usually have a better chance for education and more leisure for books than boys have—do not sink her to your level, but by study and thoughtfulness rise to her plane. . . .

Stay at home. Habitual absence during the evenings is sure to bring sorrow. If your duty or business calls you, you have the promise that you will be kept in all your ways. But if you go out to mingle with society, and leave your wife at home alone . . . you know that there is no good in store for you. . . . Home is your only retreat.[19]

THE BIBLICAL ROLE FOR WOMEN: HELPER-LOVER

Three key Scriptures outline the role of wife and mother:

> But for Adam there was not found a helper suitable for him. So the Lord God caused a deep sleep to fall upon the man, and he slept; then He took one of his ribs, and closed up the flesh at that place. And the Lord God fashioned into a woman the rib which He had taken from the man, and brought her to the man. (Genesis 2:20-22)

> Wives, submit to your husbands as to the Lord. For the husband is the head of the wife as Christ is the head of the church, his body, of which he is the Savior. Now as the church submits to Christ, so also wives should submit to their husbands in everything. (Ephesians 5:22-24, NIV)

> Encourage the young women to love their husbands, to love their children, to be sensible, pure, workers at home, kind, being subject to their own husbands, that the word of God may not be dishonored. (Titus 2:4-5)

These Scriptures make it clear that, first of all, *wives are called to be helpers for their husbands.* Every woman needs to understand just how much her husband needs her. Society considers *helper* a demeaning term; God does not.

Second, *wives are called to be submissive to their husbands.* The Greek word for submission is *hupotasso,* which means "to place or arrange under."[20] Submission is not blind obedience; neither is it silent suffering. Instead, the word connotes a voluntary subordination to a recognized authority, in this case, the divinely appointed authority of the husband.

Although the wife is responsible to God for her submission, her husband's assignment is to lead in such a way that makes it reasonable and enjoyable for her to follow.

With few exceptions, Barbara willingly has submitted to my leadership. She knows that I am eternally grateful for a wife who allows me to lead—and even to fail. Her submission is a vote of confidence in my manhood. And it encourages me to lead.

Third, *wives are called to make mothering a priority.* If you are a mom, your children need you—desperately. They need your time and attention and painstaking devotion. President Theodore Roosevelt said that "the most honorable and desirable task which can beset any woman is to be a good and wise mother in a home marked by self-respect and mutual forbearance. . . . Her very name stands for loving unselfishness and self-abnegation, and, in any society fit to exist, is fraught with associations which render it holy."[21]

HOW TO BE A GOOD WIFE

Here's the list of ideas for wives—only slightly edited—from the book *A Bond of Love:*

Reverence your husband. He sustains by God's order a position of dignity as head of the family.

Love him. A wife loves as naturally as the sun shines. Love is your best weapon. You conquered him with that in the first place.

Do not conceal your love from him. If he is crowded with care and too busy to seem to heed your love, you need to give all the greater attention to securing his knowledge of your love. Keep his love. . . .

Cultivate the modesty and delicacy of your youth. However much men may admire the public performance of gifted women, they do not desire that boldness and dash in a wife. The holy blush of a maiden's modesty is more powerful in hallowing and governing a home than the heaviest armament that every warrior bore.

Cultivate personal attractiveness. This means the storing of your mind with a knowledge of passing events, and with a good idea of the world's general advance. If you read nothing, and make no effort to make yourself attractive, you will soon sink down into a dull hack of stupidity.

Cultivate physical attractiveness. When you were encouraging the attentions of him you call husband, you did not neglect any item of dress or appearance that could help you. Your hair was always in perfect training. You never greeted him with a ragged or untidy dress or soiled hands. Keep yourself at your best. . . .

Do not forget the power of incidental attentions. A little time spent by your husband's side, without actually being busied with either work or plans or complaints, is not wasted.

Make your home attractive. This means more than furniture. It means the thousand little touches of taste that drive the darkness out of the corners, and the stiffness out of the parlor, and the gloom out of the house. Make your home so that you will feel easy in it yourself.

Study your husband's character. He has his peculiarities. He has no right to many of them, but he has them, and you need to know them, thus you can avoid many hours of friction.[22]

Wrestling with the Alligator

We wrestle with sex roles, don't we? The biblical ideals grate on our flesh and prick at our selfishness. Our obstinacy in this one area only illustrates the depth to which feminism has shaped our thoughts.

At times we feel like we're wrestling with alligators.

A few years ago, a 12-year-old boy named Michael was swimming in a small pond near his family's home in Florida. Paddling along with a snorkel and mask, head underwater, Michael didn't know that an 11-foot, 400-pound alligator was bearing down upon him.

The creature lunged for the boy's head. When its jaws snapped shut, the mask and snorkel were torn away. Miraculously, Michael's head came free from the gator's mouth; he began swimming frantically toward shore, with a hungry alligator following in his wake.

The boy's cousin, Jill, standing on the shoreline, screamed. That alerted Michael's mother. She raced to the bank just as her son reached the shore.

Then the gator clamped onto Michael's legs; his mother grabbed his hands and pulled—a fierce tug-of-war between a tenacious mother and a ferocious alligator.

Clutching Michael's hands in a death grip, his mom pulled with superhuman strength. Suddenly, inexplicably, the alligator let go and returned to the depths. Michael's mother then dragged her son up the bank to safety.

Three months later, Michael showed a friend the scene of the near-fatal attack. By then, almost all of his scars had healed. The gouge in his scalp was covered with hair; the gashes on his legs and feet had mended. Proudly, Michael showed off three small scars on the back of his right hand. Three marks of love. Those marks had been left not by the snarling alligator, but by his mother's fingernails. She had drawn blood pulling her boy to safety.[23]

Like Michael, children today are caught in the middle of a fierce struggle. Our culture, much like that hungry alligator, seeks to devour them. It demeans their value by denying the importance of the Divine imprint of *maleness* and *femaleness*. Left unchallenged, it will ultimately destroy their families.

Contrary to the prevailing cultural opinion, God-fearing, home-loving wives and their counterparts—God-fearing, sacrificing-servant husbands—are society's two greatest needs.

REFORMATION CHECKUP

Here are a few questions to prompt your thinking on the critical issue of roles. After checking your answers, refer to Scoring below.

1. How would you describe the importance to you of interdependence (seeking the insight or involvement of your spouse in most areas of your life)?
   _____ Very Important to Me
   _____ Somewhat Important to Me
   _____ Not That Important to Me

2. How comfortable are you with the biblical teaching of male headship in marriage?
   _____ Very Comfortable
   _____ Somewhat Comfortable
   _____ Not That Comfortable

WOMEN ONLY
3. How would you evaluate your success in showing your husband respect?
   _____ Very Successful
   _____ Somewhat Successful
   _____ Not That Successful

If you have children . . .
4. Based on the amount of time and energy invested, how would you evaluate the importance to you of being a nurturer of your child(ren)?
   _____ Very Important
   _____ Somewhat Important
   _____ Not That Important

5. Based on your experiences of the past year, how would you describe your commitment to teaching, modeling, and affirming biblical roles of men and women to your child(ren)?

_____ Very Committed
_____ Somewhat Committed
_____ Not That Committed

MEN ONLY

3. How would you evaluate your knowledge of the real needs and dreams of your wife?

_____ Very Knowledgeable
_____ Somewhat Knowledgeable
_____ Not That Knowledgeable

4. How effective are you at being a servant-leader for your wife (and family)?

_____ Very Effective
_____ Somewhat Effective
_____ Not That Effective

If you have children . . .

5. How involved are you in helping your wife in the care, training, and discipline of your child(ren)?

_____ Very Involved
_____ Somewhat Involved
_____ Not That Involved

6. Based on your experiences of the past year, how would you describe your commitment to teaching, modeling, and affirming biblical roles of men and women to your child(ren)?

_____ Very Committed
_____ Somewhat Committed
_____ Not That Committed

Scoring: If most of your answers were in the "Very" category, you probably have thought long and hard about the roles issue. However, if you answered many of the questions with "Somewhat" or "Not That" responses, you may be uncertain about some male-female role matters. Don't feel alone! Many in our society—including the church—are also grappling with this topic. Study God's Word to seek God's insights on this topic.

A Reformation Moment

CARLA'S NEW PARENTS

Carla Godsey could not figure out what had happened to her parents.

Weeks had passed since Debi and Jim had "found God" at the marriage conference, and although there still were many rocky moments, peace was settling on the Godsey home.

What a change from the past when take-no-prisoners verbal battles had raged and her parents' marriage was a "pile of garbage." During the fighting, Carla often ran to her room to hide and cry. Almost every argument ended with the crash of the front door—usually, Jim storming out to roam and drink for hours until his anger cooled. Carla was frightened enough during some fights to ask neighbors for help or to call 911.

But something weird was going on. Now when Carla's mom and dad got mad at each other, Jim often would stop midfight and say, "Deb, we're going to pray!" Glaring at each other, their teeth bared and jaws clenched, they would drop to their knees: "Dear God, please help us!"

And they prayed with Carla, too—or tried to. Each night Jim would come to her room for a good-night prayer, and Carla would cry. With her feelings rubbed raw after years of family turmoil, did this moment of parental intimacy seem to promise too much hope? Deep down, she still felt this "faith stuff" was fake.

Probably the most puzzling change was in her mom. Before accepting Christ, Debi was loud, outspoken, insecure—a bit wild. Carla noticed now that her mom was calmer and had more patience. Her tongue wasn't so sharp, she forgave more easily, and she had stopped wearing seductive clothing. And all of the drugs, alcohol, and pornography were gone from the house.

Jim was not himself either. Instead of backing down to Debi as before, now he was hanging in with the relationship. Instead of running out the door when tempers flared, he would stay, speak more calmly, and stand his ground. Carla liked seeing these qualities in her dad.

Most bizarre to Carla was that Jim and Debi showed genuine kindness—even affection—to each other. Could it be they actually were in love?

Before God's intervention in Debi's life, when she was suicidal, Debi had taken Carla to one of Milwaukee's top child psychologists. "I knew my ship was sinking; I didn't want Carla's to sink, too," Debi said.

A year into the counseling—about six months after the marriage conference—Carla blurted to her therapist one afternoon, "I don't need to see you anymore!"

The psychologist called Jim and Debi into the office and asked Carla to repeat what she'd said: "My parents have committed their marriage and their lives to God. I don't need to see you anymore."

"Why, Carla?" the therapist asked. "What has changed?"

"Their relationship has changed. Mom's changed."

Skeptical, the psychologist gave Carla her business card and said, "If you ever need me, call at any time." Carla took the card but never used it. Her therapy was over.

Carla's own skepticism about her parents' religion was eroding fast. And she was becoming jealous to have whatever it was that now made them so happy.

On Easter weekend 1991, after much prayer and discussion between themselves, Carla's parents concluded it was time to ask her if she wanted to give her life to God. They sensed the Holy Spirit was stirring in her heart. At Carla's request, Debi took her for a long after-dark ride, and as they cruised the empty downtown streets, Carla cried and cried. Debi understood, remembering that night six months earlier when she had felt she stood on a precipice, terrified, wondering how she could possibly let go of everything that held her fragile life together . . . and throw herself into the arms of the God she didn't know.

Finally, Debi parked the car and asked, "Carla, do you want to commit your life to Christ?"

Carla first shrugged an "I don't know," then, through her tears, she nodded her head "Yes."

Still a baby Christian herself, Debi didn't know exactly what to do or say. They agreed that Carla would make her commitment public after an upcoming church service.

The Sunday after Easter, Carla accepted the love that had saved her mom's life, rescued her dad from alcohol, and made the Godseys a family. Now she, too, knew the One whose power had transformed her nightmare into a loving home.

CHAPTER SEVEN

Parenting with a Purpose

*A child is a person who is going to carry on what you have started. . . . He
will assume control of your cities, states, and nations. He is going to
move in and take over your churches, schools, universities,
and corporations. . . . The fate of humanity is in his hands.*
—ABRAHAM LINCOLN

In the fading twilight, the headlights of an approaching car reminded
Bill to reach for the dashboard and turn on his lights. As the horde
of rush-hour cars streamed by, Bill reminisced about the teenage
daughter he had just picked up from band practice.

He smiled as he thought about all those after-school trips over
the last few years: dance classes, piano practices, the unending cycle
of softball games and tournaments. He glanced at her in the seat
next to him and thought, *She's starting to look like her mom. Her
childhood passed so quickly.*

Usually, Bill and his daughter made small talk on their brief ride
home. Not tonight. Bill was concerned about the growing emotional
distance between them. Sure, he knew this gap was normal for
teenagers and their parents. But he wasn't ready yet to surrender his
role as a parent. He hoped the conversation he was about to initiate
would help close that gap. He had prayed for an opportunity to talk
to her alone—without her three brothers around. This was it.

"Julie, how are you doing with the guys?" he asked, struggling to disguise the wobble he felt in his voice.

"Oh, okay," Julie replied in typical cryptic teenage fashion. She looked nonchalantly out her window as their car crossed a small bridge.

Bill smiled and probed: "You know, your mom and I have been talking about you and all those boys who call on the phone."

Julie squirmed uncomfortably in her seat. Realizing now where this conversation was headed, she rolled her eyes.

"Your mom and I just want to make sure you know what you stand for as you get old enough to date. You know what I mean, Pudd'n?"

Pudd'n was Bill's pet name for his daughter. He hoped it might soften her heart.

She smiled faintly.

"I would like to ask you a very personal question and give you the freedom not to answer if you don't want to." He paused, waiting for her reply.

"Sure, Dad. Why not?" she said flatly.

Bill gripped the steering wheel and shot a glance into her eyes. "Have you thought through how far you are going to go, physically, with the opposite sex?"

Whew! There, he'd done it! Bill and his wife had talked before with Julie about God's standards about sex, but soon she would be dating and making moral choices on her own. They wanted to encourage her to make the right ones.

"Uh . . . well, I guess," she replied. She was feeling even more ill at ease.

They were just a block from home, so gently but firmly, Bill pressed the final question: "Well, then, would you mind telling me how far you intend to go? Where are you going to draw your boundaries? Your limits?"

He stopped the car a few feet short of the driveway and feigned a look into the mailbox. He knew his wife always got the mail, but Julie was acting like a basketball team ahead by one point in the fourth quarter, hoping the clock would run out. She was stalling.

Bill faced Julie and waited for her response. If he had waited for a month, he wouldn't have been ready for what she said.

"No, I don't want to tell you," she said firmly.

Decision time for this dad. He deliberated, *What if I press the issue and she gets angry? Do I probe further now or double back later?*

"Okay," he replied, "I'll take that for an answer . . . for now."

A tense silence filled the car as it eased forward and stopped in the driveway.

A HIGH AND HOLY CALLING

How would you feel if you were Bill and one of your children had given you Julie's response? Would you feel successful, or would you feel like a failure?

I would say Bill was a success and give him an A+ for his willingness to address such a threatening and critical issue with his daughter. The conversation was successful because it forced Julie to think about future choices. And Bill let her know that he would not pull away from her during this pivotal season in her life. He was going to stay involved—that's what godly parents do.

Bill and his wife have a vision for Julie, and that vision has guided their parental involvement since the day she was born. Their desire is to raise a child obedient to God in every area of life; a child strong in character, able to make tough choices to maintain her purity; a child able to withstand the destructive pressures of peer influence; a child who one day will raise her own children with a similar vision.

Bill's encounter with his teenage daughter is a snapshot of what will occur in a Family Reformation. It's easy for a parent to lose this vision. We can become consumed by the demands of daily life—changing diapers, ferrying kids to activities, resolving sibling disputes, to name a few. In the muck and mire, we lose sight of God's passion and mission for our children.

Centuries ago, Otto Brunfel wrote, "For what more Christian thing could happen than that children be raised well and taught self-discipline, usable skills, and a sense of honor? What richer and better inheritance could any father give his children? If one wants to reform the world and make it Christian, one must begin with children."

Now is the time to rise above the chaos and regain a vision for parenting—biblical parenting. From God's point of view, raising children is a high and holy calling, for they are the legacy we will send to the future.

GOD'S PERSPECTIVE ON CHILDREN

God is big on kids. In Psalm 127:3, we are told, "Behold, children are a gift of the Lord; the fruit of the womb is a reward."

Two additional passages underscore the value God places on children:

> And God created man in His own image, in the image of God He created him; male and female He created them. And God blessed them; and God said to them, "Be fruitful and multiply, and fill the earth, and subdue it; and rule over the fish of the sea and over the birds of the sky, and over every living thing that moves on the earth." (Genesis 1:27-28)

> Hear, O Israel! The Lord is our God, the Lord is one! And you shall love the Lord your God with all your heart and with all your soul and with all your might. And these words, which I am commanding you today, shall be on your heart; and you shall teach them diligently to your sons and shall talk of them when you sit in your house and when you walk by the way and when you lie down and when you rise up. (Deuteronomy 6:4-7)

In Genesis, God commands parents to "be fruitful and multiply" and says that children are a blessing, a privilege, and a responsibility.

I think it's time for a heart-check about children in the Christian community. Do we truly have God's heart for children? Do we really believe children are a blessing? Or have we ever so slightly and slowly begun to adopt the world's view of children?

During the past few decades, for example, the size of families has steadily decreased because parents are choosing to have fewer children. Many people believe today that it's somehow wrong to have more than two or three kids. If you do have several children, some-one will undoubtedly express great concern: "Don't you know how much kids cost? Can you afford to send them to college?" Have you stopped to consider what a strange statement of values this is—that you'd actually decide not to have additional children because you might not be able to afford their college expenses?

Do we *really believe* that children are a gift from God? A blessing?

I'm not referring, of course, to those who desire children but suffer from infertility. And there may be valid reasons for limiting the number of children in your family. But as Christians, we must evaluate our personal beliefs *against* the truth of Scripture—God places a heavenly value on children.

Many of us also adopt the world's view in *how* we raise our kids. We believe that responsible parenting means making sure our kids go to the best schools, wear the best clothes, and participate in numerous outside activities so they'll grow into successful adults with well-paying jobs. We know we want to build character, but we don't know how to do it. So we mix in the world's values with those from Scripture. We don't want our kids to make the types of mistakes we did as teenagers, but we fail to teach them how to resist temptation and make good choices.

In short, we lack a true, biblical vision for children and parenting. In Deuteronomy 6, God reveals why He commands parents to be fruitful—not just to have children, but to have godly children *who will pass on a godly legacy by connecting one generation to the next.* The home is the best place for a child to learn about God. In a culture of weakening character and ethics, our best hope for renewal lies in the restoration of godly homes, one home at a time. God created the family circle to be the ultimate conductor of Christianity to children and to the next generation.

Although it's sobering to bring children into a decadent society, in God's timing, our children will become His agents in advancing the kingdom of God.

We need to recapture the biblical imperative that parenting is a sacred calling and that children are worth the effort! God has selected parents for a work the angels must envy—the stewardship of a child's soul.

FIVE RADICAL PRIORITIES

Family reformers possess God's perspective on parenting. They also possess a holy urgency about their assignment. This is not a time for business as usual (see 2 Timothy 2:1-4). This is not peacetime—we are in a battle for our families and their future. It's time that Christian families developed a war footing and began to retake the high ground. We will see victory as we pursue five radical priorities in our homes.

Priority #1: Radical *Selflessness*

Many parents are double-minded when it comes to children. We talk about the importance of children and say we would freely sacrifice our lives for them. But theory and practice are two different issues. In our critical choices, we demonstrate that our commitment may not be as strong as we want others to think.

I mistakenly thought, early on, that God gave Barbara and me six children so we could help them grow up. Now I believe God gave us children to help us finish the process of growing up! We have found that it's impossible to raise our children to become godly adults and be selfish at the same time. The lessons I continue to learn remind me of the bumper sticker: "MY CHILDREN SAVED ME FROM TOXIC SELF-ABSORPTION!"

The need to be selfless ought to challenge fathers who spend too much time climbing the career ladder, pursuing hobbies and sports, or following other personal interests at the expense of their kids. It ought to challenge mothers who place their young children in day-care so they can work—not out of necessity, but for self-fulfillment or a higher standard of living.

I know a couple who say they *wish* the wife and mother could stay home with her preschool-age children. Yet a quick look at this family's lifestyle raises questions about their *real* family values. They live in a new home, drive new cars, and vacation each year in San Francisco.

I fear many Christian families have bought into the Big Lie of this age:

YOU CAN HAVE IT ALL

But you and I can't.

Serious questions are emerging about the wisdom of trying to have it all: Can Christians justify choices that have been proven to be harmful to children and destructive to families? Will it be said that we sacrificed our children on the altar of materialism, greed, and self-fulfillment? Are we raising our children to be missionaries or a mission field?

Perhaps it's time we asked one another some thorny questions.

About three years ago, I called a friend and asked to have lunch with him. In our time together I expressed that I was very concerned about how much he was working—80 hours a week. His wife has a pressure-packed, prestigious job, too. I told him that I loved him, and that I wanted to challenge him to consider what his real values and responsibilities were to a wife and three children.

Our meeting ended on a cordial note, but there was a look in his eyes that made me wonder if he heard me. Maybe he did hear me and will choose to value his wife and children more than his career. Time will tell.

It's time that Christian families make some radical commitments to our children and one another:

- Couples need to commit themselves to making family a higher priority than career; if necessary, husbands and wives may need to make career sacrifices that will help their families succeed. This may lead to traveling less, working fewer hours, perhaps even turning down a promotion. But don't expect every company to support such decisions. A recent *Fortune* magazine cover pictured a mother dressed in a business suit and heading for work—with a frowning, diaper-clad toddler hanging on to her leg. The headline read, "Is Your Family Wrecking Your Career?" A haunting subtitle followed: "Sure, companies say they value families—but here's the dirty little secret. . . ."
- Upon marrying, couples should agree to establish a lifestyle that is based upon the husband's income and avoid any form of debt that would force the mother of preschool children to work. (Couples who are in bondage to debt need to seek godly counsel from their local church.)[1]

- Couples should write down their family values, then compare these stated values with how time was spent based on the past year's calendar. Civic commitments, hobbies, recreation, and entertainment that take parents away from children should be evaluated critically.
- Individuals in the Christian community need to help one another by looking out for each other's children.

The loss of community in the raising of our children is one of the most significant and harmful trends of the last two decades. When I was a teenager, my mother had spies in our community who regularly ratted on me. Not so today. We need a movement of adult Christians actively building character into one another's children, holding our Christian youth accountable, and cheering them on as they pass through adolescence to maturity.

It's time for every Christian parent to prayerfully ask: Am I dying to self so that I can be the parent God wants me to be in raising the next generation?

Priority #2: Radical *Objectives*

Students in my generation barely cracked the door of sexual freedom; today, that door is wide open—off the hinges. With three of our children in college we've heard plenty of unsettling stories about the lack of shame and the compromise of today's students—a morally frail generation whose backbone has been replaced with a wishbone, doing what feels good at the moment.

But most troubling is a generation of Christian students who seem convictionless, virtually no different from their secular counterparts. These are the husbands and wives, the fathers and mothers of the next generation—the moral guardians of the church in the twenty-first century.

Why are so many of our Christian young people indistinguishable from nonbelievers? Certainly we should not expect these young men and women to be robots in following their parents' faith. They must make their own choices. But I'm convinced that the primary reason many leave home and never make the faith of their parents their own is that many *dads and moms didn't impart God's vision for their lives—a godly vision to love others and live holy lives.* And when parents fail to paint this vision, they send their children off into a culture that takes no prisoners.

Many parents have lost sight of the goal in raising children. First Timothy 1:5 reminds us, "The goal of our instruction is love from a pure heart and a good conscience and a sincere faith." Here's how that's done:

LOVE OTHERS. Parents have a divine mandate to train their sons and daughters how to love God and others as the Bible teaches. For starters, how to keep their promises, how to build a relationship with another person, and how to seek forgiveness, forgive another, and resolve conflicts with others. Our children need to be trained in how to become "relationally literate."

LIVE A HOLY LIFE. Far too many parents are more concerned with the child's IQ than with the CQ—character quotient. In the end, it will be not the grade point but character that will be the foundation for your child's life. The Greek philosopher Heraclitus was correct when he said that "a man's character is his fate." At the heart of godly character is a desire to be holy, "just as He is holy."

It's time for Christian parents to challenge their children to encounter the living God and live holy lives. This is no small matter. Raising the bar will demand that we rethink what we believe about some age-old temptations, such as:

- *Sexual involvement prior to marriage.* How much sexual excitement should a young person experience with the opposite sex before it becomes unholy? Young people desperately need parents to help them think through where the line will be drawn with the opposite sex.
- *Movies, television, and entertainment.* How many curse words will we hear or how many times will Jesus Christ's name be taken in vain before we push back and turn off the video or walk out of the movie theater? Or stop going or viewing altogether?
- *Language in your home.* What kind of language will you allow your children to use as they talk or relate to one another?

Am I promoting a fresh brand of twenty-first-century legalism? May it never be. Jesus reserved the harshest words for those who had legalistically reduced following God to a bunch of do's and don'ts. My fear, though, is that we are sacrificing a generation of young people on the altar of so-called Christian liberty, which has become nothing more than unbridled conformity to the world. Only a daily encounter with the sovereign God of the universe will help us to live holy lives and challenge our children to do the same.

Priority #3: Radical *Modeling*

The psalmist declared, "My eyes shall be upon the faithful of the land, that they may dwell with me; he who walks in a blameless way is the one who will minister to me" (Psalm 101:6).

If there is to be a Family Reformation, then we parents must model holiness in our own lives. You and I need to experience God, know and apply His Word, and walk in the power of the Holy Spirit.

Children are like tiny radar units: They lock on. They track. They observe. And they imitate. Imagine the mixed signals from this incident: The home phone rings, and a teenager answers. It's Dad's boss. The young man finds his Christian father, and Dad says to tell the boss he's not home.

Or a mom lectures her daughter on how she should dress modestly, not worry so much about clothes, and focus on cultivating her heart. Then Mom goes to aerobics almost daily, complains about every gray hair and wrinkle, and spends hours in front of the mirror.

Or a preteen is disciplined for cheating on a test at school. The next day she watches her dad smile smugly at his "fuzz-buster" while driving 20 miles over the speed limit.

As a parent, you cannot lie and then demand the truth from your kids. You cannot cheat and then discipline a cheater. You cannot hide compromise from an all-knowing God who passes our sins down to the fourth generation (see Exodus 34:6-7). If you want a fruitful garden, don't plant a row of weeds.

Children need their parents to be models of integrity—like Dan Jarrell's father, John, was for him. Mr. Jarrell, although in his late 40s, moved his family to Oregon to take a new job. Things went well for two years, but then John's boss asked him to falsify a civil service report so that an elderly woman could be dismissed from her job. Mr. Jarrell knew the charges against the woman were false, so he refused to prepare the bogus report. The boss tried intimidation, but still John did not compromise his integrity.

Mr. Jarrell was 50 years old and had no job prospects. There were still three teenagers at home to feed, clothe, and house. But all of that didn't matter—John knew he must do the right thing.

And so without any job in sight, Mr. Jarrell did one of the hardest things he had ever done in his life: He resigned.

God blessed this man's decision in a number of ways. A month later, Mr. Jarrell was offered a more enjoyable job. But the most important outcome was the impact John Jarrell's stand had on his son Dan, who later said of his father, "His courageous decision when the heat was on is now a part of my legacy; it has marked me for life."[2]

That's what radical modeling is all about, but there is more to it than just doing the right thing. Modeling also involves admitting when you are wrong. One of my sons has heard me confess and make an offer of restitution to a neighbor for cutting down a tree not on our property. Another child heard me tearfully apologize and ask forgiveness for getting angry and acting inappropriately. All of our children have heard me ask Barbara for forgiveness for hurtful things I've said or done.

When children see a parent show true humility and demonstrate how to handle failure, this modeling is etched into their minds. Albert Einstein said, "Setting an example is not the main means of influencing another . . . it is the *only* means."

You are to be a model of holiness to your children. Are you in a war footing pursuit of becoming a holy man or woman of God?

Priority #4: Radical *Involvement*

In 30 B.C., Virgil penned these penetrating words about the formative years of child rearing: "As the twig is bent, so the tree inclines."

Every parent must do battle with the culture over the "bend" in a child's character. Peers press and push. We must compete for the privilege to shape each child's character.

Who will put the "bend" in your child? And which way will he or she lean? Character is cultivated when parents build and maintain healthy relationships with their children. This requires *involvement*.

A few years ago, our family traveled to San Francisco and toured the Golden Gate Bridge. We learned that this majestic, picturesque structure is a suspension bridge. Independent sections of the bridge are lashed together by massive cables and tightly bound steel wires. This intricate design creates a secure structure that can withstand powerful winds and crashing waves.

Wise parents lash themselves to their children with tightly bound relationships. And they begin connecting the cables at an early age by holding, hugging, and affirming their offspring. Reading to your children, getting down on the floor and playing with them, cheering for them at ball games and piano recitals—each of these experiences and a hundred others bond your children to you.

When our oldest, Ashley, was only three, she and I dressed up one night and went out on the town. I took Ashley to a smorgasbord, and we gorged ourselves on chocolate cake and chocolate ice cream. Our next stop was the theater; we watched *Bambi* and ate popcorn together.

In the car on the way home, I asked Ashley what she had liked best about the evening. I was sure she'd say "the chocolate ice cream" or "the popcorn." But resting her head against my shoulder as we rode along in our Rambler station wagon, Ashley said simply, "Just being with you, Dad; just being with you."

Early on, a child desires nothing more than simply being with Mom and Dad. Wise parents seize this opportunity and weave strong cables of love and acceptance. This tranquil period, which Barbara and I call the Golden Years, lasts through about age 10. During these years, the relationship with your child is emotionally safe. You may talk some about the birds and the bees, but the conversations generally are free of great emotional risk to the parent.

But as the calm Golden Years merge into the hormonal roller coaster years of adolescence, parents tend to allow an "emotional disconnect" to occur with their kids. We may be there physically—at the ball games, tennis matches, and school plays—but emotionally, we permit distance in our relationship because the child is pulling away.

Letting this withdrawal take place is a huge tactical error. Abandoning teenagers to set their own limits and boundaries is an unthinkable omission. We must intensify our efforts to experience deeper intimacy with our children during adolescence. When adult matters surface—issues like sexuality, manhood, womanhood, peer pressure, self-image—teenagers need our guidance to navigate the swift currents of life.

I wonder if God hasn't mysteriously given parents an opportunity to bond, soul to soul with their teen, while discussing some of the most intimate and incredibly threatening subjects known to humankind. Let me illustrate.

During high school, one of our teenagers participated in an AIDS awareness and peer counseling training program. We gave him permission to participate because we trusted the solid national reputation of the sponsoring organization. All was well until he returned from the day-long seminar and told us about the sexually explicit information presented. We were shocked.

The good news was that he shared what happened. Over the next few days, our relationship with him allowed us to talk openly and turn a potentially harmful situation into another opportunity to build character and convictions into his life. The experience further lashed our hearts together.

God has given parents an important assignment: We are called to *stay involved* in the lives of our children. This requires that we initiate discussions with them about some of life's most challenging subjects—human sexuality, masturbation, attraction to the opposite sex, modesty, dress, temptations, sexual response, kissing, touching, petting, pornography . . . the list goes on and on. As we talk, think, study, and pray our way through these topics with our kids, we will reach deeper intimacy and forge character into their souls.

Priority #5: Radical *Expectations*

Parents are the personal trainers of the next generation of spiritual warriors. Our children are our legacy.

"Like arrows in the hand of a warrior, so are the children of one's youth," asserts Psalm 127:4. God designed children to be crafted, aimed, and released for battle—spiritual battle. Some Christian young people become spiritual casualties because they were protected from battle—kept in a bunker and never trained and deployed to do battle for Christ while they were still at home.

Many parents set their spiritual sights too low for their children. How many are praying that their kids will grow up to become mature soldiers for Christ, godly men and women equipped for a kingdom assignment? How many of us desire with all our hearts that our children will have the honor to serve as pastors or missionaries?

God wants to use our children as strategic weapons in the spiritual battle for the soul of America. Millions in our nation need to hear the gospel of Jesus Christ. Our challenge is to train and move our children toward the battlefield and labor with them for the fulfillment of the Great Commission (see Matthew 28:19-20).

Encourage your children to reach out to their friends with the love of Christ. Train them to walk with God and minister to others. Give them a vision for the world by taking them to the world. As I write these words, my wife is in Moscow with our three youngest daughters, taking medicine, clothing, gifts, and the gospel to orphanages, schools, and hospitals with Josh McDowell's Operation Carelift. Undoubtedly, all four of them will *never* be the same.

In addition, we should challenge our children to fight for their families when they grow up. I recently addressed a gathering of Christian broadcasters in Michigan. Among those attending were two young ladies from a leading Christian college who were interested in Christian broadcasting. As I talked about the demise of the family and the need to return to biblical values, I turned to these two students and passionately challenged them. I spoke not as a broadcaster, but as a father, "If God calls you into broadcasting, then we welcome you and would be honored to serve the King of Kings with you. But if He calls you to marriage, then be a helpmate to your husband. Pour your life into him and into your relationship—make your marriage your priority. And if God blesses your union and grants you the unspeakable honor and privilege of becoming a mom, then I want you to know that no position in any worldwide broadcasting ministry could even compare to such a high and holy calling. Be committed as a wife and mother—to the glory of God."

The full impact of a Family Reformation may not be felt in our lifetime. But if we raise, train, equip, and send the right kind of troops from our families, battles will be won and sweeping change will occur in multiple generations.

A SPECIAL WORD FOR SINGLE PARENTS AND OTHERS

It's obvious that any Family Reformation in America must include the enthusiastic participation of many parents who are raising children outside the traditional one-woman, one-man, married-for-life family. As much as we denounce and mourn the rampant family breakdown in our society, the reality is that single parents and stepparents by the millions are doing the best they can to raise godly children.

If you are in that category, what I've just said about radical priorities applies to you, too, but I do want to offer a few special words of encouragement.

God cares just as much about you and your kids as He does for the parents and children whose lives have not been touched by divorce or other tragic circumstances. Some aspects of life may be more difficult for you, but God has the resources to help you. Use them!

If you are a single parent and the children live with you, then faithfully pray for your children and do not quit challenging them to holy living. My life has been enriched by the impact of single parents who have raised sons and daughters who now faithfully follow Christ. Expect God to do great things in you and through you that will change your children forever.

If you are a single parent and your children are not in your custody, then faithfully pray for your children and commit to be God's man or woman in your current circumstances. Speak no evil of your spouse. Seize the moments that you have with your child to read the Scriptures and pray together. Ask God to use you and your child or children in a Family Reformation.

If you are in a blended family, hold tenaciously to God's standards, but continually guard your expectations. Yours is not an ideal situation. That doesn't mean your family can't be effective. But with multiple parents and a variety of relationships in several families, you face challenges not common in the traditional home. If you expect life to be perfectly smooth in this situation, you're setting yourself up for disappointment. Keep your expectations realistic.

Regardless of your circumstances, almighty God, Creator of heaven and earth, is still working miracles. The Bible is full of stories of how God uses imperfect situations to His glory. Never lose hope. Never stop trusting Him and His Word.

BILL AND JULIE HAVE ANOTHER TALK

With the fire stoked in the fireplace, Bill sat down on the small couch. Julie sat down, too—at the other end, perhaps symbolizing the distance she wanted.

Bill countered this move by taking a half scoot in her direction.

Bill had requested this time to talk about dating. And because Julie wasn't allowed to date yet, she complied—secretly hoping for a miraculous breakthrough. As they sipped tea, Bill inquired about a young man Julie was spending time with at school.

"Just how often do you see each other?" Bill asked. "Is your relationship exclusive? Would others say you are going out? Is it a mature relationship?" The questions kept coming, and Julie kept answering.

But although Julie's answers were helpful, Bill held back several key questions. And he hadn't revealed the real reason for this chat.

Trying to ignore the knot in his stomach, he finally asked one of the crucial questions: "What's your physical relationship like, honey?"

He let her talk, listening carefully, because he knew the truth—or at least a portion of it. A couple of days earlier, another parent had called Bill's wife—expressing concern over seeing some minor, but nonetheless physical, displays of affection between Julie and the boy after school. *Ah, spies.* Bill reflected back to his childhood—his mom had run her spy network. Now it was his turn! *God felt sorry for parents,* Bill thought. *That's why He gave them spies!*

"Are you holding hands? . . . Hugging? . . . Kissing?"

Julie never blinked. Up to the challenge, neither did Bill.

She told the truth: One kiss. Regular hugs. Nothing more.

Pretty "normal" these days—but from Bill's perspective, too much, too soon.

Daughter and Dad talked for an hour on that couch. And the distance closed—physically, emotionally, and spiritually.

Bill then asked Julie if she recalled the answer she'd given that time in the car when he'd asked, "How far do you intend to go with the opposite sex?"

Yes, she remembered.

"Well, this time I want you to answer," Bill said gently. "I want you to tell me what your boundaries are. What are your standards? If you don't decide, then boys will decide for you. Do you understand?"

She was crying now, because she knew her decision to act differently from her peers would cost her at school. She would be taunted and chastised as a prude. Tears trickled down her innocent cheeks, one after another, as her answer came, "I know what I need to do. It's just that . . . it'll be so hard."

The tears came faster.

Bill was holding her now. He told her he was proud of her for wanting to stand alone, if necessary, against the crowd.

Then he did something that he'd never done with his older children. He slid off the couch to his knees in front of her. Holding her face in his hands, he looked in her eyes. Overcome with emotion, he, too, began to sob.

Julie had only seen her dad cry a decade before at her grandma's funeral. She was stunned.

He wept as he pleaded, "Oh, Julie, I don't want to make you miserable. I know this decision will cost you, but God has given me the responsibility to protect you from evil."

He cried even harder as he mentally raced to the future: "Julie, do you have any idea what it will mean to you and me to give you away to a young man on your wedding day, pure and chaste? That will be one of the most wonderful moments of your life and mine— to know that your mom and I played a part, by the grace of God, in protecting you from evil and preserving your innocence."

Hugging tighter, they both cried harder as he added, "All these painful moments will be worth it!"

They held each other for what seemed like minutes on that couch. Father and daughter. Soul to soul. One generation to the next. God was working His plan and power through an imperfect family.

REFORMATION CHECKUP

What legacy do you want to pass on to the next generation? These questions may help you focus your goals. Mark your answers, then refer to Scoring below.

1. How committed are you to the idea—"It's important to have children in a marriage"?
   _____ Very Committed
   _____ Somewhat Committed
   _____ Not That Committed

If you have children . . .
2. How consistent are you in modeling godly values for your child(ren)?
   _____ Very Consistent
   _____ Somewhat Consistent
   _____ Not That Consistent

3. How consistent, on a daily basis, are you in spending focused, one-on-one time with your child(ren)?
   _____ Very Consistent
   _____ Somewhat Consistent
   _____ Not That Consistent

4. Based on your record of consistency, how committed are you to praying for your child(ren)?
   _____ Very Committed
   _____ Somewhat Committed
   _____ Not That Committed

5. If your child(ren) is old enough to understand, how effective have you been in sharing the gospel and knowledge about God's ways with your child(ren)?
   _____ Very Effective
   _____ Somewhat Effective
   _____ Not That Effective

6. How committed are you to modeling an allegiance to the Great
   Commission and to giving your child(ren) a spiritual vision to
   reach his generation for Christ?

   ____ Very Committed
   ____ Somewhat Committed
   ____ Not That Committed

Scoring: Being a parent is tough. We'll probably never think we've
done enough to share our faith with our children. If you answered
most of your questions with "Very" responses, that's superb.
However, if most of your answers were in the "Somewhat" or "Not
That" categories, you should prayerfully consider making some
changes in your parenting goals and practices. Be sure to discuss
these issues with your spouse, too.

A Reformation Moment

RETURN TO WITTENBERG

Late on a blustery March afternoon in 1522, two travelers making their way across Germany arrived in the town of Jena. Tired from a long day of trudging over muddy roads and chilled by a cold drizzle, the two men decided to stop for the evening. After leaving their exhausted mounts at a stable, the men entered the Black Bear Inn to find warmth and a hot meal.

The inn's tiny common room was empty except for a

large, impressive diner—a knight, dressed in a scarlet cloak and wool tights, sitting at a table next to the stone fireplace. His left hand rested on the hilt of an enormous sword, and in his right hand he held a book—apparently so intriguing to him that he did not acknowledge the arrival of the two travelers.

Only after the inn's waitress greeted the new guests did the knight raise his head and respond with a hearty hello.

"Good evening, gentlemen," he said, a smile parting his untamed beard. "Would you like to join me? I have finished my meal, but you may dine at my table."

Impressed by the knight's cordiality, and also not wanting to offend a man so well armed, the travelers joined him.

"Your names?" the knight inquired.

John, the more outgoing of the two, first introduced himself, then his companion, Michael.

"And you are?" John asked.

"I go by George," the man answered with a laugh.

Michael observed that the knight's book was written in Hebrew—a puzzling choice of literature for a warrior.

After more small talk, the knight asked, "And why have you found your way to this forgotten village?"

"We are on our way to Wittenberg," John said. "We want to learn more about the professor there—Dr. Martin Luther."

The knight nodded and sipped his drink, leaving a ring of suds clinging to the whiskers around his mouth. He said nothing.

"Would you happen to know if Dr. Luther is in Wittenberg now?" John asked. "We have heard he is in great danger and hiding like an outlaw. Many want him burned at the stake."

"I know quite positively that he is not in Wittenberg, but he will be!" the knight said convincingly.

Before the conversation could continue, the owner of the inn suddenly appeared—he had been eavesdropping from his cubicle near the door. The innkeeper cupped his hand over John's ear and whispered, "The stranger at your table is none other than Dr. Martin Luther disguised as a knight!"

The knight smiled at John, his eyes twinkling. "And just what do you think of Luther?" he said, shifting his bulk in the chair.

"We believe he is a man of God, sent to help the church reform!" Michael answered, speaking at last.

"Exactly what have you heard, sir? What reforms?"

"The teaching against indulgences, and the emphasis on the supreme authority of God's written Word," Michael said.

"I have heard that they are saying parts of the Mass in German," John interrupted, "and that both the wine and the bread have been given to the people during Communion. And priests and monks have married—several of them to nuns!"

"I wonder if Martin Luther has taken a wife," Michael began—but he stopped after John's boot bounced off his shin.

"Ha! No, I don't think Luther will marry," the knight said. "He is too old and set in the ways of a monk to keep a woman charmed!"

The waitress began to clear dishes as the knight continued: "I, too, am on my way to Wittenberg—to learn what is happening with these reforms."

"Oh, then what do you think, sir, of the events at Wittenberg?" John asked.

The knight tugged at his beard. "I think it is far easier to tear down than to build up. Any brute can smash an icon or drag a priest away by his hair. But to not force someone to believe like you do, to extend respect and charity to your weaker brother—that requires true courage and is the essence of grace."

The men nodded, wiping the residue of stew from their lips with their sleeves.

His glass empty, the knight stood, as did the others. The three men exchanged parting pleasantries, and the knight left for his room. He appeared unconcerned that his table mates remained behind, eyeing him curiously.

The next morning the two visitors and Martin Luther, leaving separately, took the same rutted, muddy road to Wittenberg. For the men who had come from Switzerland, it was a journey to refine personal beliefs. For Martin, the trip was a possible death march. Leaving the security of his fortress at the Wartburg Castle, he would again publicly lead a revolution for truth.

Any reformation comes with a steep price.[1]

CHAPTER EIGHT

Courage When It Counts

We become brave by doing brave acts.
—ARISTOTLE

Jim Ryffel has never pulled a child from a burning building, nor is he a Marine who's won a medal for leading a squad of soldiers behind enemy lines. Jim is just an ordinary person like you and me, but in the war against evil, Jim deserves a "Spiritual Purple Heart" for bravery and courage.

The fortress Jim stormed was not an enemy ammunition dump but an enormous pile of X-rated, pornographic videotapes.

Jim and his wife, Linda, and their three children live near Dallas-Fort Worth. He is president of Woodcrest Management, a company that owns and manages small shopping centers in Texas. In 1995, a tenant renting space for five video stores vacated in the middle of the night, defaulting on the lease.

Jim's company took the video rental firm to court and, as part of the damage settlement, received some inventory—cases of videotapes stored in a warehouse. Jim was shocked to find out that almost all of them—about 3,500 tapes—were X-rated. Hard core. Pornography.

Jim faced a tough choice. His company needed to recoup some of its losses from the broken lease, and the inventory was worth thousands of dollars. But the sleazy covers of those tapes made Jim sick to his stomach. How could he dump such foul material into the minds of others?

Jim said, "Some people would look at that warehouse of videotapes and say, 'That's forty or fifty thousand bucks' worth.' But we looked at those videos and said, 'There's a pile of garbage. It's detrimental to our communities, it's dishonoring to our wives, families, and employees, and most important, it is dishonoring to our Lord.'"

Although it hurt to turn his back on the sale of the videos, Jim decided to destroy the porn.

About that time, I ran into Jim at a retreat. When he told me about the tapes, I challenged him not only to trash the videos, but also to make a statement. A clear statement about moral decency in his community.

And did Jim make a statement!

He decided to hold a "community celebration of decency." A press release alerted the local media, announcing the public destruction of the pornographic tapes. Our ministry's radio program, "FamilyLife Today," also promoted the event—urging local residents to go out and support Jim's decency celebration. Jim's clever plan for destroying the tapes drew widespread attention: A huge pad drum roller, the kind used to flatten hot asphalt, was loaned to Jim by a local construction company that agreed with his efforts. Jim would use the huge machine to crush the 3,500 tapes.

On the morning of November 20, 1996, Jim and his helpers piled the smutty videos in a 100-foot-long row in the parking lot of Trailwood Village shopping center in Grand Prairie, Texas. At 10:00 A.M., Jim took the driver's seat of the 13-ton, diesel-powered drum roller. His two young sons, Travis and Hunter, proudly climbed up beside him.

As TV cameras rolled and a crowd of a hundred adults and children watched, Jim opened the throttle and eased the giant machine forward, crushing the brightly packaged pornographic videos into a black soup of shattered plastic and mangled tape.

The crowd cheered, and the crunching of plastic sounded like a runaway brush fire.

Ahead of the lumbering machine, several curious men in business suits ventured near an uncrushed section of the pile for a closer look, but then recoiled—as if they'd seen a poisonous snake. The men turned back, visibly repulsed by the vile images printed on the video jackets.

Someone had asked Jim earlier, "Isn't this action—preventing people from watching what they want to watch—censorship?"

But Jim just smiled and shot back, "It's not censorship, it's citizenship."

Jim was inflicting a powerful blow against evil in his community.

Later, Jim told the press, "We believe that pornographic videos and magazines are a trap. They lead to an addiction that amounts to mental and emotional adultery. It eats at the fiber of marriages and families, and it needs to be out of our community. Pornography needs to be out of our homes."

When the huge packer finished destroying the tapes, volunteers shoveled the worthless refuse into piles that filled three dumpsters. This is the essence of a Family Reformation—taking courageous action at the spot where life and truth collide.

We need more heroes like Jim Ryffel. He faced a difficult choice and did what was right. That's the essence of courage—the willingness to do what is right. Many of us hold beliefs that we say are our convictions, yet we lack the courage to act upon those "beliefs." We must not neglect God's call to individual character.

Courage makes character visible.

It's time we realized God holds us responsible for *our* character, *our* choices, *our* acts of courage or cowardice. For a Family Reformation to occur, every Christian family needs to be marked by personal courage.

Courage begins at home.

THE IMPORTANCE OF COURAGE

Why is courage so urgently needed today? Our nation faces a crisis—the moral meltdown of our culture.

This moral decline may not seem as imminently catastrophic to our nation as an invasion by a hostile power, but is the destruction of decency, morality, and essential values not just as menacing? What about all the casualties of broken homes, alcoholism, teenage pregnancy, drug addiction, and teen suicide? Are these "corpses" of modern society any less horrifying than the fallen bodies of young men littering a battlefield?

In the struggle against evil, our generation needs men and women who can stare at critical choices and not blink. If such small acts of courage were repeated day after day by the reportedly 50 million born-again believers in America, would not the forces of evil have an enormous battle on their hands?

Evil is invading our communities and seeking to seduce and destroy our offspring. Our problem is that we have become so apathetic and intimidated by evil, and so selfish about our time, that we often don't know what to do or lack the gumption to do it!

If we dads and moms refuse to battle against evil, then who will protect our children? If grandmas and grandpas aren't willing to volunteer and use their freedom to rally decent, moral citizens against this toxic malignancy, then who will fight against it? If good men and good women who find themselves in positions of leadership of businesses and companies continue to spend their advertising dollars to fund trash on television, then will the networks and Hollywood ever become accountable? I think not.

We can no longer afford to be lazy, selfish, and cowardly.

What we are experiencing is ultimately the product of hearts that fail to move feet, an oxymoron—a convictionless Christian. It does us no good to have all the right beliefs—even private outrage—about what is wrong if we never press into the battle and push back against evil.

There is another brand of courage that may take more grit than calling a member of Congress or protesting at an abortion clinic. It's the private courage demanded to say no to a teenager; the private courage to read the Bible to your family; the private courage to pray with your mate. Or perhaps the ultimate act of private courage these days—to keep the marriage covenant when for all practical purposes the marriage is dead.

This private brand of courage should set a Christian family apart— the fortitude that turns a mom and a dad into spiritual warriors on behalf of their family.

Today, an entire generation of families and their offspring hangs in the balance. Will we trust in God and His promises and take the courageous steps necessary to protect our marriages, families, and civilization? Do we believe God can give us victory over evil? Do we believe that a parent's outrage against indecency can be effective? Can God use a man in a home and a community to restore morality and goodness?

Yes, He can.

And, yes, we can.

The question is: Will we act courageously on behalf of the next generation and do what God expects of us in our own families to bring about change one home at a time?

What Causes a Courage Deficiency?

So why is courage such a rare commodity today? Why do we not express more moral outrage within our families and communities? Why do Christians—the salt and light of any nation—also lack courage? Here are several causes of the courage deficit:

1. *We don't know or believe the truth about God and His Word.*

Courage is fueled by the truth about God and life. Truth about God bolstered Joshua's and Caleb's faith and courage when they were sent to spy out the Promised Land.

After a generation had perished in the wilderness, some 40 years later we find Joshua and the nation of Israel about to enter the land. Three times God reminded them, "Be strong and courageous" (Joshua 1:6, 7, 9). Why did He say that? "For the Lord your God is with you wherever you go" (1:9).

When we forget who God is—and forget who we are and how God wants us to live—we become religious wanderers, spiritual nomads without a country. With no moral home address, we imitate what everybody else is doing. The result: little character, few convictions, and no compelling reason to act courageously.

Why take a stand for righteousness in your life and home if God is weak or doesn't exist? Why consult the Scriptures and attempt to live according to them if the Bible is just another book? Why try to courageously raise your children to know and experience God's love and forgiveness if the truth doesn't matter?

Why not divorce? Adultery? Pornography?

But courage is fueled by biblical truth about God and life. He has put us here to proclaim and live out the gospel of Jesus Christ. We are to be spiritual warriors against evil. Soldiers for good. We are to fight the good fight of faith (see 2 Timothy 4:7). The problem is that many Christians have forgotten who the enemy is and that they are in a spiritual war for the souls of people. Only the gospel offers spiritual renewal to people with sin-sick hearts.

2. We base our lives upon "near beliefs."

I'm afraid too many of us Christians don't know what we *really* believe. Like a cork in the ocean, driven and tossed by the wind, we bounce from opinion to opinion. We've become activity junkies, seldom stopping long enough to decide what really matters to us—our core convictions. Because we're so busy, it's no wonder we never determine what's worth living for, let alone what's worth dying for.

As a result, we live our lives based upon "near beliefs." Near beliefs have just enough truth to sound like convictions, but they are too weak for courageous engagement of the enemy or for heroic assaults against evil.

Near beliefs wimp out with a teenager who is pushing you out of his life to establish his own boundaries. Near beliefs won't keep a marriage together when romance fades and reality flourishes. Near beliefs may fall silent about such issues as same-sex marriages and homosexuals adopting children.

The result? A new brand of middle-of-the-road Christianity resides in our homes and churches—a faith that has little flavor or light. And certainly few core convictions. Feathers are not ruffled, stands are not taken, absolutes are held loosely. We stand uneasily on shifting sand and, lacking solid footing, have nothing to offer the world.

Vigorous growth of courage in the human heart demands more than the shallow and infertile soil of near belief.

3. *We are more fearful of people than of God.*

We love the approval of people more than the approval of God. So often when confronted with a situation requiring courage, we say or do nothing. Abraham Lincoln once said, "To sin by silence when one should protest makes cowards of men."

Right after the Gulf War, I ran into a couple of servicemen coming out of the rest room of our family's favorite restaurant. It was apparent they were friends and had not seen each other in some time. The problem was that as they loudly greeted each other, all I heard was "Jesus Christ!" this and "Jesus Christ!" that. In a span of 30 seconds, they used Christ's name in vain at least a dozen times.

Because I abhor hearing my Savior's name used so frivolously, I turned to the two young men and said, "Guys, I really appreciate how you've protected our country and that you two are so glad to see each other. But you have just cursed the name of the One I love the most. That's very disturbing to me!"

What happened was absolutely fascinating. Both of the battle-toughened guys (either one could have snapped me in two like a twig!) dropped their heads in shame and apologized. Moments later, I was back at our table, telling Barbara and the kids what had happened.

The easiest thing to fear is what people think of you.

Courageous reformation in the family defeats fear by speaking up for the truth and living for the truth in your home and community. John Witherspoon said, "It is only the fear of God that will deliver you from the fear of men."

4. *Our lives are riddled with moral compromise.*

One of the primary reasons we cannot speak with moral outrage is that our spouses and children know the truth about our lives. It's difficult (and hypocritical) to hold your children to one standard when you live another.

How about the man who forbids his teenage son to purchase *Playboy* magazine or other pornography, yet after everyone is in bed, he is on the Internet scanning and feeding on sleazy Web sites? Or as adults, can we watch R-rated movies and then tell our teenagers that they can't?

When we fail to define our values, what our family will and will not do, the result is moral ambiguity that disorients the moral compass in our children.

Our children force us to determine what we really believe. If we keep our options open, we fail to take stands, and we give our children no model to follow. Holiness demands that we courageously define our lives—what we will and will not do. We need to learn this truth: "All things are lawful, but not all things edify" (1 Corinthians 10:23).

5. *Christian men have lost their generational vision.*

Most men today fail to see themselves as the generational protectors of the moral and spiritual health of their wives, families, and communities.

Instant gratification and a plethora of adult-oriented playgrounds of sporting events, hobbies, and other recreational pursuits have replaced the battlefield and numbed the call on men to do battle for the next generation.

Many husbands and dads long to be warriors but simply do not know what to do. So we do nothing. We don't pray about the evil that is advancing and seeking entrance into our homes. We complain about the culture and ignore the most strategic place we *can* begin to make an impact—our homes. We don't act.

Alexis de Tocqueville, the nineteenth-century French writer who came to the United States to learn the source of the country's greatness, said, "All that is necessary for evil to triumph is for good men to do nothing."

Men, we must regain our vision for the legacy we must guard, promote, and send to the future.

GROWING COURAGE

I believe the stage is being set for one of the greatest spiritual revivals in history. The darker the night, spiritually speaking, the brighter will be the dawn.

Would you like to be a part of the sunrise—the coming spiritual awakening in our country? You can, by humbly walking with God today and expressing courageous faith—first in your home, then in your community.

How can we go about growing our courage so we can make an impact on our families and the world we live in?

First, *we are to fast and pray.* I begin with fasting because I believe Jesus expects it of us. Jesus said, "And whenever you fast . . ." (Matthew 6:16-18). Not *if,* but *when.* I've found that fasting cuts quickly to the core of my selfishness. It redirects my focus and hope back to God.

If you are burdened about the spiritual vitality of your life, your marriage, and your children, I invite you to join tens of thousands who are humbling themselves and seeking God through the spiritual discipline of fasting.[1] I challenge you to fast on a regular basis—either once a week or once a month on behalf of the Christian family. Ask God to bring a spiritual awakening to Christian homes—beginning with yours.

And pray for yourself. We engage the enemy every day. Pray that you'll know how to recognize the battles and know where you are supposed to fight. Dorothy Bernard said it well: "Courage is fear that has said its prayers."

I know a woman who prayed for years that her husband would become the spiritual leader of their family. By all appearances, they were the model couple. Married for more than 15 years, they attended church regularly and were deeply involved in church activities. But until 1996, this woman's husband had never prayed with her.

He knew he should. He wanted to. He just never did it. Prayer was too threatening. Fear ruled his life. Finally, he knew what he must do. Courage subdued fear.

One morning before leaving for work, he tenderly took his wife's hand, looked her in the eyes, and asked if she would mind his praying for her and her day. Mind? She calmly told her face not to let him know that she was singing the "Hallelujah Chorus" in her soul! A set of tears trickled down her cheeks as her husband engaged in one of the most courageous acts of his lifetime—praying with his wife.

Second, *we can grow our courage by stepping out of our comfort zone and courageously stepping into divinely ordered battle zones.*

We need to step bravely into the skirmishes that God brings our way—like the one God dropped into Jim Ryffel's lap. These acts of courage may not be public confrontations with network television gurus, but family moments that count—such as intervening in the life of your teenage daughter who is being too friendly, physically speaking, with boys. Or talking to your son about how he treats girls. Or reading the Bible at the dinner table.

I received a letter from a mom who had experienced such a defining moment. Her five-year-old daughter had received a special mailing from *Sesame Street* promoting a musician who is an avowed lesbian and whose partner is expecting a child.

This mom explained to her daughter in kind and compassionate terms how it was wrong for two people of the same sex to be together and have a child. She then prayed with her daughter for this particular entertainer to repent and turn to the God of forgiveness. Next she tactfully wrote the producer of the Children's Television Network, expressing her disappointment that they were promoting immorality.

Acts of courage may not be public confrontations with network television gurus, but family moments that count.

At the close of this young mom's letter to me, she explained how satisfying it had been to step out—yes, with fear and questions—with the Holy Spirit leading her. I sensed her courage and feelings of accomplishment for taking action to protect her daughter from an immoral influence.

Actions like these will receive God's blessing and bring new power from God to millions of homes. Are there battles where your family needs you today?

Third, *we must adopt a wartime footing.* War demands personal sacrifice that is necessary for survival and victory. Consider Paul's words to Timothy: "Suffer hardship with me, as a good soldier of Christ Jesus. No soldier in active service entangles himself in the affairs of everyday life, so that he may please the one who enlisted him as a soldier" (2 Timothy 2:3-4).

Do you hear the tone of Paul's words? Paul is preparing Timothy for suffering and warning him against entanglements that would take him out of the battle. There is no end of "good things" today that can dilute our priorities and swallow our time. We need to adopt the outlook of a soldier—focused on preparing for battle and winning the war. Civilian pursuits are put on hold.

Barbara and I hammered out our wartime footing early in our marriage. We agreed that no other success would compensate for our failure to make our marriage and family a priority. But that demanded sacrifice. I gave up or postponed some hobbies I loved—hunting, fishing, and going to sporting events. She gave up painting, sewing, and pursuing numerous creative outlets that she enjoyed.

I wonder today where our marriage and family would be had we not made some tough choices more than 20 years ago.

Fourth, if we are to grow in courage, *we must have tenacious perseverance.* "Let us not lose heart in doing good, for in due time we shall reap if we do not grow weary," Paul wrote to the Galatian believers (6:9).

On D-day, General Dwight Eisenhower warned his troops in his invasion order, "Your enemy is well trained, well equipped, and battle hardened. He will fight savagely."

That's true about our enemy, too. We must resist losing heart in the battle (see 2 Corinthians 4:1). Because there is no moral consensus in our society reinforcing Christian values, we Christian parents must prepare to fight for the souls of our children with no encouragement from the culture. In fact, at points you can expect persecution—even, sad to say, from the Christian community. On some issues you will be called intolerant, narrow-minded, irrelevant. Nevertheless, persevere. Don't quit. Never give in.

Finally, *we must infect others with our courage.* Courage is contagious. As I've shared stories of those who are stepping into battle, I've sensed an incredible desire by other moms and dads, singles, and grandparents to do some combat duty on behalf of their families and others.

When you have six children, you attend a lot of activities that keep you in touch with what kids are doing. Once we went to one of our daughter's junior high dances just to check it out. We didn't go to monitor Rebecca (who was only line dancing) as much as to observe what was going on and to be a moral influence on the kids.

As we arrived, a man stopped me and said, "Have you seen *it?* Have you seen what's going on in there?" He told me of a dark corner of the cafeteria where a cluster of teens were performing an obscene dance. Listening to this disgusted and horrified man, I wondered why a parent, teacher, or administrator hadn't done something.

We must infect others with our courage. Courage is contagious.

I walked past a dozen parents near the entrance and wound my way to the dark corner of the dance floor. I had never seen *it* before—and *it* definitely was obscene. Downright filthy. The dance can best be described as simulating sexual intercourse with your clothes on. It was my turn to look disgusted and horrified. A parent or two joined me for a couple of moments before shaking their heads and walking away.

Walk away? How in the world could I do that? My hands grew sweaty and my heart beat faster as I contemplated my mission. What was wrong with *me?* Here I was—a 47-year-old man—feeling terribly afraid . . . afraid of walking up to a hormone-crazed 15-year-old boy and telling him to knock it off.

My internal battle between fear and action raged for what felt like several minutes. My mind raced: *What will they think of me? I'm Rebecca's father. If I do anything, come Monday morning they'll ridicule her out of school. They are only kids—I'm of another generation.* But indecency by any other name at any other time in any other generation is still indecent.

"May God help me," I muttered as I prayed for divine guidance. Even at 15, the first young man I approached was taller than I was. You should have seen the look on his face as I tapped him on the shoulder and said, "Knock it off!" Shock and shame visited his face. *He knew* what he was doing was *wrong!*

I gently approached the young lady he had been dancing with and appealed to her as a father, "You shouldn't be letting a boy treat you like that publicly or privately. As a woman, you are one of God's finest creations, and you need to demand that he respect you." The couple slithered off the dance floor like rats caught in the pantry.

Buoyed by my success, I moved to another couple who started to argue with me. Sensing victory was at hand, I boldly told them they should be ashamed of themselves. Because I refused to buckle to their adolescent foolishness, they caved in, too.

The events that followed were absolutely fascinating. Parents, teachers, and administrators moved in to help push back against evil. The actions of one scared-to-death, middle-aged father had strengthened the backbone of many.

THE COST AND REWARD OF COURAGE

Courage usually costs us something . . . but the return on the investment is substantial.

Jim Ryffel's courageous public stand against pornography cost him some much-desired cash for his business, but God had other changes in store for Jim's business and his personal life, too.

Later Jim reported, "This has prompted us to take a new company position. We have drawn a line in the sand. We no longer lease, renew leases, or take on any management contract where any business either distributes, sells, or leases pornographic magazines, videos, or books."

One would think Jim's actions would cost his company some business. But instead, Jim has already been contacted by a bank offering to loan him money at a point above the prime rate. The bank officials told Jim they wanted to do business with a company that takes a stand for decency.

Jim also became convinced he should give up some of the magazines he'd been looking at, and now his family is more careful about the TV programs and video movies they watch. "We have a litmus test to decide what's acceptable," says Jim. "Would we watch this with our children? Would we sit next to our mother and father and watch this? If the answer is no, we should turn it off."

Jim concludes, "I believe in Family Reformation, and I believe it's got to start with the person you see in the mirror every morning."

The "return" in Jim's life for his investment of courage is a healthier, closer relationship with his wife, Linda, as well as the wonderful joy and integrity that comes from doing what is right and taking a firm stand for God.

Courage has its rewards. We just can't be sure when they'll come—in this life or in eternity.

We live in an urgent time. Now is the time to gather our courage and to move toward the smoke of the front lines. Dare we forget that our forefathers purchased the freedom we enjoy with their blood? Should we expect that we will be able to preserve freedom by detouring around an ominous battlefield? In the words of Amy Carmichael, "We will have all eternity to celebrate the victories, but only a few hours before sunset to win them."

I refuse to believe it is too late and to do nothing. A Christian has no right to be a pessimist. I refuse to just sit back and complain as the enemy lights another fire and incinerates another family. I cannot fight in every battle, and not every battle is mine to fight. But with trust in God and His Word, I pray that I will not shrink back from those opportune moments He sovereignly brings my way.

Perhaps God will even give me the privilege of dying on the battlefield—expending my life for my wife, children, church, and community.

What about you?

A Reformation Moment

KIDS WITH NEW TOYS

Energized by her new life in Christ, Debi Godsey had a fresh perspective on her job as a bartender.

"I thought the bar was a great place to be, because now I had answers for people!" Debi said. "People will talk about God in a bar, and now since I knew Him, I could tell them there *really was* a God."

Many of her customers listened, and two of the cocktail waitresses accepted Christ.

But in spite of Debi's enthusiasm, Jim wished his wife would retire from her occupation. Several months after the marriage conference, Debi grew so sick from pneumonia that she had to quit working at the bar. After she recovered, to Jim's relief, she never went back.

The six-month trial period for the Godseys' revived marriage came and went without notice, and the divorce paperwork—hung on to just in case it needed to be copied and refiled—"got lost." Besides, because of their new faith, they felt divorce was no longer an option.

Debi and Jim's joy bubbled as they told others about the changes in their marriage, led couples' Bible studies, and shared their newfound hope in God with anyone who would listen.

"We were like kids with new toys," Debi said.

Their new road was not without bumps, but the two of them clung tenaciously to what they had learned at the conference—and every six months went back to the information they had received.

"Because the manual said 'Pray with your wife every morning,' I prayed with my wife every morning before I went to work," Jim said. When facing some sticky points in their relationship, the couple would race to their bedroom to find answers in the conference manual—and to prove "who was right."

"We had trials," Jim said, "but it was a relief to know we were both working off the same blueprint. And now we had an ally, a Friend who would help us."

In fact, friends, coworkers, neighbors, and relatives saw big changes in Debi and Jim.

"When people see anger replaced by a sparkle in your eyes, they want to know what's happened to you. So Jim and I told them about committing our lives to God," said Debi.

After years of failure, Jim was finding victory in his fight with alcoholism. His old drinking buddies and others saw Jim's success and wanted to know what was going on.

"It's like being on the other side of a fence," Jim said. "Once you cross the hurdle and find out how great it is, you can look back and shout—'Hey, guys! I know what you're going through! Come here and check this out. I know how you can get from there to here.'"

The Godseys wanted to share their newly discovered hope with everyone, but in their naiveté as new believers, they assumed the only good place to meet God was at the marriage conference.

"We didn't know you could find Christ anywhere else!" Jim said. So the Godseys began telling their spiritually hungry friends about next year's conference.

"Jim and I were trying to get everybody to go," Debi said. "I was even matchmaking! I would say: 'You've got to get married so you can go to this marriage conference and commit your life to God!'"

The recruiting for the marriage conference went well. The Godseys convinced 40 couples to join them at the October 1991 event in Milwaukee.

When the FamilyLife staff did the customary review the week after the conference, they discovered that 68 of the 80 people the Godseys had recruited had made decisions for Christ—an unprecedented response!

Eight months after the Lord rescued her, Debi exclaimed one day while praying, "God, I always told everybody I would never go through the hell of my childhood again. But if it meant I could have the peace and joy of these months of relationship with You, I would live through the whole thing again."

Debi came to identify with Mary Magdalene, another woman with a tarnished past who met the Lord, and because she was forgiven much, loved much.

Indeed, Debi loved God much. Very much!

CHAPTER NINE

Taking Responsibility: Can the Virtuous Hesitate?

A strange unaccountable languor seems but too generally to prevail at a time when the preservation of our rights and all that is dear calls loudly for the most vigorous and active exertion.
—GEORGE WASHINGTON

With each passing day the situation grew more desperate. War seemed imminent. Mother England continued to impose crushing tariffs upon the colonists; Parliament continued to greet the protests with disdain. In ever-increasing numbers, British ships, filled with soldiers, were being spotted off the New England coast. Rumors of war circulated wildly; there were skirmishes with the British in Boston and Lexington. Towns and villages throughout the colonies formed militias and stockpiled weapons and ammunition.

The politicians, believing war was inevitable, convened in Philadelphia in June of 1775 to chart a course to freedom. The first order of business was clear: find a man to command the American forces.

After debating the issue, the Continental Congress extended an invitation to a retired Virginia colonel, a tobacco farmer named George Washington. Washington's response was decisive. Only days before the invitation came, the colonel had written a letter to a

163

friend stating his intentions and bemoaning the impending loss of life. Then he had added, "But [under these circumstances] can a virtuous man hesitate in his choice?"[1]

Did he? No! History records the heroic deeds of this man who was willing to sacrifice his life for the cause of freedom.

A Different Kind of War

Today, the drumbeat of a different kind of war pounds across America. In this impending conflict, there are no harbors to secure or tree-covered ridges to protect. No visible enemy will be engaged in mortal combat, and no blood will be spilled regaining lost territory.

Nevertheless, the enemy is close at hand.

A war, *the war* for the family, rages. The battleground is the human heart; the outcome is nothing less than the spiritual destiny of the American family. Your family and mine.

But we lack, at possibly the most critical moment in our nation's history, two things: an army of volunteers—soldiers for truth; and a clear battle plan—spiritual tactics.

Washington's assessment of pre-Revolutionary America holds true today. He observed that "a strange, unaccountable languor seems but too generally to prevail at a time when the preservation of our rights and all that is dear calls loudly for the most vigorous and active exertion."[2] Our first president decried those "who think the cause is not to be advanced otherwise than by fighting."[3]

My friend, if biblical truth *truly* matters to you, then *you must fight!* If your marriage *truly* matters to you, *you must fight!* If your family *truly* matters to you, *you must fight!* If the next generation *truly* matters to you, *you must fight!*

Your enlistment into the cause of Christ—and a Family Reformation—is absolutely essential. No elected politician is going to clean up the mess; no reform-minded superintendent is going to transform the public schools; no social system or economic reform is going to solve our problems. The solution for our moral and spiritual crisis begins in your soul and your home.

As I've stressed throughout this book, the single most important reformers in America today are husbands and wives, fathers and mothers—men and women committed to personal repentance and purity, the marriage covenant, biblical roles, and parenting.

A century ago, a French poet made a prophetic statement. Looking forward to the bloodiest century in human history, and envisioning the breakdown of the family and the destruction of absolute values, Charles Peguy said: "The true revolutionaries of the twentieth century will be the fathers [and I would add the mothers] of Christian families."⁴ In other words, those with the greatest capacity to bring about change are Christian parents!

Dad and Mom, no one has as much power to effect change as you. Absolutely no one!

The only hope for your family, the only hope for the church, the only hope for your community, the only hope for America, is Jesus Christ. His minutemen are dads and moms singularly committed to the cause. Are you willing to join His army? Are you willing to make sacrifices for the good of the whole? Are you willing to spearhead a Family Reformation in your home?

A grassroots family revolution is begging for heroes who will step up and step out courageously. The time has come for us to rebuild the wall.

LET US ARISE AND BUILD

Twenty-five hundred years ago in the land of Persia, a displaced Jew named Nehemiah was cupbearer to King Artaxerxes. Some travelers returned from Jerusalem with distressing news about the Jews still living in the city of David. Two facts in particular about his homeland troubled Nehemiah deeply. First, he learned his countrymen were "in great distress and reproach." They were being victimized by a hellish culture. Second, Nehemiah discovered that "the wall of Jerusalem [was] broken down and its gates [were] burned with fire" (Nehemiah 1:3). The Jews were defenseless against their enemies.

The Jewish remnant in Jerusalem needed help. Nehemiah knew that for the people to survive, the wall had to be rebuilt. The city's defenses had to be restored.

In his Pulitzer Prize-winning book *Profiles in Courage*, John F. Kennedy wrote, "Some men showed courage throughout their lives;

others sailed with the wind until the decisive moment when their conscience and events propelled them into the center of the storm."[5] The plight of his people propelled Nehemiah into the center of the storm.

From a worldly perspective, Nehemiah's first action was superficial, even insignificant. He *fasted* and *prayed.* He confessed the sins of the nation, both collective and individual. Nehemiah invoked the promises of God and sought divine favor for the plan he was about to inaugurate (see Nehemiah 1:4-11).

Then, risking his life by approaching a powerful ruler, Nehemiah shared his burden with the king. Artaxerxes asked the cupbearer to state his objective. "Send me to Judah, to the city of my fathers' tombs, that I may rebuild it," Nehemiah said (2:5). His request was granted.

Nehemiah traveled to the great city and stood before the forlorn inhabitants of Jerusalem. In a loud voice, he cried out, "You see the bad situation we are in, that Jerusalem is desolate and its gates burned by fire. Come, let us rebuild the wall of Jerusalem that we may no longer be a reproach" (2:17).

The people responded by saying, "Let us arise and build" (2:18).

Two things grip me about this story. First are the determination and courage of Nehemiah. The masses were paralyzed. Their wall was in total ruin. Nehemiah looked and saw an opportunity to ask almighty God for deliverance.

I'm also captivated by the strategy employed to rebuild the wall. Successful construction begins with a strategic plan: The Jews were organized into teams and shared construction of different projects (see 3:1, 3, 6, 8), and many rebuilt the section of the wall *in front of their own homes* (see 3:10, 23, 28-30).

What an ingenious strategy! Where were the people *most* motivated to rebuild the wall? Near their homes!

Where are *you* most motivated to rebuild the wall? Obviously, around *your* home, *your* neighborhood, and *your* community.

That's where a Family Reformation must begin.

THE "BRICKS" OF FAMILY REFORMATION

Rebuilding a wall of protection around your family will require quality building materials. I believe the Christian community must use some critical "bricks" to construct a spiritual wall of protection.

The bricks we need are not the small, rectangular clay blocks used in building construction today. Rather, I want you to picture bricks that weigh several tons, hewn out of granite chunks the size of a car—the type of bricks used to build an impregnable wall in Nehemiah's day.

Because the process of rebuilding is not only an individual effort but also a community project, I would like to speak directly to seven audiences—each of them critical bricks in the wall we must build to restore the family:

1. Couples
2. Pastors and lay leaders in the local church
3. Leaders and workers in parachurch organizations
4. Leaders and educators in seminaries, Bible colleges, and Christian schools
5. Leaders of small businesses, companies, and corporations
6. Influencers in the media
7. City, state, and national political leaders

In the remainder of this chapter, I want to challenge Christian couples to begin rebuilding the wall around their homes. In later chapters, I'll address the other groups.

BRICK #1: CHRISTIAN COUPLES

If the wall in front of your home is to be strong, you must build it right. Flimsy construction will collapse during the first onslaught from the culture. In the following section I will list five building materials needed to construct a Family Reformation in your home. To help you clarify in your own heart the importance of these issues, I have provided a place for you (and your spouse) to sign your name as a statement of your commitment.

The Home-Building Material of Prayer

At the risk of sounding simplistic, I believe prayer is the most important factor in healing our families and bringing about a Family

Reformation. If this simple discipline were implemented, we would see a stunning difference in our marriages, families, neighborhoods, schools, churches, communities, and nation in less than *60 days.*

In the 1950s, a popular slogan was "The family that prays together stays together." Let's bring that one back! This is the single most important spiritual discipline in every Christian marriage: Husbands and wives must pray together—*daily.*

Surveys at our FamilyLife Marriage Conferences indicate that less than 8 percent of all couples pray together on a regular basis. And I suspect that less than 5 percent of all Christian couples have *daily* prayer together.

I am not exaggerating when I say that Barbara and I might not still be married had it not been for daily prayer.

In 1972, when still just a newlywed, I asked my boss and mentor, Carl Wilson, for his single best piece of advice about marriage. Carl, who had been married to Sarah Jo for 25 years and had four children, said, "Denny, that's easy. Pray daily together. Every night for 25 years we have prayed together as a couple."

An eager young husband without a clue, I immediately applied Carl's wisdom. Since that day nearly 25 years ago, Barbara and I have missed daily prayer fewer than a dozen times. That discipline has helped resolve conflicts, kept communication flowing and, most important, acknowledged our utter dependence upon Jesus Christ as the Lord and Builder of our family.

I believe that if every Christian couple would pray together regularly, our nation would experience a spiritual renewal of historic proportions. Powerful trends would emerge. Domestic disputes and the divorce rate within the Christian community would drop dramatically. Christian homes would be filled "with all precious and pleasant riches" (Proverbs 24:4), and people outside the faith would notice.

When the divorce rate drops within the church, a spiritual and moral awakening in America will have begun.

Will you make a commitment to pray with your spouse?

If you agree to pray with your spouse every day, sign here:

_____

The Home-Building Material of Scripture

Adrian Rogers, pastor of the Bellevue Baptist Church in Memphis, Tennessee, has observed that "many Christians complain that the Ten Commandments can no longer be posted in their children's public school classroom. But those same parents don't have the Ten Commandments framed and hanging in their own homes."

Is it possible that we've embraced the Bible in theory but not in practice? No spiritual trend is more alarming and dangerous than the biblical illiteracy rampant in today's Christian families. The timeless truths of the Bible must be shared in the family rooms of America. A new generation of children must learn the Word.

Three things are required for Christian families to experience this biblical renaissance:

1. Husbands and fathers must renounce passivity and take the initiative to lead their families spiritually.

Paul exhorts us, "Be on the alert, stand firm in the faith, act like men, be strong. Let all that you do be done in love" (1 Corinthians 16:13-14). A man is never more manly than when he takes responsibility for the spiritual protection and growth of his wife and family.

Wives long for this spiritual intimacy with their husbands. Children urgently need to hear the Bible read aloud by their dads.

2. The Bible must be read and family discussion held on how to apply its teachings to life.

Recently, I had the privilege of interviewing Promise Keepers founder Coach Bill McCartney and his wife, Lindy. Their story is not unlike others today. Misplaced priorities, broken promises, and wrong values all pushed their marriage to the edge of the cliff. God in His grace grabbed this couple's attention and began a work of redemption—not merely of two individuals, but of a marriage and family.

The rewards of obedience were almost instantaneous. On July 4, 1995, less than a year after Coach Mac resigned as head coach at the University of Colorado, all four McCartney children gave their parents an unforgettable gift. One after another in the McCartneys' family room, they honored Bill and Lindy by reading a personal framed tribute. Tears of honor, joy, and reconciliation streamed down the cheeks of both parents and children.

When Coach and Lindy showed me those tributes, I was profoundly struck by how powerfully the Word of God had influenced this family. Even before placing their faith in Christ, Lindy and Bill had faithfully read the Bible to their children. The Scriptures had kept hope alive in a struggling family.

Something as simple as reading from the Psalms, Proverbs, or the gospels at the dinner table will provide nourishment and spiritual direction for families. The discussion of God's standards for living will give family members a foundation for right choices.*

3. Parents must establish a family night that highlights Scripture. If Barbara and I could go back and do one thing differently, we would more vigorously protect what we call Family Night—a weekly fun time of being together as a family and learning from the Bible.

On Family Night, nothing else is scheduled, the phone is off the hook, all electronic entertainment is off-limits, and relationships and Scripture are emphasized.

Perhaps what has happened in families could best be described by the saying, "A dusty Bible will lead to a dirty life."

We must pick up the Book.

We must read the Book.

We must personally apply the Book.

If you agree to read the Bible at least once a week in your family, sign here:

The Home-Building Material of Countercultural Living

Fortunately, my wife, Barbara, was not in a hurry one particular morning. On her way to run some errands, she topped a hill on a busy highway that gently curves left. She couldn't believe what she saw—a two-year-old, diaper-clad toddler standing in the middle of the road on the yellow line.

Barbara swerved right, barely missing the child. Slamming on the brakes, she screeched to a stop, threw open her door, and ran back to get the child. The toddler's mom had heard the squealing tires

---

*At the end of this chapter I've listed some resources that will facilitate Scripture reading and discussion in your home.

and came sprinting from her home. She gathered the boy in her arms and carried him to safety.

Undoubtedly, that mom impressed her toddler with an important lesson:

THE MIDDLE OF THE ROAD IS NO PLACE TO BE.

The problem today is that too many Christian families have wandered to the middle of the road. And we don't even know we're there. As danger whizzes by, we take comfort by comparing our lives to others'. "We're no worse than anyone else," we smugly say. For the past three decades, we have taken our cues from the world, not the Word. This conformity to the culture (see Romans 12:1-2) has cost Christian families our moral and spiritual distinctives. As a result, families are not the countercultural "salt and light" influence that the New Testament challenges us to be.

Christian families cannot be considered countercultural when:

- Children from Christian homes now watch more MTV than those from non-Christian homes.[6]
- Evangelicals account for one in every six abortions in America.[7]
- Christian parents and children regularly view ungodly and degrading TV shows and movies. (In a sixth-grade Sunday school class that I teach in a strong evangelical church, consistently 30 to 40 percent of these 11- and 12-year-olds have already seen an R-rated movie, many with their parents.)
- Over half of Christian youth (55 percent) have engaged in fondling breasts, genitals, and/or sexual intercourse by the time they reach age 18.[8]
- Kids in our churches have very tolerant views toward divorce. Nearly half (46 percent) of Christian youth *disagree* with this statement: "If there are children involved in the marriage, the parents should not get divorced, even if they do not love each other anymore."[9]
- A significant majority of our Christian young people are comfortable with contemporary secular definitions of what constitutes a family. Two-thirds of our kids, when given a choice of four "family" definitions, select a description that implies a no-risk, no-commitment kind of arrangement.[10]

Actually, "middle of the road" may be a too-generous assessment of the Christian family. On many issues, the Christian family is in the wrong lane altogether.

It's time for us to reject cultural conformity and draw some boundaries around our lives and families. I would like to challenge you to consider these steps as you seek to draw the line and recapture what it means to be a Christian family. We can be different without being weird.

First and foremost, you need to look to Scripture for your personal standards of holiness.

Are there going to be some things you do not do? Why? (You'd better know the reason and explain it if you have children.) The bottom line is: What are your standards? Are you in the process of continually comparing your standards with the world's standards—and making any necessary adjustments?

You need to value what God clearly values, beginning with the Ten Commandments—such as:

- Honoring your parents. As an adult, do you honor your mom and dad regardless of their response to you? The culture blames, bashes, or ignores. How are you different?
- Rejecting adultery. Do you glorify adultery by watching movies and TV programs that promote illicit sex without guilt, blame, or regrets? Are you raising your children to be innocent of evil? Are you challenging your teenagers with boundaries that will protect their innocence and keep them out of bed with the opposite sex?
- Observing the Sabbath. How is your Sunday a day set apart unto God, a day of rest for your soul? How is it different in your reading, viewing, and recreation habits?

Second, you need to set boundaries for your family.

Experience tells me that if your children are like ours, setting boundaries won't win you any popularity contests. Therein lies part of the problem. Children don't need buddies or chums; they need heroes, leaders, and parents who are spiritual pacesetters and love them enough to appropriately "cramp their style."

Standards, limits, and boundaries are predicated on the assumption that you are aggressively building a relationship with each child. These limits and boundaries must be surrounded by something much larger—LOVE. If your children do not experience your love, then they will rebel. Guaranteed.

So how about a few boundaries? It's always easy to criticize the standards and limits of others. The more difficult task is the hard work and risk of deciding what you believe and what *your* convictions are for *your* family. If you haven't decided, then you may be in the middle of the road.

Let me suggest a few areas to prayerfully sort out with your spouse:

- How much and what kind of television are you going to let your children watch? What about movies? Are you going to decide which ones they watch as they move into adolescence? What will *you* watch?
- Will your children date? Or formally court? If so, when? With whom? Does he or she have to qualify to go out? How about the other guy or gal—do you have to approve? Will you interview a young man who is interested in your daughter?
- What kind of clothing are you going to let your children wear? Grunge? Sexy? And for the girls, what about bathing suits? Better deal with that one before they turn 13!
- Are you going to let your daughter call boys when she turns 13 or 14? Or are you going to let your 13- or 14-year-old son regularly call girls or take calls from girls?
- How about physical affection? Are you going to let your kids touch wherever they want to? Or are you going to challenge them with boundaries and limits—then regularly inspect those limits by asking how and what they are doing?
- What about the area of friendships? Are you going to determine who your 11- and 12-year-olds hang out with? If you don't, then you won't have any say in who they spend time with in their teen years. If it truly is "bad company," then are you going to step in with some limits that prevent that influence from controlling and corrupting your teen? (See 1 Corinthians 15:33.) And music? Are you going to have any say about what they absorb into their hearts and minds?

These standards may sound radical, almost Victorian. We do not need to go back in history, but we do need to go back to holiness. And perhaps a brief review of other eras is exactly what is needed! Christian families will not see their own children thrive by setting standards just a notch above the culture. That's been our problem. The Scriptures call us to not be above average, but to be holy, just as God is holy.

Will you decide what your family's boundaries are in these critical areas?

If you agree to become a countercultural family and begin the process of establishing some boundaries, sign here:

_____

The Home-Building Material of Marriage and Family Mentors

The movie *Gone with the Wind* has a scene where Scarlett is searching for a doctor to help with the birth of her sister-in-law's baby. When she finally finds the doctor, the setting is unforgettable. The camera focuses on one lone, exhausted doctor and then pans what looks like three football fields full of bleeding and dying young men.

This memorable image is similar to what every pastor faces in the local church. Surrounded by urgent marriage and family needs, he has little time to attend to those who are about to be married. The wounded must be cared for, but those who are like that newborn baby—just starting their marriages—need help, too. In reality that pastor can't and shouldn't personally meet the needs of those couples. Instead, he needs to recruit lay couples who will mentor them.[11]

I'll address this issue more thoroughly in chapter 11, but I see an urgent need for an army of church-based marriage and family mentors who will invest their lives in the next generation of families.

What if newlyweds had a marriage mentor assigned to them by their church for the formative years of their marriage? I believe that hundreds of thousands of couples in our churches would volunteer a couple of hours a week to equip our sons and daughters to survive in a culture that takes no captives.

If you agree to support or participate in a family mentor program, sign here:

_____

The Home-Building Material of Godly Patriarchy

The author of *Fatherless in America,* David Blankenhorn, jarred the nation with his profound question, "Does every child need a father?"

Contemporary society says no, but Christians should know better. After 30 years of being emasculated, feminized, and redefined, fatherhood is at best a confusing puzzle—even for a Christian man.

To counter the cultural avalanche, dads must become significant again in their families—not as authoritarian dictators, but as strong men who are powerful because they are sacrificial servant-leaders. Like Christ, who gained power and influence through humility and servanthood, men must give up their lives daily for their wives and families.

A father is never more powerful than when he is walking in the Spirit, obeying the Scriptures, becoming like Christ, serving his wife, and leading his family spiritually. I believe there is a profound need for men to regain a lost concept and position in families today—the godly family patriarch.

To become such a godly patriarch, every husband and father ought to continually refine these goals:

1. *To recommit annually to love his wife better.* The most important thing a husband can do is to love his wife. My friend Scott told me what his preschool-age daughter, Hannah, said on a recent "date" with him. He asked her if there was anything he could do better as a daddy. "Yes!" she said emphatically, with a little bit of a frown. "You can stop double-tying my shoelaces—I can't get them untied!"

Scott responded, "Sure, Hannah, I can do that. Is there anything else you want me to do for you?"

Her sweet, profound reply was, "I don't want you to love anybody more than Mom."

The command in Ephesians to "love your wives, just as Christ also loved the church" (5:25) demands a regular inventory and death to self.

Recently, after some days of prayer and fasting, I took Barbara's hands and looked deeply into her eyes and told her that I wanted to do a better job of loving and pouring out my life for her. Every husband needs to regularly revisit this sacred and solemn responsibility.

2. *To take responsibility for spiritually and morally leading his family.* To be your family's patriarch, you must assume ultimate responsibility for the spiritual and moral condition of your family. David Blankenhorn graphically points out how far we have slid:

> Over the past two hundred years, fathers have gradually moved from the center to the periphery of family life. . . . In colonial America, fathers were seen as primary and irreplaceable caregivers. According to both law and custom, fathers bore the ultimate responsibility for the care and well-being of their children, especially older children. . . . Most important, fathers assumed primary responsibility for what was seen as the most essential parental task: the religious and moral education of the young. As a result, societal praise or blame for a child's outcome was customarily bestowed not (as it is today) on the mother but on the father.[12]

3. *To be a godly and visionary patriarch as his family matures.* To explain what I mean, let me introduce you to a modern-day patriarch who lives in eastern Tennessee.

Bruce and his wife, Susan, have four married children. Success in life has always been defined around family for Bruce. Now more than ever, Bruce is deeply involved in the lives of his adult children and grandchildren.

Bruce recognizes he is moving into the last phase of patriarchal leadership of his family. He refuses to use the word *in-law* and has adopted all the spouses of his children into his family. He advises, when asked, but does not control his adult children. He invests spiritually in their lives through regular family get-togethers at his home. In fact, he and his wife kept their older, smaller home even though he could afford a bigger one, just because the grandchildren like the way it smells!

Bruce talks man-to-man with his sons and the husbands of his daughters about sex and the marriage bed. All decisions about life for him have two grids: Bible and family.

Bruce has become the patriarch of his family.

The challenges of godly patriarchy may seem insurmountable to many men, perhaps especially to those who because of divorce no longer have day-to-day contact with their children. With God's help, though, we must do what we can. Regardless of your circumstances, if you will obey God on this issue and step toward the challenge in faith, God will honor and bless that commitment. And children—and fathers—will be blessed.

Even small gains in regaining what God desires from a humble, mature, godly man will bring significant rewards for succeeding generations.

May God raise up millions like Bruce who will show us how to finish strong.

If you agree to assume the role of godly patriarch in your family, sign here:

STANDING FOR THE TRUTH

Throughout this book, I have challenged individual Christians to join in the cause of a Family Reformation. I believe that if you will ignite a fire for Christ—in your *heart,* your *home,* and your *community*—then God will restore our families. The rolling fireball of destruction about to engulf us will die out, and then our communities and our nation will experience moral, spiritual, and social rejuvenation.

But change can only occur heart by heart, individual by individual, one home at a time.

In the following chapter, I will familiarize you with a succinct description of a biblical marriage and family. This document is called the *Family Manifesto,* and I urge you and others of like mind to carefully study, discuss, and apply its content. Educating ourselves (and then adhering to solid beliefs) is certainly something all of us can do to assume personal responsibility for the return to health of the family in our churches and nation.

As James Lincoln Collier has so aptly stated in his fine book *The Rise of Selfishness in America:*

> A damaged society cannot be improved by tinkering with monetary policy or in somehow "changing the system." It is

critically important for us to understand that there is no such thing as a "system." . . . A society can only be improved when those who constitute it decide to improve it. And this means making sacrifices individual by individual for the good of the whole.[13]

Family Reformation must begin with individual sacrifice. But sacrifice takes courage. Your courage.

Your Choice: Compromise or Courage?

In the early 1970s, the Iraqi government arrested a group of American students on trumped-up espionage charges. The wicked regime of Saddam Hussein wanted confessions, and to elicit the desired admissions of guilt, the captors tortured the students.

The prisoners were told that if they confessed, they could go free: "Compromise the truth. . . . Admit to a falsehood."

The promise of freedom became irresistible. One by one, as the pressures and the pain mounted, the prisoners confessed to crimes they *hadn't* committed. Every prisoner except one.

The torture intensified for this man. The loneliness of isolation became unbearable. He came close to breaking.

Recounting his friend's story in the *Wall Street Journal,* Mark Helprin wrote,

> Then they announced that they were finished with his case, that he could simply confess or die. A confession lay before him as they raised a pistol to his head, cocked the hammer, and started a count down. He had heard executions from his cell. "Sign your name," he was told, "and you will live." But he refused. He closed his eyes, grimaced, and prepared to die. They pulled the trigger. When he heard the click he thought he was dead. The gun, however, had not been loaded.[14]

Helprin's friend was eventually released. He discovered afterward that every other prisoner who had confessed was later hanged in the public square.

Only he survived.

The moral of the story is clear: Compromise represents a far greater risk than courage. As difficult as it is to stand for truth, it is much harder to live standing in the middle of the road or with the consequences of moral failure.

My friend, when every voice around you screams, "COMPRO-MISE! SURRENDER! TAKE THE EASY WAY OUT!"—stand for the truth.

God will reward your faithfulness.

Your children will thank you.

America will be strengthened.

The virtuous must not hesitate.

Let us arise and build!

One home at a time!

Resources for Scripture Reading and Discussion in the Home

The following are family devotional materials you and your family will find helpful.

> *The Family Walk,* Zondervan
> *More Family Walk,* Zondervan
> *The Family Walk Again,* Zondervan
> *The One-Year Book of Family Devotions,* Tyndale

A Reformation Moment

THE LUTHER HOME

On a sunny afternoon in 1523, a fish wagon lumbered out the gate of a small German convent. The driver looked furtively over his shoulder while slapping the reins against the straining horses.

When the convent was out of sight, the driver turned toward his load and whispered loudly, "Ladies, you can relax now; you're free."

From among the herring barrels, several fully covered

heads peeked. Soon the 12 nuns, who had bolted to join the Protestant Reformation, were giggling and chattering. One of them, Katherine von Bora, would one day become Mrs. Martin Luther.

Not that Luther had matrimonial hopes. He had assisted the nuns' escape, and a number of his fellow ex-monks had married. But Martin was not seeking a wife. At 40, he was an old man by medieval standards. And why marry when any day you might burn at the stake and leave a widow?

One by one, a husband was found for each of the nuns—all except Katherine.

Martin visited his elderly father, and when Hans complained that the Luther family name might vanish for lack of grandsons, Martin returned to Wittenberg with a new appreciation for Katherine von Bora.

Since Katherine had earlier expressed some marital inclinations concerning Dr. Luther, no time was wasted. Soon after, on June 13, 1525, they were betrothed, and then married in a public ceremony just two weeks later. Martin was 41 and Katie—his nickname for her—was 26. Martin later wrote, "There is a lot to get used to in the first year of marriage. One wakes up in the morning and finds a pair of pigtails on the pillow which were not there before."

Because of their peasant backgrounds and lifetime service to the church, the newlyweds were nearly penniless. Martin briefly considered becoming a woodworker to help support his bride, but fortunately for the future of our faith, he continued as a Reformer; the confident and capable Katie took over the day-to-day management of the Luther home.

A hard worker, Katie tended a large garden, had an orchard, and even netted fish out of a farm pond. To make ends meet she also housed boarders.

Martin was a generous man, and the Luther home was known for its hospitality. A stream of visitors came to meet and debate with Martin, or to seek his counsel on spiritual matters.

In June of 1526, Martin and Katie had their first child, a son they named Hans in honor of Martin's father. The Luthers eventually had six children, three girls and three boys. They also raised four orphans of other family members.

Creativity, excitement, and fun marked the Luther home.

Music, art, and good conversation (including Martin's famous "Table Talks") were celebrated, and on occasion the children performed a family musical.

Martin was serious about giving biblical truth to his children. He wrote the Small Catechism to give families an outline of what should be taught. Martin believed the father's duty was to teach his children the rudiments of the faith and to check up weekly on their progress.

As in any marriage—especially one with two such strong-minded individuals—the Luthers had their tensions. Martin once said, "Think of all the squabbles Adam and Eve must have had in the course of their nine hundred years. Eve would say, 'You ate the apple,' and Adam would retort, 'You gave it to me.'"

But the couple was sincerely in love. On his frequent travels, Martin would write Katie, addressing her wittily and affectionately as "Housewife of the Heart" or "Madame Pig Marketer." He signed his letters to her, "Your Old Love Bird" and "The Willing Servant of Your Holiness."

No doubt the greatest sadness the Luthers experienced occurred in 1542. Their daughter, Magdalena, a healthy 14-year-old, suddenly fell ill with fever. Martin sat by her bed, holding her hand, praying for her healing.

"O God, I love her so," Martin exclaimed one day, "but Thy will be done."

Later, he asked her, "Magdalenchen, my little girl, you would like to stay with me, your father, but are you also willing to go to that other Father [in heaven]?"

"Yes, dear father, as God wills," she whispered.

Just a few moments passed, then with Katie sobbing nearby, "Little Lena" died, secure in her father's arms.[1]

CHAPTER TEN

The Family Manifesto

*We have plunged into a danger zone in which increasing
numbers of people—whether they are part of the body of
believers or not—are incapable of disentangling cultural mores from
fundamental Christian values.*
—GEORGE BARNA

"How can you teach such an idea?" the man said to me, his jaw
set and the red in his face betraying anger. Next to him stood
his wife, arms crossed, drilling me with a chilling stare.

"Just where are you coming from—saying that the Bible *commands* us to have children?" he asked.

I was speechless. People disagree with me—often vigorously—
but having this reaction some years ago at a Christian marriage conference was unusual. My comments on the verse in Genesis—"And
God said to them, 'Be fruitful and multiply, and fill the earth'"
(1:28)—obviously had hit a tender spot.

I explained myself more thoroughly to the couple, but I think they
left unconvinced. Reflecting on this encounter, I concluded: *Even
Christians don't know what the Bible teaches and what they believe
about children! No wonder the Christian community doesn't place a
higher value on children and rearing them.*

Because of a flawed and faulty system of beliefs, family values

185

today have become little more than a warmed-over statement from the Book of Judges: "Everyone did what was right in his own eyes" (21:25). I cannot emphasize enough how critical this scarcity of biblical definition around marriage and family is: If the truth of God's Word is not clearly stated and taught, how then can we expect Christian homes to differ from those that have no spiritual faith or biblical beliefs? Stated another way, how can you and I pass on our convictions to our children if we have not determined what we believe? Will our Christian homes be any different from others?

In the words of Jeremiah, speaking on behalf of God: "'An appalling and horrible thing has happened in the land: the prophets prophesy falsely, and the priests rule on their own authority; and My people love it so! But what will you do at the end of it?'" (5:30-31).

How can you and I pass on our convictions to our children if we have not determined what we believe?

It's no wonder the Christian family is not the brick in the wall it needs to be. It has no foundation—no solid set of beliefs that can be embraced and proclaimed.

Even as early as the 1970s, when I first entered family ministry, I noticed that the American family was steadily deteriorating—both outside and within the church.

In the two decades since then, I am pleased to have witnessed God's favor and some degree of success in family ministry: more than a half million attendees at our FamilyLife Marriage Conferences; nearly a million participants in our small-group Bible studies, HomeBuilders Couples Series®; and more than 600 full-time staff, speakers, and volunteers banded together nationwide in the FamilyLife ministry.

This all was (and is) encouraging. Yet something was missing. When I would pray, I would ask the Lord what else could be done to reverse the slide of the Christian family.

No answer came.

The puzzling silence gnawed at me. I knew He cared—the family was His creation. I grew increasingly concerned that many in the Christian community seemed to have no idea exactly what they believed about the family and issues related to it. A horde of questions goaded me:

Can Christian marriage rise above the world's view of matrimony if we aren't certain why God created marriage in the first place?

Can a person who can't articulate what a family is establish a family like God intended?

Can a man truly be a Christian husband if he is uncertain about his assignment from God? With no understanding of his responsibilities and no sense of accountability to God, why would he deny himself and serve his wife?

In a society rapidly embracing the feminist brand of egalitarianism, why would a woman choose to submit to her husband?

How could a son be raised to be a man if his father and mother are not convinced of what God expects a man to be and do? Or can a daughter be raised to be a woman if her parents don't know what the Bible teaches is the core of godly femininity?

In a culture that glorifies career success and minimizes the importance of motherhood, what would give a woman (and her husband) the courage to choose children, especially during the early years of their lives, over career?

Why would any grandparent take the time in retirement to mentor a young mother or dad unless she (or he) had convictions about a divine responsibility to mold the younger generation and call them to maturity?

And in a culture that has begun a new assault on the definition of marriage by promoting same-sex marriages, what would be the basis for a Christian response? And without a firm set of beliefs, how long would it be before Christians who believe same-sex marriages are wrong would bend and cave in? Would our children be able to stand strong and raise their children to uphold the biblical ideal of one man and one woman in a covenant relationship with God and each other for a lifetime?

If individual marriages and families were to truly become distinctively Christian, then each of these family units must know what the Bible teaches and what they believe about essential issues surrounding marriage and family.

GOD'S FAMILY VALUES

In the early '90s I concluded that if the Christian family was to endure intact and strong, its members needed to know *God's plan* for the family. They also needed to be encouraged to apply, experience, embrace, and proclaim this truth. Without a clear set of biblical beliefs, our thinking would be muddy, our behavior erratic, and our convictions virtually nonexistent—perhaps even contrary to God's Word.

The Lord impressed on me the urgent need for a written declaration of timeless principles on *real* family values. *Biblical* family values. This statement would attempt to reverse many of the negative ramifications of another statement of values first crafted in 1933 by a handful of intellectuals, educators, and philosophers. That document was called the Humanist Manifesto.

The authors of that proclamation, a group with diverse backgrounds that included John Dewey, B. F. Skinner, Sir Julian Huxley, and others, had shared a number of philosophical beliefs. First, they were ardent antitheists—men and women who disavowed the God of the Bible and the authority of Scripture. Second, they believed in the words of the ancient philosopher Protagoras that "man is the measure of all things," the final authority in heaven and on earth. Third, this group shared the conviction that reason alone can provide the solutions to humankind's most urgent problems.

Though few Americans are familiar with the Humanist Manifesto, the ideals contained therein have had a profound impact upon American society. By deifying man and humanizing God, the authors fostered the rampant self-indulgence, self-centeredness, and greed that now infect our culture. This narcissistic plague has had its greatest—and most negative—effect upon the family.

The success of the Humanist Manifesto demonstrated that a bold, courageous act by a relatively small number of people can galvanize ideas and spark a movement that can ultimately change the world.

I wanted to be part of the countermovement—a spiritual offensive that changed the world for the glory of God.

A DIFFERENT KIND OF MANIFESTO

In the fall of 1991, work began on the *Family Manifesto*. I asked Bill Howard, a friend, seminary graduate, and—at the time—staff member of FamilyLife, to help me craft such a statement of beliefs.

Fifteen months later, after 25-plus drafts had been revised by theological leaders, historians, professors, pastors, Christian leaders, and laymen and laywomen, the *Family Manifesto* was complete.

The first official signing of the manifesto was held on February 2, 1993, near our ministry's headquarters in Little Rock, Arkansas. Bill and Vonette Bright, the co-founders of Campus Crusade for Christ, joined our staff for the event and were first to place their signatures on the document.

Each section of the *Family Manifesto* was read aloud, followed by a few minutes of prayer. Most of us were on our knees, and about halfway through our time of prayer, Dr. Bright leaned over to me and said, "I believe what is happening here is historic. I predict this will change the course of millions of homes not only here in America, but around the world!"

Since that evening, a number of public signings of the *Family Manifesto* have occurred. Around our country and the world, mothers and fathers, engineers and salesmen, truck drivers and factory workers, professors and doctors, pastors and politicians have signed their names to this document and said, in effect, "I believe, and I am committed to live my life and shape my marriage and family according to these ideals." The original documents now have 679 signatures representing signers from more than 25 countries.

In our two-miles-a-minute culture, it may seem strange that I'm putting such emphasis on a written, permanent document. After all, some would say, "Don't things change too fast these days for that type of thing?" That may be one of the best reasons to write it down. In our fast-paced age, we need more stable, well-lit signposts to keep us on track. History is full of such documents, the Declaration of Independence and the Constitution to name just two. Why not have such a written statement for the family—a rallying proclamation that will guide us in the present as well as serve future generations of families?

As we enter the twenty-first century, I am more convinced than ever that we need to rally around this biblical statement about the family, because my most-feared suspicions are being confirmed. It is not only the laymen and laywomen who do not know what the Bible teaches or what they believe about the family, but also many Sunday school teachers, Christian leaders, and, yes, even pastors.

In late 1996 I attended a meeting of 20 pastors of the leading churches in a major city. When asked what we could do to help them, the nearly unanimous response from this group was, "Help us craft a clear statement of biblical beliefs around marriage and family issues." The leaders were so overwhelmed just dealing with the needs of families in their churches that they had no time to develop a "working theology" of the family.

I believe the *Family Manifesto* provides the clear statement they need.

BELIEFS YOU AND YOUR FAMILY CAN EMBRACE AND PROCLAIM

The *Family Manifesto* is reproduced on the following pages. My earnest hope is that these statements of belief will clarify convictions. I encourage you to read it, discuss it with your spouse, and then share it with others in your family.

If, after contemplating the truths of this document, you are willing to pledge your marriage and family to uphold its teaching, I encourage you to contact our offices and get a copy for framing. (Details are listed on page 202.)

If you are a leader of a church or have a burden that your church should have a service for signing such a document, larger prints with enlarged signature blocks are available for church use.

I am praying that in America alone this document will be signed and posted in one million Christian homes and in 50,000 churches across our nation.

As Dr. Bright stated, the *Family Manifesto* may well make a difference in the lives of millions of Americans. This is my hope and prayer. But I also know that such sweeping reformation must begin with a single spark. Are you willing to embrace the truth and light the fire *in your home?*

The Family Manifesto

Preface

During the latter half of the twentieth century, the American culture has suffered an unrelenting decline. Although scientific and technological advances have created an outer veneer of prosperity and progress, our inner moral values and convictions have rapidly crumbled. Once, most Americans based their sense of right and wrong on Judeo-Christian principles, which provided them with a solid, biblical foundation for life. Today, a growing number of Americans see morality and ethics as relative and subjective and have developed their own version of "morality" with little regard to absolute standards.

This idea of moral tolerance has been eroding the foundation of the American family and society. Many Americans today have little or no concept of how to maintain a successful marriage and how to raise children to become responsible adults. In addition, a growing number of educators, politicians, and members of the media are attacking and redefining the family, creating a vast amount of confusion about what a family is. Many people today proclaim that "family values" are important, but the gradual shift to moral relativism has led to a great debate about what "family values" ought to be.

Abraham Lincoln once said, "The strength of a nation lies in the homes of its people." It is our conviction that the family is the backbone of the Christian church and of society as a whole. History shows that, if any society wants to survive, it must uphold, strengthen, and continue to build upon the biblical institutions of marriage and family.

The Bible begins in Genesis with the marriage of a man and a woman and ends in the book of Revelation with the marriage of Christ and His bride, the church. In between, God provides timeless blueprints for family life, which, if followed in a spirit of humility and obedience, provide us with the only true way to maintain healthy family relationships.

The following document affirms this biblical model and challenges us to consider how we should live within the walls of our own homes. It is offered in a spirit of love and humility, not of judgment or contention. Furthermore, it is not intended to be a comprehensive doctrinal statement about what the Bible says about marriage, family, and related subjects.

Unquestionably, this document attempts to face critical cultural issues. We invite response from anyone who wishes to affirm the truths of marriage and family from the Scriptures. It is our hope that this document will serve to accurately represent the truth God has revealed to us in Scripture, will provide insight into what a biblical family looks like, and will show how we can honor and glorify Him in our family relationships.

We freely acknowledge that we, like all people, have often denied the biblical truths of family life by the way we live. We desire, however, to live by God's grace in accordance with the principles stated herein and to pass these principles on to future generations so that He will be honored and glorified as our families reflect His character.

The Bible

We believe the Bible was written by men who were divinely inspired by God the Holy Spirit, and we believe it to be authoritative and errorless in its original autographs. We believe the Bible contains the blueprints for building solid marriage and family relationships. It teaches principles for marriage and family life that transcend time and culture. We are committed to communicating biblical truth in order to strengthen and give direction to a marriage and family. (2 Timothy 3:16; 2 Peter 1:20-21; Hebrews 4:12.)

Family

We believe God is the originator of the family. It was established by God in His inaugural act of the marriage between a man and a woman. The Bible further defines the family through God's instruction for married couples to have children, whether by birth or by adoption. We believe the purpose of the family is to glorify and honor God by forming the spiritual, emotional, physical, and economic foundation for individuals, the church, and any society.

It is at home that children see manhood and womanhood modeled. It is at home that moral values are taught by parents and placed into the hearts of their children. It is at home that people see the reality of a relationship with Jesus Christ modeled. It is at home that people learn to live out their convictions. Therefore, we are committed to upholding the concept of family as God's original and primary means of producing a godly offspring and passing on godly values from generation to generation. (Ephesians 3:14-15; Genesis 1:26-28; Romans 8:15,23; John 1:12; Galatians 3:29; Psalm 78:5-7; Deuteronomy 6:4-9.)

Marriage

We believe God, not man, created marriage. We believe marriage was the first institution designed by God. We believe the Bible teaches that the covenant of marriage is sacred and lifelong. The Bible makes it clear that marriage is a legally binding public declaration of commitment and a private consummation between one man and one woman, never between the same sex. Therefore, we believe God gives a wife to a husband and a husband to a wife, and they are to receive one another as God's unique and personal provision to help meet their mutual needs.

We believe God created marriage for the purpose of couples glorifying God as one flesh, parenting godly children, and enjoying sexual pleasure. We believe that as iron sharpens iron, God uses marriage to sharpen a man and woman into the image of Jesus Christ. Just as the Trinity reflects equal worth with differing roles, we believe God created a man and a woman with equal worth but with differing roles and responsibilities in marriage.

Finally, we declare the marriage commitment must be upheld in our culture as that sacred institution of God in which men and women can experience the truest sense of spiritual, emotional, and physical intimacy, so that the two can become one. (Genesis 2:18-25; Ephesians 5:30-32; 1 Corinthians 7:3; Matthew 19:4-6,

22:30; Mark 10:6-9, 12:25; Proverbs 27:17; Romans 1:26-27, 8:29; Hebrews 13:4; Deuteronomy 24:5; Song of Solomon.)

Husbands

We believe God has charged each husband to fulfill the responsibility of being the "head" (servant-leader) of his wife. We believe God created a man incomplete, and as a husband, he needs his wife as his helper. We believe a husband will give account before God for how he has loved, served, and provided for his wife. We reject the notion that a husband is to dominate his wife. Likewise, we reject the notion that a husband is to abdicate his responsibilities to lead his wife. Rather, we believe his responsibility is to love his wife. This love is characterized by taking the initiative to serve her, care for her, and honor her as a gift from God. We believe his responsibility is to protect his wife and help provide for her physical, emotional, and spiritual needs.

We also believe a husband is to seek after and highly regard his wife's opinion and counsel, and treat her as the equal partner she is in Christ. Therefore, we are committed to exhorting and imploring men not to abuse their God-given responsibilities as husbands, but rather to initiate a sacrificial love for their wives, in the same way Jesus Christ initiated sacrificial love and demonstrated it fully on the cross. (Genesis 2:18-25; Ephesians 5:22-33; Colossians 3:19; 1 Peter 3:7; 1 Timothy 5:8.)

Wives

We believe God has charged each wife to fulfill the responsibility of being her husband's "helper." We believe a wife will give account to God for how she has loved, respected, and given support to her husband. We uphold the biblical truth that she is of equal value with her husband before God. We reject the notion that a wife should assume her husband's leadership responsibilities. Likewise, we reject the notion that a wife should passively defer to the dominance of her husband. We believe that her responsibility is to willingly and intelligently affirm, respect, and submit to her husband as the leader in the relationship and in his vocational calling. Therefore, we are committed to exhorting a wife to be in support of her husband by accepting and excelling in her responsibility as his helper. (Genesis 2:18-25; Ephesians 5:22-33; Colossians 3:18; 1 Peter 3:1-6; Proverbs 31:10-12.)

Sexual Union

We believe the Bible clearly states that marriage is the only context for sexual intimacy. We believe contemporary culture is pressing single people to engage prematurely in acts that are intended only for the context of marriage. Our culture has rejected God's plan for intimacy by promoting sexual promiscuity of various kinds and, as a consequence, has brought upon itself sexual diseases and relational dysfunctions. We believe in sexual purity and fidelity.

Therefore, we are committed to training parents to teach their children at an early age to respect their sexuality and to preserve their virginity and purity until marriage. We are committed to communicating the message to teenagers, single adults, and married couples that sexual intimacy is available only in the context of marriage. (Genesis 1:24-25; Romans 1:24-27; 1 Thessalonians 4:3-8.)

Fathers

We believe God has charged a father to execute the responsibilities of a family leader. He is accountable before God to lead his family by sacrificially loving his wife and children and by providing for their physical, spiritual, and emotional needs. We believe the greatest way a father can love his children is to love their mother. We believe children gain much of their concept of God from their fathers. We believe a father should teach his children, by instruction and example, truth from the Bible and how to apply it practically in daily life. Therefore, a father should spend a quantity of time, as well as quality time, with each child.

We believe a father should demonstrate godly character revealed in humility, tenderness, and patience toward his children. We believe a father should demonstrate love by practicing consistent discipline with each child. Therefore, we are committed to turning the hearts of fathers back to their children by emphasizing the importance of their role as "father." We are committed to exhorting every father to model a love for God and His Word, to model love for his wife, and to love his children. (Malachi 4:6; Ephesians 6:4; Colossians 3:20-21; Deuteronomy 6:4-9; 1 Timothy 3:4-5, 5:8.)

Mothers

We believe God has uniquely designed women to be mothers. We believe the greatest way a mother can love her children is to love their father. We also believe God has created a woman with an innate and special ability to nurture and care for her children.

Therefore, we believe mothers are the primary people who execute the vital responsibilities of loving, nurturing, and mentoring children. We believe these responsibilities should be met before a mother contemplates any other duties. We believe our culture has devalued the role of a mother by placing greater significance on activities outside the home than on those inside the home.

We realize there are cases where a mother will find it necessary to work outside the home (e.g., financial distress, single parenthood); however, we also believe some couples have made career and lifestyle choices that result in de-emphasizing the mother's role as nurturer. Therefore, we are committed to presenting a biblical framework through which couples can rightly evaluate their priorities in light of a mother's role. We are committed to elevating motherhood by rightly assessing its exalted value in God's economy of the family. We are committed to exhorting mothers to model love for God and His Word, to model love for her husband, and to love her children. (Titus 2:4-5; 1 Thessalonians 2:7; Proverbs 14:1, 31:1-31; Deuteronomy 6:6, 11:19; Ezekiel 16:44-45.)

Children

We believe children are gifts from God and should be received and treated as such. We believe a child's life begins at conception. We believe children have a special responsibility to God in obeying and honoring their parents. We believe a child's identity and spiritual growth are either helped or hindered by his or her parents' devotion to God, to one another, and to him or her. Parents should see themselves as God's ambassadors, working to build strong character in the lives of their children through consistent godly living, nurturing, discipline, and teaching them right from wrong. We are committed to God's plan for passing His love down through the ages by encouraging parents to love their children "so the generations to come might know" the love and forgiveness of Christ. (Ephesians 6:1-3; Colossians 3:20; Psalms 78:5-8, 127:3-5, 139:13-16; Proverbs 4:1, 6:20.)

Childless Couples

We believe God has allowed some couples to be without biological children according to His sovereign plan in their lives. We believe couples without children are of no less value before God than those with children. We believe in encouraging childless couples to consider adoption as a family alternative. We are committed to encouraging childless couples to pass on a godly legacy through involvement with children in their immediate families, churches, and communities. (Luke 1:6-7; Romans 8:28-29.)

Grandparents

We believe grandparents are to be honored as valued family members. We believe their wisdom in living should be sought and passed on to their children and their children's children. We also believe that grandparents have the responsibility of teaching and modeling to their grandchildren how to know Jesus Christ and grow in a relationship with Him as well as passing along biblical principles for godly living. The Old Testament is filled with examples of grandfathers and grandmothers who excelled in their roles of grandparenting.

Therefore, we are committed to giving honor to grandparents by encouraging their children and grandchildren to listen to their voices of wisdom. We are also committed to exhorting grandparents to pray for and become actively involved with children and grandchildren whenever it is possible. (1 Timothy 5:4; Genesis 18:18-19; Proverbs 17:6; Psalm 78.)

Church

We believe the family and the church are interdependent. A primary responsibility of the church is to help build godly families, and godly families also help build the church. We believe the family supplies the relational rudiments of the local church. We believe the local church is the spiritual home where families should corporately worship God. It is the place where the knowledge and love of God may be communicated to fathers, mothers, and children.

Therefore, we are committed to exhorting families to support the local church through their involvement. We are also committed to exhorting the local church to uphold the priority of helping build godly marriages and families. (1 Timothy 3:15; Ephesians 5:22-33; Philemon 2; Colossians 4:15.)

Divorce

We believe God's plan for marriage is that it be a lifelong commitment between one man and one woman. We believe God hates divorce. We believe divorce brings harm to every person involved. Therefore, reconciliation of a marriage should be encouraged and divorce discouraged. We also believe that God allows for divorce in certain situations, not because He wills it, but because of the hardness of people's hearts. We believe the Bible teaches that God allows for divorce in the case of adultery and in the case where an unbelieving spouse has chosen to abandon the commitment of marriage.

We believe, however, that it is God's priority that marital oneness be restored and that, through the power of the gospel of Jesus Christ, forgiveness and reconciliation be experienced. We believe that in the unfortunate cases of abuse and abandonment, God has provided protection for an abused spouse and provision for child support through the church, civil law, godly counselors, prayer, and other practical measures. We believe God can restore broken people and broken marriages by His grace, by the power of His Spirit, and by His practical truths found in the Bible. (Malachi 2:16; Matthew 5:31-32, 19:3-9; Mark 10:6-12; Luke 16:18; Romans 7:1-3, 13:1-5; 1 Corinthians 7:15.)

Single Parents

We believe that, ideally, a child needs the influence of both a father and mother for healthy development in life and relationships. At the same time, we recognize that God's grace is sufficient and that He is a father to the fatherless and a husband to the husbandless. We also believe He is a guardian to children without a mother and a friend to a husband who has lost his wife.

We believe God, by His grace, can use the void left from a missing parent to accomplish His eternal purposes of building Christlike character in single parents and their children. We believe a single parent and his or her children are a family and that the Bible contains principles for them to grow as a family. We believe the local church should be a home for single parents, providing their children with godly people who serve as role models in place of the missing parent.

Therefore, we are committed to exhorting Christians within the local church to creatively help meet the needs associated with single-parent homes. We are committed to comforting and encouraging single-parent families by providing resources and developing biblical principles to assist those who struggle in the role of a single parent. (Psalm 68:5-6; 1 Corinthians 7:32; James 1:27; 1 Timothy 5:3-16; Romans 8:28-29; Luke 18:3-5.)

Broken and Blended Families

We believe God has allowed men and women, either by circumstance or by choice, to endure difficult and painful consequences in their marriages and family relationships. We also believe God gives abundant grace to the broken, blended, and single-parent families.

Therefore, we believe He can and does enable them to carry out His functions and principles for healthy family life. We are committed to comforting, encouraging, and teaching these families

God's principles of marriage and family life. We are also committed to exhorting the local church to help with the burden of the broken family. (James 1:27; 1 Timothy 5:16; Philippians 4:13.)

Work and Family

We believe work is an important and necessary aspect of one's service to God and one's responsibility to provide for the needs of the family. We also believe security and significance cannot be found through pursuing career goals or financial achievement apart from one's responsibility to God and one's spouse and family. Instead, we believe those needs are best met in the warmth of a home where parents and children are experiencing harmony in their relationships with each other and with Jesus Christ. Therefore, we are committed to challenging any person or couple to rearrange their priorities so that over the course of a lifetime they can be successful at home and not merely successful in their careers. (Revelation 3:14-22; Ephesians 6:7-8; Matthew 6:33; 1 Timothy 5:8; 1 Thessalonians 4:10-12.)

Mentors

We believe in the biblical admonition for older men and women to teach younger men and women. We believe younger couples today should seek out older couples for their wisdom and counsel in matters of marriage and family. We believe older couples should be taught and encouraged to mentor younger couples, and we believe this is best accomplished through the local church. Therefore, we are committed to establishing a strategy for mentoring that the local church may implement and use to build strong marriages and families. (Titus 2:3-5.)

Marriage Education

We believe single adults who choose to marry should be taught the biblical principles of marriage. We also believe the education of a married couple does not end after the wedding ceremony is over, but continues throughout life.

Therefore, we believe that both premarital and postmarital education are helpful and essential in a couple's growth toward and in oneness. We are committed to elevating, establishing, and teaching the precepts of marriage by which single adults can rightly evaluate their relationships and equip themselves for marriage. We are committed to providing the teaching and training necessary to equip married couples to live a lifetime together as one. Finally, we are committed to showing couples how their marriages can be used by God to give others the hope found only in Jesus Christ. (Titus 2; 2 Timothy 3:16-17; Acts 16:31-34; John 4:53.)

The Deceiver and Culture

We believe there is a living Devil who is God's enemy and whose nature and objective are to lie and deceive. We believe the Devil has attacked God's plan for the family from the beginning of mankind until now. We believe the Devil uses the various aspects of the culture to promote personal independence, distort the differences between men and women, confuse their roles, and elevate personal rights over marital responsibilities. We believe the Devil seeks to persuade people to move away from God's plan for intimacy and oneness and toward isolation and divorce. (John 8:44; Genesis 3; Isaiah 14:12-14; Ezekiel 28:12-18; 1 Peter 5:8; Ephesians 6:12; 1 John 2:15.)

God—the Creator of the Family

Father

We believe in the Fatherhood of God. The title "Father" implies that God is a relational being. The Bible reveals God has four primary relationships as Father: He is the Father of creation, of the nations, of the Lord Jesus Christ, and of all believers. We believe the Bible presents the title "Father" as one of the primary names Christians should use in addressing and relating to God. In doing so, Christians identify themselves as children who belong to the family of God. We are committed to proclaiming and demonstrating this truth about who God is and who we are, so that God will be glorified, and that He might use us to bring others into His family through a personal relationship with His Son. (John 1:12; Exodus 3:14-15; Ephesians 3:16; Matthew 6:9; Romans 8:15; Acts 17:24-28.)

Son

We believe God the Son, fully revealed in the person of Jesus Christ, was God's final sacrifice for the sins of man through the shedding of His blood on the cross and His resurrection from the dead. We believe He is the only way to know God the Father and to experience His plan for marriage and family. We are committed to introducing people to Jesus Christ in order that, by faith, they might personally receive Him, be born into the family of God, receive forgiveness and eternal life, and begin a relationship with God that is essential in marriage and family life. (John 1:4, 12; 17:3; 1 John 2:23-24; Ephesians 2:19-22; Colossians 1:13-18; Hebrews 1:1-4.)

Holy Spirit

We believe God the Holy Spirit is the agent and teacher of a godly marriage and family. We believe when Christian couples and their children consistently yield to His control and power, they will experience harmony in their marriages and families. Therefore, we are committed to sharing the ministry of the Holy Spirit with people so they may know God better, make Him known to others, and appropriate His power in fulfilling their duties in marriage and family relationships. (John 14:26, 15:26, 16:5-15; Ephesians 5:18-21.)

Commitment

In recognition of and in full agreement with these biblical principles regarding marriage and the family, I, by the grace of God, commit myself to adhere to, practice, and teach what God has made clear are my responsibilities within His design of marriage and the family.

---

*Full-size, frameable copies of the *Family Manifesto* are available from FamilyLife. For more information, call 1 (800) FL-TODAY or write to FamilyLife, 3900 North Rodney Parham Rd., Little Rock, AR 72212.

A Reformation Moment

KIDZ IN THE 'HOOD

Debi Godsey eventually learned that God had a unique job in mind for her.

Because the Godseys live in an inner-city neighborhood of Milwaukee, they see all the problems found in urban America: violence, kids without dads, drugs, unwed mothers, unemployment—a dark place desperately needing light.

When Jim and Debi returned from the marriage conference in 1990, they were so aglow that they just had to shine some of that light on others.

God sent them needy kids and families from their neighborhood. In fact, so many came that eventually their home became the focal point for a full-time, informal ministry they call Kidz in the 'Hood.

Small groups of inner-city kids stop by after school for help with homework, a meal, or a shoulder to lean on. Debi makes herself available to meet their needs, whatever they may be. She also makes sure the kids get to know God through learning the Scriptures and prayer.

Jim's job at a paper mill limits his availability, but he repairs bicycles and assists with evening Bible studies. Groups of children are loaded in a donated van and regularly taken camping in the forest to learn more about God through first-hand exposure to creation. But more than anything, Jim and Debi just live their faith and tell others what the God of hope has done for them—and can do in anyone's life.

"We tell them about Jesus, because the food and the clothing wear off, but Jesus won't," says Debi. "He's given us the privilege of introducing a lot of broken, hurting, crushed, depressed people to Him."

Over the years, hundreds have experienced God's arms of love and hope in the Godsey home. Debi draws on her painful past to identify with the wounded and help knit together broken hearts.

"There's nothing these little kids have been through that I haven't been through," Debi says. "God just used all the garbage of my past to reach out to all these hurting kids. I've had to escort girls to the hospital for exams and to make sure they get proper medication and medical attention. I've seen fathers put in prison for what they did to their little girls."

After nearly everyone on their block accepted Christ, the Godseys reached out to many others throughout the city. Several hundred children, youth, and adults have committed their lives to Christ since 1990.

At the time of this writing, daughter Carla was in her last year of high school, and a National Honor Society member considering a major in marine biology in college. She loves horses and helps out with the Kidz in the 'Hood—many times using the middle of the Godseys' street to teach neighborhood girls a worshipful ballet for the Lord.

Carla's life is marked by spiritual multiplication. She also occasionally ministers on her own, traveling in the Wisconsin and northern Illinois area to speak to youth groups about worshiping God.

Jim and Debi continue to drive flocks of people to FamilyLife Conferences: Debi estimates she hands out 500 conference brochures a year. Hundreds of couples have been cajoled to attend. "I stopped keeping track long ago," Debi says. "I feel like a spiritual paramedic. I still never leave the house without a stack of brochures."

It's not all roses for Debi and Jim. The Godseys promised themselves early on that they would keep going back to the marriage conferences about every six months to learn more— they have attended nine times.

"Sometimes we barely make it six months," Debi says with a grin. "We would be lying if we told you that our relationship is always smooth; it's not."

"I'm a slow learner," Jim adds.

"Only in my wildest dreams would I have imagined that I would be loved as I am by Jim," says Debi. But the key element has been her acceptance and love by God. "When you're loved by God, then there is no insecurity about whether you are loved by your husband or not."

"There was no way I could fill the needs that Deb had. It was too great for a man to fill," Jim says.

"Everybody needs hope," Debi adds. "I need God. You need God. We all need God."

CHAPTER ELEVEN

Living Bricks

Our problems in America today are primarily problems of the heart.
The soul of our nation is the sum of our individual characters.
Yes, we must balance the federal budget and there are a lot of other
things we need to do at the federal level, but unless we change our
hearts, we will still have a deficit of the soul.
—SENATOR SAM NUNN,
FROM AN ADDRESS GIVEN AT THE 1996 PRESIDENTIAL PRAYER BREAKFAST

During the height of the Greek Empire, the city of Sparta was a military stronghold, a place where the citizens felt secure. Extremely safe.

An ambassador from another country once visited the king of Sparta to find out why the city was so secure. Because of Sparta's reputation, the ambassador expected to find a city surrounded by a mighty wall and fortified by legions of armed soldiers. Surprisingly, the visiting dignitary found no such visible stronghold, and he exclaimed to his host, "King, you have no fortifications for defense. Why is this?"

"Come with me tomorrow," the king replied confidently, "and I will show you the walls of Sparta."

The next morning, the king and his diplomatic guest arose early and traveled on a dusty road to a plain near Sparta where the king's army stood in complete battle array. Pointing to the thousands of soldiers standing proudly at attention, the king said, "The city is well fortified which has a wall of men instead of brick!"[1]

Today, many "bricks"—men and women—are needed to erect a wall of protection around our families, our communities, and our nation. But unlike the king of Sparta, who boasted of the military might of his army, our confidence must be in God, who will deliver us from our enemies and grant us victory. The prophet Daniel described the kind of bricks we need today: "The people who know their God will display strength and take action" (Daniel 11:32).

In chapter 9, I spoke of the first brick needed to rebuild the wall—the husbands and wives, moms and dads who, through their courageous efforts inside the home, play *the* pivotal role. Here my focus shifts *outside* the family unit to another critical brick—like the family, ordained by God—the church.

BRICK #2: PASTORAL AND LAY LEADERS OF CHURCHES AND DENOMINATIONS

Spiritually, the church is God's number one choice for offensively enriching and equipping the family as well as defensively protecting its members. Yet for the most part, in the church today there is no strategy for rescuing the family, and sadly, no offensive battle plan for recapturing lost territory.

"Many churches have no strategy to help families except referring them to self-help books," says Dan Simpson of the Charles E. Fuller Institute of Church Growth. "Seminaries focus on academic studies and preparing sermons, but pastors have little training in helping families."[2]

Over the past two decades, I've interacted with hundreds of pastors, lay leaders, and their wives about how to rebuild the Christian family. Two conclusions are painfully clear: First, pastors and lay leaders in the church have enormous needs *in their own marriages and families*. And second, these church leaders *are not equipped to handle* the crisis in the Christian family.

Divorce and its ramifications are crushing most pastors and church staff. I am a member of an effective church that aggressively attempts to equip marriages and families. The staff numbers 62. Yet, as I was writing this book, our senior pastor, Robert Lewis, made a startling pronouncement when reviewing the church's budget with our members: "There is not anything that we deal with in the local church that takes as much time as those contemplating divorce, those going through a divorce, or those recovering from divorce. In fact, divorce issues now take more time from our staff, more effort and expense, than *all the other issues in the church combined!*"

That is a profound observation.

The needs of the sheep have so overwhelmed the shepherds that only a handful of the largest churches have a clear vision of goals to accomplish with their families. The needs of the hurting are so emotionally compelling and exhausting that there is little time or energy left to grapple with the core issues church families face.

Certainly, a portion of every church's mission must be to care for the brokenhearted. But think of it: If we could wipe out the plague of divorce within the Christian community, our professional clergy would gain up to 50 percent of their time back for more proactive ministries.

It's time for another D-day. The church must declare war on divorce!

THE NEED OF THE HOUR

Howard Hendricks, a friend and one of my seminary professors and spiritual mentors, tells a compelling story of how a spiritual and Family Reformation began long ago in one local church:

> Richard Baxter was a great man of God who took a very wealthy and sophisticated parish. For three years he preached with all the passion of his heart without any visible response. Finally . . . he cried out, "O God, You must do something with these people or I'll die!"
>
> He said, "It was as if God spoke to me audibly, 'Baxter, you are working in the wrong place. You're expecting revival to come through the church. Try the home.'"
>
> Richard Baxter went out and called on home after home. He spent entire evenings in homes helping parents set up family worship times with their children. He moved from one home to another. Finally, the Spirit of God started to light fires all over until they swept through the congregation and made it the great church that it became—and made Baxter a man of godly distinction.[3]

It has been said that a leader is a person you will follow to a place that you wouldn't go by yourself. I believe people in the pews are waiting to follow, to be stirred to action in their own homes by godly shepherds like Richard Baxter.

But not much will happen until pastors and lay leaders set the example by humbling themselves and making their families a visible priority within their congregations. If you are a pastor or pastor's wife, this is where a Family Reformation must begin—in your relationship with God, your spouse, and your children.

The church needs leaders similar to the sons of Issachar—"men who understood the times, with knowledge of what Israel should do" (1 Chronicles 12:32). Our churches cry out for those who understand the need of the hour, know what to do, and then *do it!*

Of course, I do not pretend to have all the answers. But I will propose several strategic initiatives I believe are critical as we deploy troops in a battle that only God can help us win.

Strategic Initiative #1: Pastors and Lay Leaders Must First Love and Lead Their Own Families

If church leaders choose to fight on behalf of families, they must first shout the war cry in their own homes. Passionate sermons cannot be preached with integrity if we are not fervently leading and loving our wives and children.

For many pastors and lay leaders, the ministry is a mistress. Wives sit silently in pews, knowing they are emotionally divorced from their husbands. Children are abandoned by clergy fathers doing "the will of God."

I recall what the daughter of a famous Christian leader once said, "Daddy and God made a deal. Daddy would take care of God's sheep . . . and God would take care of Daddy's sheep at home. Unfortunately, the deal was Daddy's and not God's." The descendants of that family still bear the marks of the father's workaholism.

The army of God will never be enlisted and unleashed if its field generals fail to visit the front lines and battle against the enemy by leading in their own marriages and families.

In 1996, Promise Keepers leader Randy Phillips led a time of prayer for Christian husbands at the Fasting and Prayer Congress in St. Louis. Instead of saying a generic prayer for all husbands everywhere, Randy asked those of us who were leaders and speakers at the Congress if we needed to confess publicly our failure to love and lead our wives.

His challenge was on target. How can we with integrity urge those we shepherd to lead and love their families if we neglect our own? We can't!

Pastor, elder, deacon, staff member, or lay leader—these questions (primarily targeted to men) need to be pondered before the living Lord God almighty, who sees all and knows all:

- Do you regularly pray with and for your wife?
- Do you read the Bible together and lead her spiritually in the truth?
- Are you passionately loving God's most holy human gift to you—your wife?
- Are you spiritually leading, loving, and protecting your children?
- Do you model a humble and teachable heart for God by asking for forgiveness when you've wronged a family member?

Could it be that the spiritual awakening that is begging to sweep our nation will begin in the homes of the spiritual leaders of our churches?

Strategic Initiative #2: Proclaim a Solemn Assembly for the Family

During Old Testament times, Judah had been devastated by an invasion—pillaged and plundered, its people left vulnerable. The prophet Joel likened the invasion to that of an army, but no humans were involved. The soldiers were swarming locusts.

We, too, have been invaded by a cloud of immoral "locusts." Joel's words describe how most Christian families feel—overrun by evil: "They march everyone in his path. When they burst through the defenses, they do not break ranks. They rush on the city, they run on the wall; they climb into the houses, they enter though the windows like a thief" (Joel 2:8-9).

Like Judah, we have been laid waste. And the prophet's solution for them is an appropriate one for the church: "Gird yourselves with sackcloth, and lament, O priests; wail, O ministers of the altar! Come, spend the night in sackcloth . . . Consecrate a fast, proclaim a solemn assembly; gather . . . all the inhabitants of the land to the house of the Lord your God and cry out to the Lord!" (Joel 1:13-14).

Am I an alarmist? Is this too radical? I don't think so! The locusts of divorce, immorality, violence, abuse, drugs, perversions, murder, and materialism are marching through our communities, neighborhoods, and homes. How much worse does it need to get before we declare a fast—a solemn assembly? Is there an issue in the church any more important than resurrecting godly families?

It's time to declare an annual gathering and cry out for God to exterminate the locusts that are in our land and our homes. For more than symbolic reasons, I suggest that we use Father's Day for such an assembly in our churches. Perhaps God will withdraw His judgment and grant us favor in battle. Perhaps God will bring healing to the walking-wounded generation of divorce and restore the years the locusts have eaten (see Joel 2:20-25).

Your church could be the first brick in your community—go to your pastor and share this idea with him. An offer to help with the service or the special day may be all that's needed.

Think of it: What if tens of thousands of the estimated 300,000 churches in America began to set aside one Sunday a year, every year, for the next 40 years as a Solemn Assembly for the Family? I believe God yearns for us to humble ourselves and cry out to Him for help. I believe this kind of long-term commitment will bring the change in homes that is needed.

Strategic Initiative #3: Reclaim the Sanctity of Marriage Vows

Across the country, in community after community, the sacredness of the marriage covenant is high ground just waiting to be recaptured by the church. Even those who are not religious long for someone—anyone—to remove the tarnish and restore the brilliance of the scriptural ideal of marriage: one man and one woman under God's authority, committed to each other in an unbreakable marital covenant *for a lifetime.*

The time has come to compassionately, yet firmly, push back against the culture of divorce that is slowly eradicating the relational, moral, and spiritual compass in our children. The Christian community needs to lead the charge to put the *fault* back in no-fault divorce.

Consider this: What is no one's fault is no one's responsibility. It's time for divorce to become shameful again. In ridding divorce of shame, we aborted the dignity and sacred nature of the covenant.

As citizens, every promise we make—whether it be father to son, employee to employer, doctor to patient, teacher to parent, neighbor to neighbor, or businessman to businessman—is undermined and eroded by a culture that cannot keep its promise to stay married. Certainly, a huge portion of our national cynicism is traceable to the seeds of distrust sown at home.

Divorce is costing us far more than we realize.

As the church takes on this bitter enemy, we must do so in a way that embodies the love of Christ for those who are already divorced. We must compassionately speak the truth—always in love (see Ephesians 4:15). But we must speak the truth. Where should church leaders begin?

- Exalt the biblical ideal of the sacred nature of the marriage covenant from the pulpit. We need to talk more about the meaning and permanence of the vows and talk less about the exceptions. Vows could be reviewed and recited publicly once a year during a church service. Regularly honor couples who have long-term marriages. Plato wrote, "What is honored in a land will be cultivated there."
- Publicly read, pray through, and have a solemn ceremony for church members to sign the *Family Manifesto* (see chapter 10). Frame the document and publicly hang it so that it will be a reminder of our most solemn pledge to our families and to one another.
- Pray for our church bodies to be cleansed from Christians divorcing one another. We need to ask God that the divorce rate would drop by 90 percent in the church over the next 40 years. Pray for the leaders of churches to be

courageous and push back against the pressure to conform to the world's mold.

- Entreat Christian counselors, both professional and lay, to stop running toward divorce as a solution and start challenging struggling couples to honor their covenant and aggressively seek reconciliation. We need to surround hurting couples with love *and* truth.

- Ask couples getting married to publicly sign a covenant saying they will marry for a lifetime. Copies should be kept on file at the church and given to the families of both the newly married husband and wife. Refuse to marry any couple who signs a prenuptial agreement.

- Aggressively equip couples, especially newlyweds, to know how to fulfill their vows. Sunday school classes and small-group studies need to be taught by older couples who will help these couples establish their home early in their married life.*

- Commission adult church members to work to restore and reconcile hurting marriages. Helping all marriages succeed within the church needs to become more than the pastor's responsibility; it must become the church body's responsibility.

- Revive church discipline for those who refuse to honor the truth of Scripture and divorce their spouses (see Matthew 18:15-17). Church or denominational leaders need to craft a statement of how they will deal with individuals who divorce and leave one church and try to attend another.

We need to do more than just set theological or emotional speed bumps between married couples and divorce. Instead, fortified walls of people must be erected that protect and ensure the permanence of marriage for generations to come. By creating a climate within the church that honors the marriage covenant and equips couples to keep their covenant, we will see divorce in the church diminish.

---

*For information on a church starter kit for Sunday schools and small groups, call 1 (800) FL-TODAY.

While we must mount an offensive against divorce, at the same time we must not neglect the needs of those left hurting in divorce's wake. Our brothers and sisters who are single parents or who are part of a blended family deserve our total love and acceptance. This tension between reclaiming the biblical ideals of marriage and family while at the same time helping the hurting is difficult, but we must press into the pain for the sake of God's kingdom.

Strategic Initiative #4: Establish Church-Based Mentors for the Life Cycle of the Family

Recently, I commissioned a professional firm to lead a focus group on the needs of Christian families. I sat behind a mirror, watching and listening to husbands and wives, moms and dads, as they articulated their needs.

Their opinion was unanimous! Two things were desired: a marriage and family mentor from their local church, and training/equipping for the major phases and needs during the life cycle of their families.

These couples wanted help from someone with skin—a real, breathing, older person who had negotiated the turbulent stretch of river they were currently navigating. They wanted a trustworthy person—someone willing to share successes and failures—who had the biblical wisdom and Christian maturity to answer their questions and instruct them.

Further proof of the need for mentoring and training comes from pollster George Barna, who reported a 10 percent drop in church attendance in just one year. He discovered that the Baby Boomers have looked to the church for equipping in the major commitments in life. Apparently, significant numbers of them haven't found it, so they've left.[4]

I'm convinced the church can bring these families back by providing the hands-on tools they're looking for: practical, biblical principles that equip couples to solve the needs of the family—presented through a wisely crafted, lay-led strategy. And although these family mentors may need some training to build their confidence, I believe they are waiting for the call to battle on behalf of younger families.

This intergenerational ministry begs for massive expansion in our churches. The largest volunteer "army" in America must enlist mentors to rescue and train the next generation of families.

THE LIFE CYCLE OF A FAMILY

In response to that focus group of couples, we began crafting what became The Life Cycle of a Family.

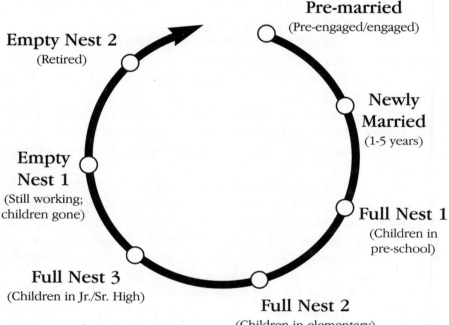

Predictably, every family goes through well-defined seasons, and with multiple children, may be in two or more seasons at the same time. Although each marriage and family is unique, I believe that 90-plus percent of the issues faced in each phase are the same for most. Every couple who wants instruction should have a qualified mentor during each phase of the family cycle. I believe this ministry would spiritually revitalize and galvanize the local church—a ministry that would enlist many older couples who need to share their wisdom.

A PLAN FOR MENTORING:
FOLLOWING THE LIFE CYCLE OF A FAMILY

Question: Where should a church start?

Answer: Before the marriage begins.

Nationally, 73 percent of marriage ceremonies are held in either a church or a synagogue.[5] This provides a strategic opportunity for the church to insist on well-planned, helpful, and mandatory pre-marital counseling.

Because the divorce rate is highest in the early years of marriage (over 40 percent of all divorces in a 30-plus year period occur in the first five years of marriage—see graph below[6]), it is to the church's strategic advantage to target a key group: newly marrieds. Slashing the divorce rate will require churches to go upstream to the head-waters of marriage. Ideally, a mentoring couple would begin helping a couple during their engagement—or shortly after the marriage—and walk them through the critical first years.

As the graph vividly illustrates, the "seven-year itch" in marriage is a myth. Couples start "itching" in the first year, and many are already divorced by year five.

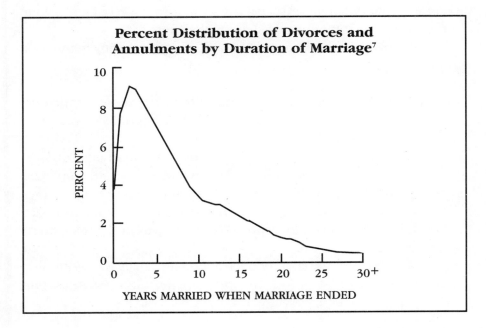

Percent Distribution of Divorces and Annulments by Duration of Marriage[7]

John Schmidt, a minister at Frazer Memorial United Methodist Church in Montgomery, Alabama, has trained dozens of couples to mentor nearly marrieds. These mentors help lead small groups of engaged couples through an eight-week course on the biblical model of marriage. As a result of the course, some couples have decided they should cancel or delay the marriage.

Each mentoring couple helps an average of three engaged couples at a time, leading them through the course and meeting with them individually for encouragement and counseling. Many mentoring couples then continue their involvement after the training ends.

Frazer Methodist will take as many as 120 engaged couples through this course in a year. Several other churches in Montgomery are considering the same program.

With so many people growing up today in broken or dysfunctional homes, many new couples have little knowledge about the key issues in Christian marriage, such as resolving conflict, handling money, defining roles of husband and wife, and raising godly children.

I believe hundreds of thousands of church laymen and laywomen, if challenged properly, would form a mighty volunteer army to equip younger families. Once a Family Reformation begins in your home, you have something to share with others.

Additional groups who would benefit from mentoring within our churches include:

- Single parents. There are more than 18 million of them in the United States who have children aged 18 or under in their homes.[8]
- Blended families. Forty-six percent of all marriages in 1990 involved one spouse who'd been married before—up from 31 percent in 1970.[9]
- Urban families. Eighty-seven percent of black children are likely to spend at least some of their lives in a single-parent home.[10]
- Couples in need of reconciliation (Jim Talley has written an excellent book on this subject entitled *Reconcilable Differences*).

Mentoring couples and families may well be *the* single most important strategy the church can implement to retrain and bring healing and hope to a generation wounded by divorce, dysfunctional families, and the culture. And I believe that marriage and family issues are *the* most strategic opportunity to proclaim the gospel in the new millennium.

Strategic Initiative #5: Establish a Community-Centered Coalition of Churches for the Family

Has the condition of Christian marriages and families become acute enough for us to lay aside denominational distinctives and join as one under the Lord and Captain of the army, the Lord Jesus Christ? I think so. The world seems united in its lies against the church; isn't it time for the truth to unite us?

By forming community coalitions, our combined voice could be effectively heard. The purpose of these coalitions would be fourfold:

1. Sign a document that upholds the truth about the family and related issues. (The *Family Manifesto* may provide a beginning point for discussion.)

2. Establish a Community Marriage Policy that sets minimum preparation requirements before a couple can be married in any church or synagogue. (See Appendix for more information.)

3. Annually join together with other churches on Father's Day for a Solemn Assembly for the Family. As a statement of shared commitment, perhaps advertise and meet in a stadium for this citywide event.

4. Bring training resources into the community and share in the equipping for family life of pastors, mentors, counselors, and pre-married and newly married couples.

The Bible promises spiritual leverage when we join others in battle. It's time for the body of Christ to experience the promise of Leviticus 26:6-9:

> I shall also grant peace in the land, so that you may lie down with no one making you tremble. I shall also eliminate harmful beasts from the land, and no sword will pass through your land. But you will chase your enemies, and they will fall before you by the sword; five of you will chase a hundred,

and a hundred of you will chase ten thousand, and your enemies will fall before you by the sword. So I will turn toward
you and make you fruitful and multiply you, and I will con-
firm My covenant with you.

According to the equation (five will chase 100), mathematically
speaking, 100 should cause only 2,000 to flee, not 10,000. But with
God's power, a group of united Christians has an exponential spiritual advantage that's five times more effective. What if just 10 percent of the churches in your community shared resources and
united in prayer for the family?

Before us is the opportunity of a lifetime! A generation of people
is broken, lonely, and looking for help. The world has no answers. I
am absolutely convinced that the church is *the* answer. We must help
the church succeed in its mission!

A GENERATIONAL COMMITMENT

Edwin Land was not only an inventor, but a brilliant businessman
and thinker as well. In addition to creating the Polaroid camera, he
built a financial empire with his vision and leadership.

Land once made a statement about his vision that can be applied
to the church as it addresses the needs of the family: "My motto is:
Don't do anything that someone else can do. Don't undertake a project unless it is manifestly important and nearly impossible. . . . If it is
manifestly important, then you don't have to worry about its significance. Since it's nearly impossible, you know that no one else is likely
to be doing it, so if you do succeed, you will have created a whole
domain for yourself."[11]

Looming before us, the needs of families represent an immense
opportunity. Reconstructing society's most basic building block, the
family, certainly constitutes a significant task. With God's favor,
Christians can strategically offer help and hope to all families. And by
doing so, Christians can seize an opportunity to preach the gospel
of Jesus Christ and the Scriptures as the solution to hurting, hopeless, and lost sheep.

The need is clear. The solution is spiritual. Jesus Christ and His

Word are the answers. But our nation's families did not fall in this deep ditch overnight. We will not climb out of this ditch overnight either. That's why I believe we need to declare a generational commitment (in the Old Testament, a generation is generally spoken of as 40 years) to rebuild and restore the Christian family.

> ## *Our nation's families did not fall in this deep ditch overnight. We will not climb out of this ditch overnight either.*

In the near future, Christians and churches could prepare strategies, train people, and garner resources for an all-out assault beginning in January of 2000. The years between 2000 and 2040 could be declared The Era for a Family Reformation.

Important? Absolutely! Our children and grandchildren are at risk.

Nearly impossible? Without a doubt. If God does not grant us favor in this battle, I fear for succeeding generations. But "the things impossible with men are possible with God" (Luke 18:27).

I'm reminded of a scene in C. S. Lewis's *Chronicles of Narnia*. The mystical country of Narnia had been frozen under the grip of evil. But suddenly, everything in Narnia began to thaw. The Lion, Aslan, who represents Jesus Christ, had given his life to break evil's spell.

I will never forget the phrase that resonated hope in Narnia— and brought chills to me as a reader: "Aslan is on the move."

Today there is fresh evidence that God is "on the move." Individual Christians are getting right with God. Christian leaders in city after city are coming to the conclusion that something must be done to reverse the downward spiral of the Christian family.

The family is God's smallest battle formation. The battleground for the soul of the church lies in the homes of its people. The church's impact on the culture will never rise above the spiritual condition of its families.

It's time for the church to become a solid brick in the wall. For the sake of our children and our children's children, may God grant us favor and success.

A Reformation Moment

A Song in the Morning

Martin Luther's courage had inflamed a revolution of faith, but this morning the great Reformer could not raise himself from bed.

Exhausted by another sleepless night, he felt his reddened eyes burning, and an ache throbbed throughout his skull.

Martin forced himself from under the covers and made his way to a chair. He tried to pray, but his mind wandered. By sheer will, he picked up his Bible and turned to the

Psalms, a source of such comfort when the blackness assailed him from all sides.

During the darkest moments of the previous night, when hope was but a misty memory, Martin had cried out for his God but heard only silence.

His eyes attached to the opening of Psalm 46: "God is our refuge and strength, a very present help in trouble. Therefore we will not fear."

Yes, of course, how could he have forgotten, even in the thick, numbing grip of depression? His only hope was in God.

"Hmmm," Martin said aloud, "Ein feste Burg—A mighty fortress . . . is my God."

A man who loved words with a poet's passion, Martin grasped a pen and scribbled phrases on a sheet of paper . . . "A mighty fortress is our God, a bulwark never failing. Our helper He amid the flood, of mortal ills prevailing."

The words, filled with life and power, lifted Martin's spirit. Line after line took shape, soon making a verse. A second followed, then another—finally four in all.

The ink was still wet when Martin began humming tunes. The first melody, reminiscent of a theme heard recently at an opera, he discarded as too light and flimsy. Then a more solemn melody played in his mind. The beat was resolute. He could almost hear the sound of soldiers' boots on the cobblestones.

"Dum dum dum da-da-da, da-da-da DUM!" he sang out.

The morning's first smile lit his jowly face. Martin picked up his lute and plucked several notes. Then he both played and sang, his baritone rattling a windowpane—exploding the quiet of the chilly room: "A MIGHTY FORTRESS IS OUR GOD, A BULWARK NEVER FAILING!"

Martin smiled . . . and laughed. He must find Katie and share the new song—this might work in Sunday worship. Martin saw sunlight flooding the room. This would be a better day. Grabbing paper and lute, he bolted from the room.

"Our helper He amid the flood," the voice boomed in the hallway, "of mortal ills prevailing!"

The Reformer had written a battle anthem for all time. Even in our day, the words of this resounding hymn contain seeds of truth that will sprout and grow into a Family Reformation.[1]

A mighty fortress is our God,
A bulwark never failing;
Our helper He amid the flood
Of mortal ills prevailing.
For still our ancient foe
Doth seek to work us woe—
His craft and power are great,
And armed with cruel hate,
On earth is not His equal.

Did we in our own strength confide,
Our striving would be losing,
Were not the right man on our side,
The man of God's own choosing.
Dost ask who that may be?
Christ Jesus, it is He—
Lord Sabaoth His name,
From age to age the same,
And He must win the battle.

And though this world with devils filled,
Should threaten to undo us,
We will not fear, for God hath willed
His truth to triumph through us.
The prince of darkness grim,
We tremble not for him—
His rage we can endure,
For lo, his doom is sure:
One little word shall fell him.

That word above all earthly powers,
No thanks to them, abideth;
The Spirit and the gifts are ours
Through Him who with us sideth.
Let goods and kindred go,
This mortal life also—
The body they may kill;
God's truth abideth still;
His kingdom is forever. Amen.

—Martin Luther, 1527
Translated by Frederick H. Hedge

CHAPTER TWELVE

Special Forces

Never fight a battle if you do not gain anything by winning it.
—GENERAL GEORGE PATTON

Persian Gulf, 24 February 1991, 0100 hours...
Fifteen miles off the coast of Kuwait, two speedboats carrying a platoon of American SEAL commandos roared to a stop. The boat engines idled as a dozen men, wearing wetsuits and armed with silenced submachine guns, grenades, and an assortment of knives and handguns, transferred their gear and a cache of explosives to several Zodiac raiding craft.

The SEAL contingent then moved stealthily through the darkness, the waves slapping the hulls of the rubber boats. Within an hour, the small armada halted, just 500 yards from the shoreline.

The SEALs slid on their masks, attached other gear and weapons, and on signal slipped without a splash beneath the surface. The men who stayed behind in the small boats scanned the coastline. Just over a quarter mile away, a large force of enemy soldiers was dug in on the beach. The Iraqis knew the ground war could begin at any time, and this very beach south of Kuwait City was a likely attack point for an Allied amphibious operation. The Iraqi soldiers expected the U.S. Marines.

Heavily armed, the Iraqis waited in fortified bunkers along an enormous trench line. The beach was littered with mines and protected by barbwire. Artillery and tanks stood ready to the rear. Enemy soldiers, their eyes scanning the sea, paced up and down the beach.

The SEALs swam furtively toward a 200-yard-wide stretch of beach. The tide was in but would recede soon. Closer and closer the invaders paddled until the surf was only a foot deep. Working in teams and using only hand signals, the men carefully lined the 600-foot corridor with plastic explosives, placing the small charges just below the surface of the water. The commandos were so near the beach that they could hear the enemy soldiers on shore eating, talking, joking, and moving about.

The explosives placed, the SEALS swam back out to sea, halting just long enough to place the blue-and-white buoys that would guide amphibious units and their landing craft to the spot of attack.

Back safely in their speedboats, only one of the boats zoomed near the beach, splattering the Iraqi positions with .50-caliber machine-gun fire and 40-mm grenades. Simultaneously, Allied jet aircraft roared in, hammering the beachfront with rockets and bombs. Finally, with the tide flowing out, the satchel explosives detonated on cue, shaking the ground and spewing plumes of sand into the air.

Convinced that the ground offensive had begun, the Iraqis hurried to return fire and ordered two armored divisions to redeploy from the interior to defend the coastline.

Their mission accomplished, the SEAL combat unit roared off into the darkness in their speedboats.

Three hours later, at 0400 hours, the long-awaited ground offensive of Desert Storm began—not at this beach south of Kuwait City, but inland, many miles to the west. The SEALs' mission had been a ruse, a special forces operation to confuse the enemy and divert its forces away from the point of actual attack.[1]

AN ARMY OF SPECIALIZED FORCES

As this operation in the Gulf War illustrates, every successful army requires a variety of special units to perform critical tasks in advancing the war effort. *The* army of armies—the church—is no different. As the war for the family is fought, a number of such uniquely skilled units must come alongside the church to perform strategic combat assignments.

As we work together to rebuild the wall of the family, important and specialized bricks must be set in place by key groups—special forces attacking at strategic points to bring about a Family Reformation. Structurally the wall will demand many more bricks than just those provided by individual couples and the church. As with the previous two bricks mentioned in previous chapters, these additional five bricks are critical for success and must be firmly set in place.

BRICK #3: LEADERS AND WORKERS IN PARACHURCH ORGANIZATIONS

Throughout church history, entities outside the walls of the church—parachurch organizations—have been raised up by God for strategic purposes. Today, 80,000 such ministries are listed on the Internet. Because of the strength and resources these organizations represent, it's time to consider how to use them to strengthen families in the local church. Two critical actions are needed.

First, all family-related parachurch organizations must review how we are coming alongside the local church and helping it accomplish the mission of equipping marriages and families.

Urgent times demand radical analysis. At FamilyLife, our leadership team has decided to focus our attention on helping the local church build families. The fate of millions of marriages and families desperately depends on the church's success.

Perhaps the spiritual revolution we all long to see will be fueled by selfless leaders in organizations and churches who have decided it's time we all work together. What would happen if every family-related parachurch organization (and perhaps even some that are not presently in family ministry) began to prayerfully strategize about how to help the church equip marriages and families?

That leads me to a second critical action that must occur.

Parachurch organizations and churches must forge innovative partnerships. It's time that church leaders and parachurch leaders sat down at a table and admitted the truth: There is tremendous competition between local churches, between churches and parachurch organizations, and between parachurch groups. I'm sad to report there are territorialism, distrust, bitterness, and division—to name a few problems.

It's time to repent. Perhaps this repentance needs to begin in the parachurch sector. We need to ask ourselves some tough questions:

1. Are we truly coming alongside the church—or are we building ministries at the church's expense?

2. How are our current strategies focused on helping the church succeed?

3. How can we correct our focus to truly serve pastors and help them in one of life's most challenging vocations?

It's time to confess our failures to one another and seek forgiveness. The walls that divide us must be torn down. Then we'll begin to open our ministries to one another and ask God how we might work together.

Partnerships that need to be formed would include:

National Coalition for the Family (or a CoMission for the Family)

This national alliance of church and denominational leaders, as well as parachurch organizations, would form strategic working relationships *to serve the local church.* Much of the expertise, materials, and training needed to equip families is already in place in churches and parachurch organizations. We've got to find out who is doing the best job in each phase of family life development and pass on this expertise to entire communities of churches.

As an outgrowth of the activities of this national coalition, a national congress focused on the church and family could be held every two years. An international congress could be held every five years. The purpose of these gatherings would be to measure progress in stemming the tide against divorce, to share resources, to help churches share their family strategy, and to encourage and motivate one another.

Church Partnerships in Communities

A partnership of churches in a community could be developed

that would unite churches locally to impact marriages and families. The larger National Coalition for the Family could then serve these community partnerships by providing consultations, outstanding resources, and citywide training. This partnership concept is already developing in communities with parachurch ministries like Marriage Savers (see Appendix) and Intimate Life Ministries.[2]

Family and Church Think Tank

A group of the finest theological minds and strategic thinkers should address the real needs and issues of a church that has been devastated by divorce and dysfunctional families. Pastors who shepherd local churches need wise counsel as they compassionately represent the truth of God's Word to broken people. This think tank could provide pastors much needed encouragement and biblical guidance as they rebuild and equip the family (see Isaiah 58:10-12). Thorny issues, such as divorce and remarriage, could be addressed by this group.

In short, we've got to amass and assemble the most serious offensive battle plan for the family in the history of the church. This is not peacetime. This is not time for business as usual. This is war.

We must work together.

BRICK #4: LEADERS AND EDUCATORS IN SEMINARIES, BIBLE COLLEGES, AND CHRISTIAN SCHOOLS

Family Reformation is primarily a work of individuals and families. But for the reformation to succeed, undergraduate and graduate Christian schools, Bible colleges, and seminaries must help raise their section of the wall. The next generation must study the biblical blueprints of the Christian family.

The Christian education movement is a severely underutilized strength in the Christian community. Approximately one million students are enrolled in evangelical Christian schools.[3] Undergraduate and graduate Christian institutions abound, and our seminaries prepare thousands of men and women for the ministry annually. These educational institutions must assist by providing the catalytic leadership in the biblical reengineering of the Christian family.

Two important steps are essential for this to occur. First, *young people must receive biblical training in the basics of the Christian family.* Divorce has shattered the biblical ideals of family for too many of our youth. An entire generation of students lacks a fundamental, consistent model for marriage and family. As students progress through these educational institutions, they need to develop a comprehensive, Christian view of the marriage covenant, roles, and a godly legacy.

Many students have grown up in biblically illiterate homes. We must create biblical courses on marriage and family issues. Topics—such as marriage fundamentals, conflict resolution, masculine and feminine identity, biblical roles in marriage, finances, and Christian parenting—should be taught by parents at home. But supportive courses at school would reinforce these basics. This family-focused educational reform movement will demand a new generation of Christian family life textbooks.

An entire generation of students lacks a fundamental, consistent model for marriage and family.

Christian colleges and seminaries should insist on marriage and family course offerings for students preparing for ministry. In rebuilding the Christian family, it would be dangerous to assume that these future pastors, leaders, and Christian workers have adequate understanding and practical skills for strengthening their own families. Many of them need insight and healing from their own family wounds. Students must be implored to know, apply, experience, embrace, and proclaim God's truth about the family *before* they make their own marital commitments and become parents. Seminary graduates should be able to articulate what they believe about the Christian family.

Second, *we must establish a theology of the family and require all seminarians to formulate their beliefs and convictions about the family before graduation.*

Pastors who lead local churches are desperate for biblical counsel on marriage and family issues. Excellent theology has been developed on divorce, remarriage, and marital roles, but there is no comprehensive evangelical doctrine of the family—what I would term *oikosology* (oikos in Greek means "household" or "family").

I asked my friend Dr. John Hannah, chairman of the Church History Department of Dallas Theological Seminary, why a doctrine of the family has never been written. He gave two reasons. First, historically most church doctrines have come from a need for clear and thorough teaching on a specific issue. Perhaps there was a heresy or disagreement on a particular subject. That disagreement drove scholars to thoroughly analyze what the Bible taught on a subject like sin, the Holy Spirit, or the Second Coming. Until recently, such a doctrinal need never surfaced regarding the family.

A second reason, according to Dr. Hannah, is that the Christian family throughout the ages has generally been strong. There was no compelling need for a comprehensive doctrine on marriage and family.

The needs of families have changed dramatically in the last 25 years. If we don't biblically define and address critical issues concerning the family, then the culture will continue to do it for us. A team of evangelical scholars needs to craft a Christian Magna Carta for the family. Evangelicals ought to be *the* leaders in shaping a comprehensive theology of the family. It's time.

The commitment and the influence of every Christian educational institution in America are needed if the next generation of Christian marriages and families is to have a chance to succeed in this culture.*

At this point I also want to address the evangelical Christians who have been divinely and strategically placed in secular schools, colleges, and universities. I commend those who are already sharing their faith in the classroom in relevant ways. If you are a faculty member of a secular institution, I challenge you to use your influence to give students an accurate representation of what the Bible says about marriage, family, and related issues. Students hunger to have

---

*It may be appropriate to give a copy of this book to the board members of your child's school or to some other educational leader in a position of influence at a Christian or secular university.

role models and to hear men and women with conviction defend the biblical family. As you know, they definitely hear from people with other views on the family.

BRICK #5: LEADERS OF SMALL BUSINESSES, COMPANIES, AND CORPORATIONS

God has sprinkled His "salt and light" in the workplace by placing men and women in leadership positions in companies to spiritually impact their employees and peers. If families have ever needed some "combat smart" leaders to exhibit courage on their behalf, today is the day.

A pair of such leaders decided they wanted to use their influence and money to provide scholarships for some of their employees to a FamilyLife Marriage Conference.

Charlie Monroe and his cousin-in-law, Lewis Card, Jr., started Card Monroe Corporation (CMC) in Chattanooga, Tennessee, in 1981. The company manufactures carpet machinery and employs 140 people.

One day Charlie's secretary, Jamie Gilbert, came into his office crying. Her marriage was in trouble, and she wanted to make her boss aware of the situation at home. She had filed a restraining order against her husband of nine months, Chuck. He also worked at CMC.

Charlie offered to pray for her and her marriage and family. Then he told her about a FamilyLife Marriage Conference coming to the city in about six weeks and offered to pay for the registration and hotel room for Jamie and Chuck. The Gilberts agreed to go, and six other couples from the company went as well.

After attending the weekend conference, the Gilberts showed up in Charlie's office on Monday morning. They asked him to pray with them and to witness their signing of a Oneness Covenant received at the conference.

Over time, Jamie's and Chuck's lives and marriage were radically changed by Jesus Christ and the Bible's blueprint for their family. Charlie Monroe was so impressed by what happened to the Gilberts and the others that he hosted a luncheon for other Christian business leaders in his community—hoping to encourage them to send their employees to a marriage conference. Invitations were sent to 33 businesses, and 27 responded.

At the luncheon, Charlie shared his testimony as an employer: "We have all had ladies in our office crying. It is a very stressful time, and we don't know what to tell them. We don't know how to counsel them about personal matters."

Charlie went on to share what a privilege it had been to make the conference available to his secretary. He recognized that fixing problems in marriage is far more expensive than preventing them. When Charlie realized the cost of what was going on in Jamie's life—including that restraining order—he felt that he was making an investment in the "quality of life," not just for her but for all his employees.

The Gilberts also shared their testimony at the luncheon. They said, "Combined, we had been married 21 years and had three children before we ever met each other." At the conference, they finally connected heart to heart.

As a result of that luncheon with business owners, 110 people received scholarships from their employers to a marriage conference in Chattanooga. Several owners of local companies are trying to get every one of their employees to a FamilyLife Marriage Conference.

More than 270 companies, businessmen, and ministries—including Boston Market, McCoys Lumber Co., Touch One, Chick-Fil-A, Promise Keepers, Gordon Foods, Prince Corporation, Thomas Nelson Publishers, and Amway—have paid the way for their employees to attend FamilyLife conferences.

Tens of thousands of small business owners and corporate leaders in America could do similar things that would positively influence marriages and families.

A Family Reformation will be hastened by individual leaders visibly taking a stand for the family. Such courage is contagious among business executives, and when leaders become burning lights for Christ, incredible ministry opportunities abound in their companies.

BRICK #6: INFLUENCERS IN THE MEDIA

A growing number of Christians now work in the media—television, radio, print, the Internet, and the motion picture industry. Two groups have a strategic niche to fill as we rebuild the family—first, Christians involved in the secular media, and second, those employed in Christian media. Both groups are critical family brick layers.

Secular Media. Christians employed in this arena certainly know how Daniel felt in the lions' den. Across the nation, a substantial number of Christians, working in various media industries, yearn to do something courageous for Christ. (To be certain, many are already taking courageous steps; but more need to step out.)

First, pray that God will give you the wisdom to be "shrewd as a serpent and innocent as a dove." Next use your influence to call leaders in your company and industry to promote moral decency and discriminate in favor of the family. Challenge leaders to evaluate their work on the basis of how it's either strengthening or weakening the family. Tactfully appeal to their conscience on behalf of children. Finally, if your voice is not heard or heeded, prayerfully consider resigning.

Scott, who was 31 years old at the time, reported to the president of one of the top computer on-line companies in America. Courageously, he used his influence to challenge the company's distribution and promotion of pornography by linkage to the Internet. After nearly three years of fighting what became a losing battle, Scott turned in his resignation. Scott and his wife are now raising financial support and will join our staff at FamilyLife.

Christian Media. Over the past 20 years Christian media—primarily radio, television, book publishing, and recording—have shown remarkable growth. The number of Christian-formatted radio stations has almost quadrupled since the '70s. During the 1980s, the number of religious television programs showed similar growth.[4]

Christian record companies market $550 million worth of CDs and cassettes every year, and Christian artists sell another $10 million in concert tickets. Christian book publishers will move more than 150 million books this year, with sales totaling more than $1 billion.[5]

Christian media, which began years ago as a fledgling industry with essentially ministry goals, now make up a huge business sector. A rash of corporate buyouts has left some original companies in the hands of secular interests who are attracted by the profit potential, but not necessarily a ministry vision. As a result, there is a need for a thoughtful spiritual analysis: Is our primary objective ministry or money?

I say this as one who has become a part of Christian media, with a daily radio program airing in hundreds of cities across the country and with books sold in Christian bookstores. We need to revisit our mission and standards—to ask ourselves (and one another) some tough questions:

Do we live in private what we preach, publish, and promote in public?

Are we being led by the Holy Spirit in a spiritual mission, or has the bottom line become our mandate?

Are we chewing up families in our workplace/ministry, or are they better off for having worked in our operation?

Are the people we promote, broadcast, and publish the models of holy living after whom we want our constituents (and our children) to model their lives, marriages, and families? And if we wouldn't want our children to emulate the people we promote, then we need to ask ourselves, why are we promoting them?

Do we pray with our spouses? Children? Do we live by the Scriptures in our homes?

Are we promoting authors and artists whose marriages are in question and look suspiciously like their secular counterparts? Is there a higher standard for those who are given the responsibility of public ministry? If so, what is that standard?

As we pursue Christlikeness, being holy and compassionate, are we going to draw the line on certain sins and refuse to publish, broadcast, or promote people who have fallen into such sins? Any sinner who repents is forgiven and restored in fellowship with God. But does that mean we immediately return a fallen Christian leader, author, or artist to a position of authority or prominence? In our efforts to extend grace, are we confusing the body of Christ and further reducing our standards when we are quick to restore a fallen leader's platform?

In the midst of our repentance, there is the need to return to what A. W. Tozer called a "gentle dogmatism." He wrote, "Moral power has always accompanied definitive beliefs. Great saints have always been dogmatic. We need right now a return to a gentle dogmatism that smiles while it stands stubborn and firm on the Word of God that liveth and abideth forever."[6] Selah.

BRICK #7: CITY, STATE, AND NATIONAL POLITICAL LEADERS

The significance of the family institution must be restored in the public square and political arena. We need to elect Christians to public office, and once there, they need to use their influence on behalf of families. I want to extend five challenges to political leaders who serve from the school board to the halls of Congress.

1. *Make your home and family a priority.* Based on the counseling I've done with the spouses and children of politicians, politics is not a family-friendly occupation. Are you abdicating your responsibility at home to fulfill your duty to politics? We need Christian leaders to model and speak about strong marriages and families. Your life, marriage, and family must be different because you are a follower of Christ.

A couple of suggestions: Give others (godly men and women) access into your life to hold you accountable and keep you on track with your marriage and family. Vigorously protect Sunday for your family. Let your constituents know that your family is a priority.

2. *Spearhead divorce law reform.* State and national leaders must lead a nationwide movement to eliminate no-fault divorce laws. Laws need to be written and passed that will make divorce much tougher. And greater pressure must be applied to make deadbeat dads pay alimony and child support.

In a town hall meeting sponsored by a conservative Washington, D.C., think tank, I was asked for ideas that would strengthen families. When I answered, "How about a tax on divorce?" the room became very quiet. Unworkable? Perhaps, but the question remains: How radical are we willing to be to save the next generation?

3. *Hold the high ground against same-sex marriages.* The Scriptures forbid such relationships. Bear in mind the words of Noah Webster: "The moral principles and precepts contained in the Scriptures ought to form the basis of all our civil constitutions and laws. . . . All the miseries and evils which men suffer from vice, crime,

ambition, injustice, oppression, slavery and war, proceed from their despising or neglecting the precepts contained in the Bible."[7]

If we further allow marriage to be dumbed down, where will we draw the line—two brothers marrying each other? Two 13-year-old girls who aren't mature enough to know better? This attack on the family must be won quickly and decisively.

4. *Punish the networks and Hollywood for profiting from moral pollution they pump into homes and communities.* A national crusade led by government leaders should be mounted to call the media to moral goodness. More political leaders should use the "bully pulpit" God has provided to uphold biblical family values.

5. *Call the private sector, especially churches, to a purposeful and all-out commitment to rebuild urban families.* An extensive network of partnerships between suburban churches and urban churches (as well as parachurch organizations) needs to be formed to resource and rescue this segment of society, which the evangelical community has often ignored. Responsibility for this initiative must be passed down to the spiritual leaders of communities.

There are enough Christians holding government offices at every level to make an immediate difference in the family landscape. Why not join together in a bipartisan statement speaking out for marriage and family and speaking against divorce? A little leadership from Christians in politics will reap substantial gains. Speak out with courage for your ideals and lead the citizens you represent in a godly way back to the biblical family.

THE FINAL ELEMENT

Now that we've examined some of the bricks needed to rebuild the family into a mighty fortress, one additional, mandatory element is required for victory. I've mentioned it several times already: God-infused *courage*—a courage born out of conviction that we must act now on behalf of the next generation.

People are waiting . . . for leaders.

Leaders who will compel them to action. Leaders who will challenge them with a clear vision of what we must do. Leaders who won't quit, but will plead with God for victory.

Without God's favor we are in deep trouble—the outlook is hopeless. With Him we're empowered—hope is boundless.

The war on the family rages. You and I feel the heat of the battle. Many times it seems enemy fire has us pinned down. What are we going to do?

What are *you* going to do?

At Omaha Beach in 1944, some Allied soldiers faced a similar choice. Many of the soldiers on D-day never made it out of the water, and many more died on the sand. But those who found a temporary place of safety faced another moment that tested their character.

Behind them on the few yards of beach they had crossed, the cries of death were everywhere. As they looked forward, they saw nothing but barbwire and entrenched nests of lethal German machine gunners.

It was grim.

It was war.

At moments like these, true leaders step forward, and that's what happened at Omaha Beach. In one case, a lieutenant and a wounded sergeant exposed themselves to gunfire so they could inspect an entanglement of barbwire.

The lieutenant slithered on his belly back to his men and asked, "Are you going to lie there and get killed or get up and do something about it?"

Nobody moved, so the lieutenant and sergeant—still under enemy fire—blew up the barbwire themselves. That got the men moving, and eventually 300 made it through that section of the German lines.

Those of us concerned about the family may find ourselves facing a decision similar to that of those troops caught on the battle-field. We may be in a place of temporary comfort. We may ponder, *Why take the risk?* Or we may question our ability to fight and win. But if we don't face our fears, seek God's help, and move into the firefight, we're doomed to failure anyway.

It's time to plead for God's favor, to lock arms, and to do something. Nehemiah challenged the people to rebuild the wall and they responded, "'Let us arise and build.' So they put their hands to the good work" (Nehemiah 2:18).

Does God expect anything less from us today?

CHAPTER THIRTEEN

The Fruit of Reformation

There are three phases to any worthwhile enterprise:
Impossible . . . Difficult . . . Done.
—**Hudson Taylor**

A young man ran across the barnyard of a well-tended farm near Wittenberg, Germany. Several portly sows, rooting for corncobs in the snow and mud, grunted at the red-cheeked lad. Ahead, leaning against a wood fence, he saw the familiar rotund form, the man's huge shoulders sagging with age.

"Papa, Papa," the youth yelled. "Word has come from Eisleben. The counts of Mansfield want you to visit them—soon!"

"Yes, Martin, tell John to prepare the wagons and horses," the man answered. "You and your brothers need to pack—each must have an extra coat for this cold. Does Mother know? We will leave in the morning."

"Yes, Papa! I will tell the others!" Martin Luther, Jr., waved to his father, then the 15-year-old bolted toward the house, once more scattering the pigs with angry squeals and snorts.

A smile curled the old man's lips, and the famous glint flashed in his eyes. "Ah, the enthusiasm and strength of the young," he said softly, his breath exhaling wisps of white cloud into the frigid air. "If only I could send the wisdom of an old man in a box with them to Eisleben—I would stay here with my dear Katie."

Martin started slowly toward the house, then turned and veered away. He would take the longer route, savoring a few more moments of solitude before he entered his clamorous home. In wintertime, especially on cold January days that kept everyone in near the fire, bedlam prevailed in the Luther home. Besides his beloved wife and the five kids, as always there were numerous relatives and guests, many of them wanting "just a few words with Dr. Luther."

Martin rounded the barn and headed toward the orchard. There, the snow was deeper, with no trail packed by other boots. Martin took several steps and stopped. He struggled to breathe, and his knees trembled. There was no point in trying to go farther; he must return to the house and rest. He gazed longingly at the fruit trees, the garden, and the vineyard on the hill. He wondered if he would again see the passing of winter's brown-gray to the vibrant green of spring.

"Get behind me, Devil!" Martin shouted, chasing the morbid thought from his head. Small step after small step, he trudged back to the house.

Slipping in a back door, the famous Reformer escaped detection and arrived at his small study. A fire snapped and popped in the fireplace, and after shedding his heavy cloak, Martin pushed two fresh logs on the blaze. He warmed his hands, then sat down at his desk.

Picking up the pen, he began another letter—the sentences sparkling with the usual wit and warmth. The letter half done, Martin paused. Tears filled his eyes. Seeking comfort, he whispered the Lord's Prayer, the sound of the familiar words obscured by the crackling fire. Several phrases he repeated—two or three times as if to ensure they had been heard: "Thy will be done" . . . "Forgive us our trespasses" . . . "On earth as it is in heaven. . . ."

Tomorrow he would leave on another journey, not to engage in some theological battle, but to help mend fences among the squabbling rulers of his old hometown.

Martin leaned back in his chair. *Has my life really counted for much?* he thought. *Why, God, have You allowed me to live to old age when others—younger men—suffered a martyr's death?*

He remembered the summer day more than 20 years before when word had come about the two men in Brussels burned at the stake—the first martyrs of the Reformation. That afternoon he had sensed such a death was his fate. Why, then, had he been spared?

Martin reminisced, remembering the small triumphs sprinkled among many setbacks. He recalled the constant struggles to fan the fire of renewed faith he had helped ignite—on the one hand battling the enemies of the gospel, while on the other calming the excesses of the fervent believers.

And what would the future bring his family after he was gone? Thousands were still dying from the plague, and class war and other chaos threatened Germany. Above all else, Martin felt tired. Perhaps it was time to go home. . . .

"Do not run in the halls!" a woman shrieked, jarring Martin from his dark mood. "How many times must I tell you? Running is for outside!"

"Yes, Mama!" several young male voices answered. "So sorry. We won't run!" The three boys passed Martin's door, whispering excitedly about tomorrow's trip, trying to rein in their happy feet.

Martin laughed. A pot clanged in the kitchen, then clanged again. Perhaps he should go check on his precious Katie. Did she need a word of encouragement?

His heart still skipping erratically, Martin pushed against the desk with his arms and rose to his feet. As he turned toward the door, his gaze fell on a large object on the corner of his desk. Tears came again to the old man's eyes as he looked longingly at the book. His voice breaking, he said, "Ja, God, that alone makes a life worthwhile."

Martin leaned forward and rubbed the book's spine, his shaking finger tracing the letters. This book was his crowning achievement—the Bible, Old and New Testaments, translated so lovingly and skillfully into the language of his people. Now all could read the Word of God for themselves and know the truth—the cook, the maid, the farmer, the housewife, the servant, the child, the lawyer, the king.

"To God be the glory!" he whispered and left for the kitchen.

―

On a balmy July evening, a van bulging with passengers rumbled down the lane of a remote, heavily wooded acreage in the Kettle

Moraine area of southern Wisconsin.

The vehicle entered a clearing and stopped in front of a wood frame house. A man and a woman, smiling and waving, walked briskly out from the front porch.

"Hi, Grandma Sonny! Hi, Grandpa Robert!" voices shouted, the sounds scattering birds perched in the towering oaks nearby.

A dozen or more children from Milwaukee's inner city poured from the van's side door and ran to surround their hosts.

"Come inside! Wash up! Supper's nearly ready," Sonny said, turning to head back to her kitchen. Two small girls walked with her, their arms wrapped tightly around her waist.

Robert waited for the driver and his wife to emerge. "Hi, Debi and Jim," he said, reaching out to hug both Godseys. "Good trip?"

"You betcha," Jim said, grinning.

"I'll go help Sonny," Debi said.

Jim and Robert unloaded the van, piling the food boxes, sporting gear, and paper sacks on the sandy driveway.

Soon everyone was enjoying an abundant supper around large tables in the house. Then after some outdoor play, the group gathered for a Bible study in the living room. Robert read Scripture, and Debi and Jim led a discussion—explaining why everybody needs Jesus and how the Bible is *the* truth, God's perfect plan for living right.

The kids paid attention as best they could, but after the sun set, excitement for the evening's final event threatened to overwhelm them. The group prayed, then with flashlights and sweatshirts in hand, rushed out into the fragrant summer night. It was time for the Friday night tradition—a midnight hike!

The Godseys in the lead, the small troop walked deeper and deeper into the lush vegetation of Kettle Moraine State Forest. Flashlights turned off, the kids chattered and laughed nervously, awed by the total darkness and eerie stillness. For many of them, it was a world never before encountered—almost a voyage to another planet. Here, thoughts of their homes in the inner city—with its foul smells, glaring lights, sounds of gunfire, screams, boom boxes, and automobiles—faded. In the forest a person could discover God in a new way, through the stunning beauty of His creation.

Hours later, the group returned, exhausted and ready for bed.

As the excited kids headed for the sleeping lofts in the house, Debi and Jim exchanged a quick, knowing glance and smiled. Both knew what the other was thinking—no need to say it: *Can you believe what has happened in our lives? Just look at what God has done!*

———

On January 23, 1546, Martin Luther left with his sons and an attendant for Eisleben, the town of his birth. The trip in the heart of winter was arduous, and they were delayed several days at the Saale River by flooding.

The negotiations with the counts of Mansfield were trying, but by mid-February Martin successfully arranged an agreement. Only days later while preaching, Martin became ill. He hurriedly ended his sermon and retired to his room.

Martin stayed in bed for two days, and by the evening of February 17, he felt stronger. But just hours later, at 1:00 A.M. on February 18, Luther awakened in terrible pain. He knew he was dying. Word spread quickly, and soon a small crowd surrounded his bed. As death approached, Martin repeated over and over, "For God so loved the world that He gave His only Son. . . ."

With Martin failing rapidly, his close friend, Justus Jonas, asked, "Martin, do you want to die standing firm on Christ and the doctrine you have taught?"

Luther's body shifted, and then for a scant moment, the familiar, confident, booming voice filled the room—*"Ja!"*

Moments later, the man whose life had brought the hope of Christ alive to thousands slipped into eternity.

On February 20, with 50 mounted horsemen serving as an escort, Luther's procession left for Wittenberg. Crowds lined the road as the casket passed, just as they had 25 years earlier when Luther had journeyed triumphantly across Germany to the Diet at Worms.

The group arrived in Wittenberg two days later. After the funeral was held before an overflowing audience at Castle Church, the Reformer was laid to rest—his body lying near where he had preached, and only paces away from the door punctured nearly three decades earlier by a nail bearing the 95 Theses.

—

At a sky-blue lake in Wisconsin, the sounds of splashing, laughter, and screams of delight blended into a chorus of joy. With the sun blazing, the cool water provided relief for Debi and Jim Godsey and their campers.

A few miles away, Sonny and Robert Heinz worked together on preparations for the Saturday evening meal, enjoying moments of calm before their energetic guests returned.

It always happened by about this time each camp-out weekend—several of the visitors had stolen the hearts of "Grandpa Robert" and "Grandma Sonny." At first many of the children were shy, but once they sensed the love and acceptance in this home, their bright smiles were followed by hugs. Finally, voices were heard begging, "It's my turn to sit in your lap!"

For years both Robert and Sonny had wanted their undeveloped Wisconsin land to be used by God for a special purpose.

As a child, Sonny had dreamed of growing up to become a foreign missionary, but as a teenager and adult, she had drifted away from God. Her marriage ended in divorce.

Robert, too, had faced disappointments, his marriage and family falling apart. Full of regret, he had longed for another opportunity to be a more loving and responsible husband and father.

Sonny and Robert had met and married, then moved to the beautiful 20 acres adjoining the state forest. For 12 years Sonny prayed for God's insight on how to share the land with others, and Robert, the green thumb of the two, had planted large gardens—harvesting the produce to help feed poor people in the city. But prayers for a fuller ministry to others had remained unanswered.

Unknown to Robert and Sonny, 50 miles away in Milwaukee, Debi and Jim Godsey began to pray in 1990 that God would provide a place in the country where they could take inner-city children from their Kidz in the 'Hood ministry for a wilderness experience. No answer came, so Jim and Debi continued to pray—waiting on Him.

One Sunday the Godseys and the Heinzes—who did not know each other—met at church. After the two couples discovered their common interests, they decided to spend a weekend together at Sonny and Robert's place. The Holy Spirit bonded their hearts, and they agreed to give their shared vision for ministry a try.

A date for the first camp-out was set. Before that weekend, Debi sent Sonny a card, earnestly promising not to bring any children who had head lice or were currently in trouble with the law. She also said she would check all the bags of clothes for roaches!

Reading that, Sonny froze: *Just what were she and Robert getting into?* "Okay, Lord," she remembers praying. "You'll have to give us the love to see this through."

The first group arrived, and after just a few minutes of ice-breaking, Robert and Sonny knew the Spirit had provided the love they needed. "It was such a joy, such an uplift," Sonny says. "Helping those groups of kids—for five years now—has been the highlight of my spiritual life. I *am* a missionary now."

Debi and Jim Godsey, and their vans full of kids, were the answer to Sonny's prayers. And now Robert had plenty of waiting mouths—at his own table—for the vegetables growing in his fruit-ful garden.

———

A young man carefully closed the front door of Castle Church behind him and walked down the center aisle, stopping in the front near the elevated pulpit. A solitary fly buzzed high above, banging hopelessly into the stained glass windows. The summer sun streamed gold through the glass, pooling at his feet.

Martin Luther, Jr., cried. Someday he might comprehend the impact of the man whose passion for God and His Word had ignited a movement that shook Europe and ultimately touched a new world when the Pilgrims set foot on a distant shore.

This day, though, young Martin just wanted a few moments to be alone with his memories. Minutes later, he forced his tear-filled eyes to look at the writing on his father's tomb, here inside Castle Church. He mouthed the words silently, then said them aloud, his voice echoing in the empty room: "A mighty fortress is our God!"

Martin turned and walked to the back of the church. "Good-bye, Papa," he said, then firmly closed the door.[1]

—

Late on Saturday night, Debi and Jim Godsey finally had a moment alone. After watching excited kids romping in the Wisconsin countryside for nearly 15 hours, they were beat.

"Deb, let's step outside for a minute," Jim said.

Debi sighed but managed a tired smile. "Sure, why not?"

Holding hands, the ex-bartender and the ex-alcoholic went to look at the clear Wisconsin sky. Here, away from the city lights, the stars shone brightly—vast fields of white, heavenly dust.

The weekend had been a success. Early tomorrow they would pack up and drive to Milwaukee, arriving at Eastbrook Church in time for worship.

They stood quietly, close to each other, feasting on their view of the Creator's handiwork.

"After all these years since I met the Lord," Debi said, "I still can't get over that He's there, seeing me, liking me."

"It's pretty cool, Deb."

After a hug and some exhausted yawns, the Godseys went into the house and fell soundly asleep.

—

Martin Luther, a hero of history. And to a group of street kids and families in urban Milwaukee, another pair of heroes in the making— Debi and Jim Godsey. Each of their lives proclaims the incomparable gospel of Jesus Christ. Indeed, *He still changes lives.*

Throughout history, God's methods may change, but He always uses people to accomplish His mission. He starts first with the reclamation of individuals, then He moves on to touch others nearby— like a family. Their joy and ministry tumble into the lives of friends and neighbors, and finally, even outsiders get caught up in a ministry that cannot be contained.

Do you long to be used like this by God? Are you one of a growing number who wants to finish strong?

There is still time.

Time to see and experience God at work in your life, your marriage, and your family. Time to pray and ask God to restore your first love for Him—time to experience His grace, forgiveness, and love. Time to yield to God and experience the indescribable privilege of being used by Him in touching another's life.

Do you long to be used by God?
Are you one of a growing number who
wants to finish strong?

We have His promise that He will use us. Paul reminds us, "For we are His workmanship, created in Christ Jesus for good works, which God prepared beforehand that we should walk in them" (Ephesians 2:10).

Will you be God's man? God's woman? Will you enlist in the Family Reformation army?

Will you and your family become the next brick in a Family Reformation?

You know what you can expect. War is costly. Ugly at times. Battles are fought and won by wounded, exhausted soldiers on the front lines. Hardship is to be endured. Commitment, sacrifice, and perseverance are the companions of war heroes.

But it's worth it.

God speaking through the prophet Isaiah promises us,

> And if you give yourself to the hungry, and satisfy the desire of the afflicted, then your light will rise in darkness and your gloom will become like midday. And the Lord will continually guide you, and satisfy your desire in scorched places, and give strength to your bones; and you will be like a watered garden, and like a spring of water whose waters do not fail. And those from among you will rebuild the ancient ruins; you will raise up the age-old foundations; and you will be called the repairer of the breach, the restorer of the streets in which to dwell. (58:10-12)

Wouldn't you like that to be said of you? Wouldn't you like to be a part of a movement of God that brings His timeless principles *home?*

If we trust in Him alone, summon our courage, work together, and persevere, it will happen. A Family Reformation.

Perhaps the promise of God spoken through Isaiah will be fully experienced in our lifetime: "'And as for Me, this is My covenant with them,' says the Lord: 'My Spirit which is upon you, and My words which I have put in your mouth, shall not depart from your mouth, nor from the mouth of your offspring, nor from the mouth of your offspring's offspring,' says the Lord, 'from now and forever'" (59:21).

May God's favor be upon us—one home at a time.

Appendix

A COMMUNITY MARRIAGE POLICY

The divorce rate in every community in America could be reduced if local church leaders—ministers, priests, and pastors—of all denominations agreed to more carefully prepare individuals for marriage.

To put it bluntly, it's often too easy for a couple to find someone at a church to do a wedding ceremony. Since the vast majority of marriages are still performed by clergy, if minimum standards for marital preparation could be agreed to by church leaders in a community, some high-risk marriages would be canceled or postponed—and those who do marry would benefit from the marriage preparation they received.

A leader in the movement to see communities adopt marriage policies is Michael McManus, a syndicated newspaper columnist and author of the book *Marriage Savers.* In the mid-1980s, McManus (along with a local pastor named Jim Talley) was instrumental in initiating a community marriage policy in Modesto, California. Since then a number of other cities throughout the nation have adopted the Modesto Community Marriage Policy—or some variation of the Modesto plan.

The Modesto Community Marriage Policy is reproduced here. I urge you to be a leader in implementing such a policy in your community.[1]

COMMUNITY MARRIAGE POLICY

I. CONCERN: "Marriage is holy."

One concern as ministers of the gospel is to foster lasting marital unions under God and to establish successful spiritual families. Almost 90 percent of all marriages are performed by pastors, and we are troubled by the nearly 50 percent divorce rate. Our hope is to radically reduce the divorce rate among those married in area churches.

It is the responsibility of pastors to set minimal requirements to raise the quality of commitment in those we marry. We believe that couples who seriously participate in premarital testing and counseling will have a better understanding of what the marriage commitment involves. As agents of God, acting on His behalf, we feel it is our responsibility to encourage couples to set aside time for marriage preparation, instead of concentrating only on wedding plans. We acknowledge that a wedding is but a day; a marriage is for a lifetime.

II. SCRIPTURE: "What therefore God hath joined together, let no man put asunder" (Matthew 19:6, KJV).

God has established and sanctified marriage for the welfare and happiness of the human family. For this reason, our Savior has declared that a man shall leave his father and mother and be joined to his wife, and the two shall become one. Through His apostles He has instructed those who enter into this relationship to cherish a mutual esteem and love; to share in each other's infirmities and weaknesses; to comfort each other in sickness, trouble, and sorrow; to provide for each other and for their household; to pray for and encourage each other; to live together as heirs of the grace of life; and to raise children, if there are any, in the knowledge and love of the Lord.

Malachi 2:13-16 says that God hates divorce, and in Ephesians 5 the image of marriage is that of Christ and His church.

III. IMPLEMENTATION: These are the minimum expectations.

Waiting Period: A minimum of four months from the initial marital appointment until the wedding date.

Premarital Counseling: Minimum of two sessions that would include a relational instrument, inventory, or test (e.g., Meyers/Briggs or TJTA) to help the couple evaluate the maturity of their relationship objectively.

Scripture: Teach biblical doctrines on morality, marriage, and divorce. Encourage couples to memorize key verses on marriage.

Engagement Seminar: Encourage the couple to participate in a concentrated period of joint introspection.

Helping Couples: Provide as needed a mature married
couple to meet with them to assist in the concept of marital
"bonding."

Post-Marital: Commit ourselves to counseling the couple as
needed.

IV. COVENANT:

I covenant to build successful, spiritual families.

I covenant to follow Scripture and to implement these minimum
preparations for the couples that I marry to substantially reduce the
divorce rate in our area.

I covenant to join with other spiritual leaders to encourage couples to seriously participate in premarital preparation.

Signed	Date

Notes

Chapter One

1. The incidents and setting of this moment in Martin Luther's story are true, although some elements have been fictionalized. There is no record of a mouse named Tetzel, and the great man's thoughts during the night of October 30 are conjecture. However, I believe this retelling of one of history's most important moments captures faithfully the personality, apprehension, and courage of Martin Luther. A number of sources were consulted for background information on Martin Luther—in this chapter as well as throughout the book. Four of the most helpful were Roland H. Bainton, *Here I Stand* (New York: Meridian, 1995); James M. Kittelson, *Luther the Reformer* (Minneapolis: Augsburg Publishing House, 1986); Hanns Lilje, *Luther and the Reformation* (Philadelphia: Fortress Press, 1967); and Leopold von Ranke, *History of the Reformation in Germany,* Vol. 1 (New York: Frederick Ungar, 1966).

2. I greatly appreciate the cooperation and assistance of Debi and Jim Godsey in telling portions of their miraculous story in this book. The Godseys have reviewed the material for accuracy and given their permission for its use.

Chapter Two

1. Ernest W. Lefever, "Reforming Gomorrah," *Christianity Today* (11 November 1996): 58.

2. William J. Bennett, "The National Prospect," *Commentary* (November 1995): 29.

3. "Halting the Decline," *Modern Maturity* (November/December 1995): 12.

4. Norman Maclean, *Young Men and Fire* (Chicago: University of Chicago Press, 1992), 120.

5. In 1996, respected researcher and author George Barna published an insightful book entitled *The Index of Leading Spiritual Indicators* (Dallas, Texas: Word Publishing). Although we independently settled on the same term and share many conclusions, our methods of analysis differ. I highly recommend Mr. Barna's book.

6. Don Feder, *Who's Afraid of the Religious Right?* (Washington, D.C.: Regnery, 1996), 261-62.

7. Will and Ariel Durant, *The Lessons of History* (New York: Simon & Schuster, 1968), 51.

8.   Gerald Kreyche, "The Age of Disrespect," *USA Today* magazine (September 1995): 20.

9.   Josh McDowell, *Right from Wrong* (Dallas: Word Publishing, 1994), 246.

10. Sheila Muto, "From Here to Immodesty: Milestones in the Toppling of TV's Taboos," *Wall Street Journal* (15 September 1995): B1.

11. Ibid.

12. "So Long Family Hour . . . ," *The American Enterprise* (May/June 1996): 11.

13. Michael Novak, "The National Prospect," *Commentary* (November 1995): 90.

14. These figures derive from three sources: (1) *Historical Statistics of U.S. 1789-1945,* Supplement to Statistical Abstract of U.S., copyright 1949, Bureau of the Census, Department of Commerce; (2) *Historical Statistics of U.S. 1920-1970;* Colonial Times to 1970, Part 1, Bureau of the Census; Department of Commerce; (3) *Historical Statistics of U.S. 1970-1990,* Statistical Abstract of the U.S. 1995, Department of Commerce, Economics and Statistics Administration; Bureau of the Census.

15. "Marriage in America," Institute for American Values Report (1995): 1.

16. William R. Mattox, Jr., "God Hates Divorce," *World* (28 October 1995): 25.

17. Pitirim Sorokin, cited in *Table Talk* magazine.

18. John Piper, "A Vision of Biblical Complementarity," in *Recovering Biblical Manhood & Womanhood: A Response to Evangelical Feminism,* ed. John Piper and Wayne Grudem (Wheaton, Ill.: Crossway, 1991), 33.

19. Cited in *Why Johnny Can't Tell Right from Wrong* by William Kilpatrick (New York: Simon & Schuster, 1992), 246.

20. Nancy R. Gibbs, "Life Without Father," *Time* (28 June 1993): 55.

21. David Murray, "Poor Suffering Bastards," *Policy Review* (no. 68, spring 1994): 11.

22. "Great Transitions: Preparing Adolescents for a New Century," Carnegie Corporation of America (October 1995): 9.

23. James Lincoln Collier, *The Rise of Selfishness in America* (New York: Oxford University Press, 1991), 252.

24. Patrick Fagan, "The Real Root Cause of Violent Crime," address delivered to Hillsdale College, 5 February 1995.

25. Maclean, *Young Men and Fire,* 73-74.

26. Ibid., 100.

Chapter Three

1.   Page Smith, *A New Age Now Begins,* vol. 1 (New York: McGraw-Hill, 1976), 872.

2.   Many Christians dismiss the teachings of Confucius for religious reasons. They fail to realize that Confucius was, first and foremost, a social philosopher. His thoughts on the family—as the chief component of

social organization—are profound. Historians credit Confucius for the high value placed upon the family in the Far East. This quotation is taken from Will Durant, *The Story of Civilization: Our Oriental Heritage,* vol. 1 (New York: Simon & Schuster, 1935), 668.

3. David S. Shrager, *Trial* (March 1984): 6.
4. Richard Price, "Violence Spreading Like Wildfire," *USA Today* (9 May 1994): IA.
5. Personal correspondence from Dave Johnson, a police officer in San Jose, California.
6. Neil Postman, *The Disappearance of Childhood* (New York: Delacorte Press, 1982), xi.
7. Michael Golay, *To Gettysburg and Beyond* (New York: Crown Publishers, 1994), 157.
8. Ibid., 158, 163.

A Reformation Moment: "Here I Stand!"
1. Martin Luther's appearance before the Diet of Worms was certainly one of the most important events of the Middle Ages. The retelling here is based extensively on the excellent biography by Roland Bainton (*Here I Stand*). Also of assistance was Kittelson, *Luther the Reformer.*

Chapter Four
1. Jerry White, *The Power of Commitment* (Colorado Springs, Colo.: NavPress, 1988), 55.
2. Keith J. Hardman, *The Spiritual Awakeners* (Chicago: Moody, 1983), 21.
3. C. C. Goen, ed. "The Works of Jonathan Edwards," in *The Great Awakening* (New Haven, Conn.: Yale University Press, 1972), 4:146.
4. Ibid., 4:151.
5. Hardman, *The Spiritual Awakeners,* 15-16.
6. Harold K. Moulton, *The Analytical Greek Lexicon Revised* (Grand Rapids, Mich.: Zondervan, 1978), 266.
7. John Calvin, *Institutes of the Christian Religion,* vol. 1, ed. John T. McNeill (Philadelphia: Westminster, 1960), 597.
8. J. I. Packer, *Evangelism and the Sovereignty of God* (Downers Grove, Ill.: InterVarsity, 1961), 72.
9. Personal correspondence.
10. Copyright © 1995 by Nancy Leigh DeMoss, 2000 Morris Drive, Niles, MI 49120. Used by permission.

Chapter Five
1. Lee Covington, *How to Dump Your Wife* (Seattle, Wash.: Fender Publishing Co., 1994), 7.
2. Ibid., 49.

3. Ibid., 47-48.
4. Judith S. Wallerstein and Sandra Blakeslee, *Second Chances: Men, Women, and Children a Decade after Divorce* (New York: Ticknor & Fields, 1989), 20.
5. Personal correspondence.
6. Gary Sprague, *My Parents Got a Divorce* (Elgin, Ill.: David C. Cook, 1992), 18.
7. Ibid., 22.
8. Ibid., 26.
9. Quoted in Wallerstein and Blakeslee, *Second Chances*, xxi.
10. Christine Lyons, "Modern Marriage: Booking a Lawyer Before the Minister," *New York Times News Service*, published by *Arkansas Democrat-Gazette* (15 March 1995).
11. Reported in *Discipleship* 94 (1996): 16.
12. Quoted in Michael McManus, *Marriage Savers* (Grand Rapids, Mich.: Zondervan, 1995), 50.
13. I want to thank Dr. Dan Allender for insight furnished on this topic during a personal conversation.
14. Personal correspondence.
15. Prepared by Tom Clagett, "Is FamilyLife Effective?" Effectiveness Study, FamilyLife, 1995.
16. James Humes, cited in Richard Exley's *The Making of a Man* (Tulsa, Okla: Honor Books, 1993), 37.
17. W. Peter Blitchington, *Sex Roles and the Christian Family* (Wheaton, Ill.: Tyndale, 1984), 165.
18. Bud Greenspan, "100 Years of Great Olympic Moments," *Sports Illustrated* (26 February 1996): 26.
19. Robertson McQuilkin, "Living by Vows," *Christianity Today* (8 October 1990): 40.
20. Robertson McQuilkin, "Muriel's Blessing," *Christianity Today* (5 February 1996): 34.

Chapter Six
1. "Collar ID Points Out Hungry Thief: Gator with Taste for Hunting Dogs," *Arkansas Democrat-Gazette* (29 August 1995): IA.
2. W. Peter Blitchington, *Sex Roles and the Christian Family* (Wheaton, Ill.: Tyndale, 1984), 49.
3. Susan Moller Okin, cited in *Fatherless in America* by David Blankenhorn (New York: BasicBooks, 1995), 91.
4. George Gilder, *Men and Marriage* (Gretna, La.: Pelican, 1986), 115.
5. Quoted in Blitchington, *Sex Roles and the Christian Family*, 174.
6. James Dobson, *Straight Talk, Revised Edition* (Dallas: Word, 1991), 23.

7. Alice Schwarzer, *After the Second Sex: Conversations with Simone de Beauvoir* (New York: Pantheon, 1984), 73.
8. Theodore Roosevelt, Presidential Address Before the National Congress of Mothers, Washington, D.C., 13 March 1905. Cited in *Presidential Addresses and State Papers,* vol. 3 (New York: P. F. Collier & Son, Publishers, n.d.), 283, 287.
9. Brenda Hunter, *Home by Choice* (Portland, Ore.: Multnomah, 1991), 98.
10. Ibid., 98, 100.
11. Gilder, *Men and Marriage,* 105.
12. Blitchington, *Sex Roles and the Christian Family,* 109.
13. Ibid.
14. Christine Gorman, "Sizing Up the Sexes," *Time* (20 January 1992): 42.
15. Ibid., 44.
16. Ibid., 42.
17. John Piper and Wayne Grudham, *Recovering Biblical Manhood & Womanhood* (Wheaton, Ill.: Crossway Books, 1991), 43.
18. From an interview with Patrick Goldstein, *Los Angeles Times,* 5 May 1991. Calendar Section, 7.
19. Anonymous, *A Bond of Love* (Chicago: United Bible House Publisher, 1900).
20. Harold K. Moulton, *The Analytical Greek Lexicon Revised* (Grand Rapids, Mich.: Zondervan, 1978), 419.
21. Roosevelt, Address Before the National Congress of Mothers, 285, 291.
22. Anonymous, *A Bond of Love.*
23. Henry Hurt, "From the Jaws of Death," *Reader's Digest* (April 1987): 117.

Chapter Seven

1. An excellent resource for information on personal finances is Crown Ministries, 530 Crown Oak Centre Dr., Longwood, FL 32750.
2. Personal correspondence.

A Reformation Moment: Return to Wittenberg

1. The incident with the two travelers from Switzerland at the Black Bear Inn is detailed in Bainton, *Here I Stand* (p. 165). It is also mentioned in Kittelson, *Luther the Reformer* (p. 181). Although based on fact (for example, it was reported that the inn's host did whisper to one of the Swiss men that their table companion was Martin Luther), a transcript of the conversation does not exist and is fictionalized here.

Chapter Eight

1. For more information on fasting, see the excellent book by Bill Bright, *The Coming Revival* (Orlando, Fla.: New Life Publications, 1995). Or you may also obtain information from FamilyLife, P.O. Box 25114, Little Rock, AR 72221-5114.

Chapter Nine
1. Charles Cecil Wall, *George Washington: Citizen-Soldier* (Charlottesville, Va.: University Press of Virginia, 1980), 39.
2. Douglas Southall Freeman, *George Washington: A Biography,* vol. 4 (New York: Charles Scribner's Sons, 1951), 408.
3. Ibid., 435.
4. Cited in *Idols for Destruction* by Herbert Schlossberg (Washington, D.C.: Regnery Gateway, 1990), 333.
5. John F. Kennedy, *Profiles in Courage* (New York: Harper & Brothers, 1961), 21.
6. George Barna, *The Barna Report* (Ventura, Calif.: Regal Books, 1993), 124.
7. Michael Horton, *Beyond Cultural Wars* (Chicago: Moody Publishers, 1994), 167.
8. Josh McDowell, *Right from Wrong* (Dallas: Word Publishing, 1994), 9.
9. Ibid., 60.
10. Ibid., 62.
11. My gratitude to Kirk Greenstreet, an associate with FamilyLife, who shared this illustration/metaphor with me.
12. David Blankenhorn, *Fatherless in America* (New York: BasicBooks, 1995), 12-13.
13. James Lincoln Collier, *The Rise of Selfishness in America* (New York: Oxford University Press, 1991), 264.
14. Mark Helprin, "To the New Congressional Majority," *Wall Street Journal* (3 January 1995): 8.

A Reformation Moment: The Luther Home
1. Primary sources: Bainton, *Here I Stand;* Kittelson, *Luther the Reformer;* and Lilje, *Luther and the Reformation.* The actual words Martin spoke at Little Lena's deathbed were recorded and preserved. Although Martin entered marriage somewhat reluctantly, he came to greatly enjoy and cherish his wife, Katherine, their children, and their boisterous household.

Chapter Eleven
1. Portions of this story may be fictional. However, King Lycurgus of Sparta did make the final quote, recorded in Plutarch, *The Lives of Noble Grecians and Romans,* the Dryden Translation, edited and revised by Hugh Clough, vol. 1. (New York: Modern Library, 1992), 70.
2. Jan Johnson, "How Churches Can Be Truly Profamily," *Christianity Today* (6 February 1995): 33.
3. Howard G. Hendricks, *Heaven Help the Home!* (Wheaton, Ill.: Victor Books, 1990), 95-96.
4. George Barna, *The Barna Report 1992-93—America Renews Its Search for God* (Ventura, Calif.: Regal Books, 1992), 92.

5. Johnson, "How Churches Can Be Truly Profamily," 35.
6. "Divorces and Annulments by Duration of Marriage at Time of Decree: Divorce Registration Area and Each Registration State, 1988," *Vital Statistics of the United States* 1988, volume III—Marriage and Divorce (Hyattsville, Md.: U.S. Department of Health and Human Services, 1996), 31.
7. Ibid. This graph is based on sample data from 32 of the 50 states.
8. Statistical Abstract of the United States, 1996, The National Data Book, U.S. Department of Commerce, table no. 85.
9. "I Do Is Repeat Refrain for Half of Newlyweds," *USA Today* (15 February 1991).
10. Rod Little, "Black Fathers: Finding Families," *USA Today* (17 June 1992).
11. Subrata N. Chakravary, "The Vindication of Edwin Land," *Forbes* (4 May 1987): 83.

A Reformation Moment: A Song in the Morning
1. Primary source: Bainton, *Here I Stand* (pp. 270-71). Luther loved music and was considered a poet. The hymn was written in 1527 (first published in 1529), a year during which Luther suffered from intense depression. He once wrote, "The Devil, the originator of sorrowful anxieties and restless troubles, flees before the sound of music almost as before the Word of God" (Daniel Poling, A *Treasury of Best-Loved Hymns* [Pickwick Press, 1942], 95). Although factually based, the specifics of the writing of the hymn as told here are conjecture.

Chapter Twelve
1. This operation, the retelling here slightly embellished for dramatic effect, is reported in several sources, including Rick Atkinson, *Crusade: The Untold Story of the Persian Gulf War* (Boston: Houghton Mifflin, 1993), 369-70, and Greg Walker, *At the Hurricane's Eye: U.S. Special Operations Forces from Vietnam to Desert Storm* (New York: Ballantine/Ivy Books, 1994), 185-86.
2. You may contact Intimate Life Ministries at P.O. Box 201808, Austin, TX 78720; phone: (818) 881-8008.
3. Ronald Nash, *The Closing of the American Heart* (Dallas: Probe Books, 1990), 128.
4. Tina W. Ferguson with Josephine Lee, "Spiritual Reality," *Forbes* magazine (27 January 1997): 71.
5. Ibid., 72.
6. Quoted by John Armstrong in *Reformation and Revival Update* vol. 5, no. 6 (November/December 1996).
7. Noah Webster, *The History of the United States* (New Haven, Conn.: Durrie & Peck, 1832), 309.

Chapter Thirteen

1. The events of Martin Luther's final days, the procession across Germany, and his funeral are well documented. Primary sources: Kittelson, *Luther the Reformer* and Lilje, *Luther and the Reformation.* The incidents at the Luther farm and with young Martin Luther, Jr., in the church at Wittenberg are fictionalized, although based on fact. However, Martin Luther is buried in Castle Church and the first line of "A Mighty Fortress Is Our God" adorns his tomb.

Appendix

1. I want to thank Michael McManus for his efforts in divorce prevention and for continuing to advance the cause of community marriage policies. I highly recommend his book *Marriage Savers,* available from Zondervan Publishing House. Dr. Jim Talley has an extensive ministry in the areas of relationships, marriage preparation, marital reconciliation, and divorce recovery. He continues to urge communities to accept marriage policies and furnished the Modesto policy reproduced here. He may be contacted through the Internet at drtalley.com or via e-mail at drtalley@drtalley.com.

Resources

The following list is not intended to be exhaustive. There are many other excellent resources available through churches, ministries, and bookstores.

MARRIAGE

Books

Communication: Key to Your Marriage, H. Norman Wright (Gospel Light).

Dr. Rosberg's Do-It-Yourself Relationship Mender, Gary Rosberg (Focus on the Family).

52 Dates for You and Your Mate, Dave and Claudia Arp (Thomas Nelson).

The Five Love Languages: How to Express Heartfelt Commitment to Your Mate, Gary Chapman (Moody Press).

400 Creative Ways to Say "I Love You," Alice Chapin (Tyndale).

Getting Away to Get It Together, Bill and Carolyn Wellons (Wellons).

Growing a Healthy Marriage, Mike Yorkey (Focus on the Family).

Holding on to Romance, H. Norman Wright (Gospel Light).

Husbands Who Won't Lead and Wives Who Won't Follow, James Walker (Bethany).

If Two Shall Agree, Carey Moore and Pamela Roswell Moore (Baker Book House).

Intended for Pleasure, Ed Wheat, M.D., and Gaye Wheat (Baker).

Intimate Allies, Dan B. Allender and Tremper Longman III (Tyndale).

Love for a Lifetime, James Dobson (Word).

Love Life for Every Married Couple, Ed Wheat, M.D., and Gloria Okes Perkins (Zondervan).

Moments Together for Couples, Dennis and Barbara Rainey (Regal Books).

The New Building Your Mate's Self-Esteem, Dennis and Barbara Rainey (Thomas Nelson).

The Questions Book for Marriage Intimacy, Dennis and Barbara Rainey (FamilyLife).

Rocking the Roles, Robert Lewis and William Hendricks (NavPress).

Staying Close, Dennis Rainey (Word).

Tightening the Knot, Susan Yates and Allison Yates Gaskins (NavPress).

The Triumphant Marriage, Neil Clark Warren (Focus on the Family).

Audio
"Building Your Mate's Self-Esteem," Dennis and Barbara Rainey (FamilyLife).
"Creating a More Romantic Marriage," Dennis and Barbara Rainey (FamilyLife).
"FamilyLife Marriage Conference," Various Speakers (FamilyLife).
"2=1: Why God Created Marriage," Dennis Rainey (FamilyLife).

Video
"Raising the Standard in Our Marriages," Various Speakers (PromiseKeepers).

FAMILY/PARENTING

Books
Different Children, Different Needs, Charles Boyd (Questar).
Discipline Them, Love Them, Betty N. Chase (David C. Cook).
Do I Have To? Patricia H. Sprinkle (Zondervan).
Drug-Proof Your Kids, Stephen Arterburn and Jim Burns (Gospel Light).
The Duties of Parents, J.C. Ryle (Gospel Mission).
God's Design for Sex Series:
>   *The Story of Me,* Book 1, Stan and Brenna Jones and Carolyn Nystrom (NavPress).
>   *Before I Was Born,* Book 2, Carolyn Nystrom (NavPress).
>   *What's the Big Deal? Why God Cares About Sex,* Book 3, Stan and Brenna Jones (NavPress).
>   *Facing the Facts: The Truth About Sex and You,* Book 4, Stan and Brenna Jones (NavPress).
>   *How and When to Tell Your Kids About Sex—Parents' Companion* (To God's Design for Sex Series), Stan and Brenna Jones (NavPress).
Heaven Help the Home, Howard G. Hendricks (Scripture Press).
Home-Grown Heroes, Tim Kimmel (Multnomah).
How to Really Love Your Child, Ross Campbell, M.D. (Chariot Books).
How to Really Love Your Teenager, Ross Campbell, M.D. (Chariot Books).
The Hurried Child, David Elkind (Addison-Wesley).
Let's Make a Memory, Gloria Gaither and Shirley Dobson (Word).
Little House on the Freeway, Tim Kimmel (Questar).
The Little House on the Freeway Home Maintenance Manual, Tim Kimmel (Questar).
Making Family Memories: A Family Night Planner, Rich and Bonnie Skinner (Fulton Press).
The One-Year Book of Family Devotions, Volume 2 (Tyndale).
Parenting: An Heir-Raising Experience, Mary Glynn and Sam Peeples (Peeples).
Preparing for Adolescence, James Dobson (Regal Books).
Prodigals and Those Who Love Them, Ruth Bell Graham (Focus on the Family).
Raising Kids Who Turn Out Right, Tim Kimmel (Questar).

Raising Money-Smart Kids: How to Teach Your Children the Secrets of Earning, Saving, Investing, and Spending Wisely, Ron and Judy Blue (Thomas Nelson).

Real Family Values, Robert Lewis and Rich Campbell (Vision House).

The Strong-Willed Child, James Dobson (Tyndale).

Tough Parenting for Dangerous Times, Andy Bustanaby (Zondervan).

The Tribute, Dennis Rainey with Dave Boehi (Thomas Nelson).

Watchmen on the Walls: Praying Character Into Your Child, Anne Arkins and Gary Harrell (FamilyLife).

The Way They Learn, Cynthia Tobias (Focus on the Family).

Audio

"A Biblical Approach to Spanking," Dennis and Barbara Rainey (FamilyLife).

"Building a Relationship With Your Child," Dennis and Barbara Rainey (FamilyLife).

"Dad," Dennis Rainey (FamilyLife).

"Guiding Your Child Through Peer Pressure," Dennis and Ashley Rainey (FamilyLife).

"Love, Sex, and Marriage," Dennis Rainey (FamilyLife).

"Principles for Effective Parenting," Dennis and Barbara Rainey (FamilyLife).

"Teaching Your Children About Sex," Dennis and Barbara Rainey (FamilyLife).

Other

"Resurrection Eggs®," A FamilyLife Resource (FamilyLife).

Step-Parenting

Living in a Step-Family Without Getting Stepped On, Kevin Leman (Thomas Nelson).

Resolving Conflict in the Blended Family, Tom and Adrenne Frydenger (Baker).

MEN

The Effective Father, Gordon MacDonald (Tyndale).

Guard Your Heart, Gary Rosberg (Questar).

How to Be Your Daughter's Daddy, Dan Bolin (NavPress).

How to Be Your Little Man's Dad, Dan Bolin and Ken Sutterfield (NavPress).

How to Be Your Wife's Best Friend, Dan Bolin and John Trent (NavPress).

If Only He Knew, Gary Smalley (Zondervan).

Locking Arms, Stu Weber (Questar).

The Silence of Adam, Larry Crabb with Don Hudson and Al Andrews (Zondervan).

Tender Warrior, Stu Weber (Multnomah).

Promise Keepers resources are available by calling 1(800) 265-6023.

WOMEN

For Better Or For Best, Gary Smalley (Zondervan).
Home By Choice, Brenda Hunter (Questar).
How to Be Your Husband's Best Friend, Cay Bolin and Cindy Trent (NavPress).
Mom, You're Incredible, Linda Weber (Focus on the Family).
The Mommy Book, Karen Hull (Zondervan).
*A Mother's Heart: A Look at Values, Vision, and Character for the Christian
    Mother,* Jean Fleming (NavPress).
*Partners in Promise: Discovering Your Role in Your Husband's Spiritual
    Quest,* Mary Jensen (Questar).
Women Leaving the Workplace, Larry Burkett (Moody).

CHILDREN

Arch Book Series, (Concordia).
Benjamin's Box, Melody Carlson (Questar).
Caution: Dangerous Devotions, Jackie Perseghetti (Chariot Books).

SINGLES

Books
Becoming a Friend and Lover, Dick Purnell (Tyndale).
Before You Say "I Do," Wes Roberts and H. Norman Wright (Harvest House).
Finding the Love of Your Life, Neil Clark Warren (Focus on the Family).
Free to Love Again: Coming to Terms With Sexual Regret, Dick Purnell
    (Thomas Nelson).
Passion and Purity, Elisabeth Elliot (Baker Books).
Quest for Love, Elisabeth Elliot (Baker Books).

Audio
"Before the Wedding Night," Ed Wheat, M.D. (Scriptural Counseling).
"Preparing for Marriage," Dennis Rainey (FamilyLife).

STUDY/WORKBOOK MATERIALS

The Financial Planning Workbook, Larry Burkett (Christian Financial Concepts).
The HomeBuilders Couples Series®, Various Titles and Authors
    (Gospel Light).
School Choice: Making Your Decision and Making It Work, A FamilyLife
    Resource (FamilyLife).
*Understanding One Another: A Personalized Guide to Better
    Communication,* A FamilyLife Resource (FamilyLife).

GENERAL

The Book of Virtues, William J. Bennett (Simon & Schuster).
The Gift of the Blessing, Gary Smalley and John Trent (Thomas Nelson).
How to Deal With Powerful Personalities, Tim Kimmel (Focus on the Family).
Knowing God by His Names: A 31-Day Experiment, Dick Purnell
    (Thomas Nelson).
The Knowledge of the Holy, A. W. Tozer (Spring Arbor).
A Passionate Commitment, Crawford W. Loritts (Moody Press).
Recovering Biblical Manhood and Womanhood, Wayne Grudem and John
    Piper (Crossway).
Right from Wrong, Josh McDowell and Bob Hostetler (Word).
What the Bible Says About Healthy Living, Rex Russell, M.D. (Gospel Light).
When Life Is Changed Forever, Rick Taylor (Harvest House).
The Wounded Heart, Dan B. Allender (NavPress).

FAMILY LIFE HOMEBUILDERS
COUPLES SERIES

The HomeBuilders Couples Series® are the fastest growing small-group studies in the country. This series is designed to help your relationship build and grow on the solid biblical principles found in God's Word.

Building Teamwork in Your Marriage
by Robert Lewis
Understand your differences are gifts from God, and learn how you are the unique person equipped to complete your mate.

Building Your Marriage
by Dennis Rainey
Discover and apply God's basic blueprints for a strong, healthy marriage that will last a lifetime.

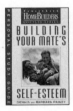

Building Your Mate's Self-Esteem
by Dennis and Barbara Rainey
Learn how to encourage each other, and experience new levels of love and fulfillment.

Expressing Love in Your Marriage
by Jerry and Sheryl Wunder and Dennis and Jill Eenigenburg
Express God's love in your marriage—seeking His best for one another.

Growing Together in Christ
by David Sunde
Discover all the power and joy you and your mate can find together by developing an exciting daily relationship with Christ.

Life Choices for a Lasting Marriage
by David Boehi
Identify the key choices for a lasting marriage and renew your minds with the truth of God's Word.

Managing Pressure in Your Marriage
by Dennis Rainey and Robert Lewis
Make better choices, plan for the future, and find new solutions for your life and marriage.

Mastering Money in Your Marriage
by Ron Blue
Discover how you can make money matters a tool for growth instead of a bone of contention in your marriage.

Resolving Conflict in Your Marriage
by Bob and Jan Horner
Learn to transform conflicts into opportunities to energize your marriage and increase your love for your mate.

For more information on these and other FamilyLife Resources contact your local Christian retailer or call FamilyLife at 1-800-FL-TODAY. A free HomeBuilders Information Pack is also available through the FamilyLife "800" number.

FAMILYLIFE™
Bringing Timeless Principles Home

P.O. Box 23840 • Little Rock, AR • 72221-3840
(501) 223-8663 • 1-800-FL-TODAY
http://www.familylife-ccc.org

A division of Campus Crusade for Christ

"A Weekend to Remember"

Every couple has a unique set of needs. The FamilyLife Marriage Conference meets couples' needs by equipping them with proven solutions that address practically every component of how

to build a better marriage. The conference gives you the opportunity to slow down and focus on your spouse and your relationship. You will spend an insightful weekend together doing fun couples' projects and hearing from dynamic speakers on real-life solutions for building and enhancing oneness in your marriage.

You'll learn:

- *Five secrets of a successful marriage*
- *How to implement oneness in your marriage*
- *How to maintain a vital sexual relationship*
- *How to handle conflict*
- *How to express forgiveness to one another*

Our insightful speaker team also conducts sessions for:

- *Engaged/Pre-marrieds*
- *Men only*
- *Women only*

FAMILYLIFE
MARRIAGE CONFERENCE

To register or receive a free brochure and schedule, call FamilyLife at 1-800-999-8663 or connect to the FamilyLife web site at http://www.familylife-ccc.org

FAMILYLIFE™
Bringing Timeless Principles Home